AF248901

St. George's School

A History: 1896 - 1986

Gilbert Y. Taverner

Published by St. George's School
Newport, Rhode Island

Paper: 70 lb Monadnock Dulcet Smooth, Bennington, New Hampshire

Type: Times Modern, AM Varityper 6400

Printed by Reynolds-DeWalt Printing, Inc., New Bedford, Massachusetts

Copyright © 1987 by St. George's School, Newport, Rhode Island 02840

Library of Congress Catalog Card Number: 87-60966

ISBN 0-9618397-0-8

Dedicated to
George Williamson Wheeler '27
and his wife
Margery Borden Wheeler

Who represent everything
St. George's School holds valuable

The St. George's School Shield

From an original design by
Pierre La Rose in 1939

The Shield features the red Cross of St. George and black and white fusils (diamond-shaped designs) reflective of the name of the Founder, the Rev. John Byron Diman.

The School motto: *Sapientia Utriusque Vitae Lumen,* is most commonly translated as, "Wisdom, the light of every life." It was suggested in 1900 by William Binney, one of the School's original incorporators.

FOREWORD   PAGE v

CHAPTER 1   PAGE 1
"FROM THE SMALLEST OF BEGINNINGS" – 1896-1901

"Mr. Diman's School for Boys," 1896 • The Rev. John Byron Diman • Emily Diman, Faculty and Staff • St. George's School • Economic pressures • Swann Villa Days, 1897-1901 • School chartered, 1900.

CHAPTER 2 – GROWTH AND CHALLENGE – 1901-1907   PAGE 21

The move to the Hilltop, 1901 • Faculty • Facilities – Old School, The Cottage, Sixth Form House and Gymnasium • Enrollment growth • Early Hilltop life • "The Pie House" • Chapel at St. Columba's • School servants • Tension over athletics • Diman offered a position at St. Paul's • School crowded.

CHAPTER 3   PAGE 39
THE REV. JOHN BYRON DIMAN'S LAST YEARS – 1907-1917

Diman's dreams for the School, 1907 • Arden and King Hall • Benefactors • Second Charter, 1907 • Affiliation with the Protestant Episcopal Church • Strict academics and behavior • Prefect system instituted, 1908 • Hilltop life • The Little Chapel, 1911 • Diman Vocational School, 1912 • World War I and the School • Diman's resignation, 1916 • His conversion to Roman Catholicism, 1917.

CHAPTER 4 – A HALCYON ERA – 1917-1928   PAGE 67

Search for a Headmaster, 1917 • Unitarian, Stephen P. Cabot, appointed • Cabot the scholar • The Faculty • World War I ends • Delays completing the Memorial Schoolhouse • Announcement of gift of School Chapel 1922 • Cabot's resignation over Chapel • Clergyman/Layman Headmaster issue • Russell H. Nevins, Headmaster, 1926-1928 • Social stratification • Student life.

CHAPTER 5   PAGE 85
THE CRUCIBLE OF THE GREAT DEPRESSION – 1928-1943

The ebullient Spring of 1928 • School Chapel dedicated • J. Vaughan Merrick, III, new Headmaster • First married Headmaster • School life • The Great Depression and severe economic problems • Enrollment crises • World War II begins • Merrick taken ill • 1930's and 1940's exhausting years • Chapel Spotting Station.

CHAPTER 6   **PAGE 101**
COLLISION AND RESTORATION – 1943-1961

Dr. Willet L. Eccles, Headmaster • Innovations to increase enrollment • Collisions with tradition • Changes in types of boys at School • Faculty • World War II ends • Fiftieth Anniversary, 1946 • William A. Buell '14, Headmaster, 1951-1961 • Relationship with Faculty • School Chaplains • Turn-around to better days • Growth in facilities and prestige • School life • Buell's retirement.

CHAPTER 7   **PAGE 131**
CHARTING NEW COURSES IN CHANGING TIMES – 1961-1972

St. George's a select independent school • Archer Harman, Jr., Headmaster 1961-1972 • Questions as to School's direction • Trustees • Prime years to teach at St. George's • Business aspects of School • Student life • Black and minority students • Coeducation • Seventy-fifth Anniversary • Persistent Church School issue • Harman decides to leave.

CHAPTER 8   **PAGE 155**
CONSOLIDATION AND FURTHER PROGRESS – 1972-1986

All aspects of School brought together • Improved finances • Anthony M. Zane, Headmaster, 1972-1984 • Inflation upsets finances • Enrollment growth • Unique time for students • The "different" students of the 1970's to mid-1980's • A female Senior Prefect • Coeducation and its effects • Day students • Faculty, teaching and changes • Deaths • Trustees closer to School • Alumni • The Rev. George E. Andrews, II, Headmaster, 1984-   • Emphasis on students • Deans of Students' roles • Facilities improved • Church School issue • Reaching out to the community • Collegial style.

AFTERWORD   **PAGE 175**

APPENDICES   **PAGE 176**

A. Faculty

B. Trustees

C. Alumni Leadership

D. Students Killed in Wars

E. Senior Prefects

F. School Prayer, Hymns and Portraits

G. Chronology of Buildings

PHOTOGRAPHS

Inside front cover, *1920's aerial view of the School*
Inside back cover, *1980's aerial view of the School*
Between pages 84 and 85
George and Margery Wheeler
The Rev. John Byron Diman; Miss Emily Diman
Headmasters: Cabot, Nevins, Merrick, Eccles, Buell, Harman, Zane, Andrews
Headmasters' Wives: Merrick, Eccles, Buell, Harman, Zane, Andrews
The Hunter Avenue houses; The School in 1899
Building Memorial Schoolhouse; First Gymnasium-become-Schoolroom; Interior Schoolroom
Early Hilltop Tennis Courts; School Battalion in 1919
Little Chapel, 1911; Diman Hall Cubicles
Drama, 1905; Drama, 1985
Faculty, 1936; Faculty, 1986
Study Hall, 1951; Viking Ship, 1983
Library-become-Student Center; Girls in Astor Hall
School Chapel Interior; Exterior
The Dragon Statue; Christmas Festival
Frostbite Picnic; "Geronimo"
Coeducation; Parents
Prize Day; Alumni Dinner
Crew; Basketball; Hockey (before Rink was covered); Football
Girls' Field Hockey; Baseball; Cross Country; Soccer
Page 189, detail of the *Processional Cross*

SKETCHES

Pages: 9, *Swann Villa;* 20, *Old School;* 25, *Sixth Form House;* 38, *King Hall;* 66, *Architectural sketch of Chapel;* 84, *St. George cartoon;* 100, *The Studious Dragon;* 154, *Untitled;* 188, *St. George and the Dragon.*

FOREWORD

Those who know St. George's School best will succumb to the irresistible temptation to rewrite this book as they read it. This is as it should be. Those of each succeeding generation who have known "The St. George's Experience" will amplify the factual data of the School's history with memories known only to them. The decision to provide this History was to preserve and understand St. George's first ninety-years in terms of its major events and their impact. Thus, this book is a point of departure not a point of arrival.

An ever-lengthening list of people contributed information to this History – one that would consume several pages. To as great an extent as possible their contributions are included in these pages. The preparation of the manuscript has been guided by the School History Committee: G. Danforth Hollins, Chairman; Mrs. George W. (Margery) Wheeler, RAdm. John R. Wadleigh '33, W. S. R. Rogers '44, Eleanor T. Howard, and the Rev. George F. Andrews, II. Former Headmasters, Archer Harman, Jr. and Anthony M. Zane, also read the book-in-progress, offering valuable ideas.

I am indebted to members of my family for their patience and support. My daughter, Nancy E. Adelman, has given expert advice. Above all others, my wife, Elizabeth (Bette), deserves the highest recognition. Her research, editorial and proof-reading talents have been of inestimable value.

The Board of Trustees has generously funded this History in appreciation of all who have truly made St. George's history over the years.

To all, a resounding "Thank You!"

As Catherine Drinker Bowen wrote her history books, she kept over her desk: "Will the reader turn the page?" This volume has been written with the hope that readers will both turn its pages and be stimulated to remember afresh a splendid Hilltop School and all that it means to them.

Gilbert Y. Taverner

February 1987
Middletown, Rhode Island

CHAPTER ONE

From the Smallest of Beginnings
1896 - 1901

> **INSTRUCTION**
>
> ## Mr. John B. Diman
> ### WILL OPEN A SMALL
> ## Boarding School For Boys
> In Newport, in September, 1896. For information,
> address 300 Angell Street, Providence, R.I.
>
> *Newport Daily News,* April 24, 1896

IN 1896 the Rev. John Byron Diman decided to open a college preparatory school for boys in Newport, Rhode Island. In keeping with a common practice at the time, it was for boys in Forms I through VI (grades 7 through 12). The decision drastically changed his life and affected generations yet unborn. Mr. Diman's School for Boys, to become known as St. George's School, was first announced to the public in newspaper advertisements in April 1896. The notice that Diman intended to open a "boarding school" in September told something about the man. Allowing himself four months to collect students, equip and start a School, may have seemed brash to some but not to Diman. At thirty-three, he brought three years teaching experience at the University Grammar School in Providence (1892-1895), a newly-earned M.A. from Harvard, but most of all, an amazing ability to organize people, overcome circumstances, and undertake risks which he turned into successes. He was a young man of considerable self-confidence.

From the time he announced his intention to open a school, Diman was dogged by frustration and disappointment. A dozen years later, with visible successes achieved, he would recall:

"As early as the April preceding I had put notices in two papers that a school would be opened on the first of the following October.* And then I laid back for the boys to come in. The months went by, however, and not a single boy turned up. I had some very queer letters from strange out of the way places, but none of them materialized into even the prospect of a boy."

By August he had only one "live" admissions prospect, so he postponed the School's opening to October 1st. Frank Howland was the "live" prospect and Diman has recalled him as an exceptional "find":

"[The first boy] was Frank Howland, who became very closely identified with the first years of the school and may be said to have had a very distinguished career in it, for he was captain of about all the athletic teams we had in those days, and at the end of the course entered Yale with the highest honors that could be taken."

Diman, painfully searching for students, made what must have been for him a major concession — in the late summer and fall he advertised his School as both a "boarding and day school." He likewise resorted to hyperbole, rare for him, understatement being more his style. He claimed for his forthcoming school "Preparation for any college or scientific school." He had only three students at the time, but he was sure of his faculty: N. Henry Black, a gifted young Harvard graduate, teaching mathematics and science, and himself, grounded in the classics and English.** Two rented houses on Deblois Avenue (later Hunter Avenue), Newport, were awaiting his occupancy. But from every perspective, the situation was bleak.

Nevertheless, Mr. Diman's School for Boys did open on October 1st. There were about a dozen students, roughly half boarders and half day students. The young founding Headmaster was never to forget the early months of the School:

"Besides the Armistead Cottage we had taken...a very little house next door [Elizabeth Hunter's Cottage at

---

*Diman was well-known for his somewhat unreliable memory. He seems to have forgotten that (as verified by actual advertisements in the *Newport Daily News*) he had set September as the opening date of his school.

**See Appendix A for a list of Faculty, 1896-1986.

> 57 Deblois Avenue]. There we had a very small school-
> room, one recitation room and a laboratory. The impres-
> sion of that first year is very distinct in my mind and is
> made up of pictures which bespeak the very smallest of
> beginnings of things. Rooms so draughty that the bed-
> room floors were half covered with snow in the winter,
> hardly any athletic field at all, [but] a pleasant jolly lot of
> boys who seemed utterly unacquainted with the deficien-
> cies of the equipment and who helped to lay the founda-
> tions upon which all the future years were to build."*

That the school survived its first year of trial and testing was a tribute to Diman's unflappable strength. But this alone did not do it. His sister, Emily, was there that first year. Warm, outgoing, beloved by the boys, she was an alter-ego to her brother's undeniably stern, reserved, if also kind, demeanor.

Nellie Brown was there that first year as cook, to begin her long, faithful and famous service to the school. Edward Howland, one of the first boys, was twelve-and-a-half at the time. Fifty years later he was to recall the supper Nellie Brown cooked and served (wearing a red kerchief), which included squash muffins and stewed apples with lemon peel.

Sam Ross was there, to become "Old Sam" in time, handling the maintenance of buildings, a handy-man, friend of boys, to give devoted service to the school for thirty-five years.**

Henry Black, with Diman, established from the beginning the school's insistence on a rigorous, no-nonsense curriculum. He was also an exciting teacher. G. Andrews Moriarty was a "first boy" and reflected a half-century later:

> "...geology was the high spot. The field work delighted
> me [and others.] Every Saturday morning we started out
> with Mr. Black on bicycles with our lunches and geology
> hammers to study the exceedingly interesting rock forma-

---

*See Appendix G for a list of St. George's buildings.

**In the social structure of the 1890's and early 1900's, Nellie Brown and Sam Ross were highly respected and much loved "servants." Nellie Brown was honored in 1932 for her "inspiration to others" and the high regard in which she was held by the St. George's Family. Sam Ross was to be remembered by a head-and-shoulders bust, given by Barbara Woodworth Scully in 1934, and kept in the Faculty Room.

tions in the vicinity.

> "I remember especially the thrill I used to get digging
> out fossils from the slate at Wood's Castle on the
> Sakonnet River. We all liked Mr. Black, even if he did
> teach mathematics."

It was clear that Black compensated for what the School lacked in proper laboratory facilities by using the surrounding fields and seacoast as a living laboratory.

Black was to remain from 1896 until 1898, an all-too-brief tenure, but a brilliant one. He later became a professor of science at Harvard and the author of textbooks on physics.

There was an international flair that first year, 1896-1897. Once a week, Jean Louis Marie Pierre d'Ancourt came down from Providence to teach French. Edward Howland remembered him as given to extremes in colorful clothing and:

> "His classes were a series of small riots [not] a fair
> example of our general instruction, as Mr. Diman and
> Mr. Black were splendid teachers."

Frank McCloskey was there the first year, teaching violin. He was to remain until 1928.

To ask "What was John Byron Diman like as a teacher?" is to receive mixed reviews. The bulk of his teaching was confined to the earliest days of the school (except for Sacred Studies).

Moriarty was positive about Diman's teaching, as he experienced it that first year:

> "Mr. Diman, as became a scholar who was the son of a
> famous clergyman and professor of *Belles Lettres,**
> taught the *Literae Humanitores,* which consisted of
> Latin and English...
> "In Latin we used Collar's *First Latin Book,* and read
> *Urbis Romae ius Neopos.* In English we read Macauley's
> *Lays Of Ancient Rome* and Scott's *Marmion...*"

By and large, however, it was Diman the Headmaster, not Diman the Master, who was to be remembered.

---

*Moriarty's memory slips a cog here. The Rev. J. Lewis Diman, D.D., taught History and Political Economy at Brown University. The slip is understandable, however, in that he was also known for his fluent use of language and breadth of scholarship.

The School's first students were soon aware of Diman's accent on Mathematics and Science, as well as the more familiar classical studies of Latin, Greek and Ancient History. Charles Darwin had spurred both an interest in science and an emphasis on disciplined intellectual thought in men like Diman. In the nation at large, curriculum was taking on better defined and focussed direction. Even in that first year, without anything approaching proper facilities, Mr. Diman's School for Boys had a demanding academic program.

The collage unfolding for that first year, 1896-1897, revealed a rugged, difficult, yet successful one. Diman, always reticent about his personal affairs, had neither the inclination nor the time to leave a written contemporary record of the year. It has all surfaced later in other contexts, in letters and documents reflecting how the School actually had its very small beginnings.

John Byron Diman's choice of Newport for his school was fortuitous. He had made his first mark upon the city and Aquidneck Island not as an educator but as a clergyman. Having completed Brown in 1885, he matriculated at the Cambridge (later Episcopal) Theological School, Cambridge, Massachusetts and, upon completing his divinity degree, was ordained a Deacon in the Protestant Episcopal Church in 1888. There was no indication then of his later interests in education as he became Deacon-in-Charge of The Berkeley Memorial Chapel (known more familiarly in later years as St. Columba's Episcopal Church), on Indian Avenue, Middletown.

He was a breath of fresh air to the tiny chapel. It had been for four years a summer colonists' chapel (it even lacked a furnace.) The young twenty-four-year-old Deacon established the church as a year-round parish and poured into it his visible drive, energy and superior management abilities. He put on a coon-skin cap and a pea coat to join the men of the parish in venturing to Tiverton to cut greens for the church's Christmas decorations. Well-liked and greatly respected, he became known as an up-and-coming young clergyman.

It was at the Berkeley Memorial Chapel that he met, and served, people who were to be instrumental in the life of his future School. Bishop Thomas March Clark, aged but alert, was associated with the parish. Julien T. Davies and George Gordon King, generous supporters of the later School were there, as was the Sturtevant family, important in the life of the School over many years.

Diman was important to the life of Aquidneck Island as a clergyman, a factor intrinsic in his choice of Newport for his school.

The personal education which John Byron Diman brought to the founding of his School was largely that of a clergyman, with the significant addition of his Master of Arts degree from Harvard in 1896.

His secondary education was acquired at the English-Classical School in Providence, a private school with excellent credentials, which was to be absorbed into the University Grammar School in 1890 (the school at which Diman taught from 1892-1895.) This later became known as the University School; begun in 1764, it had an intermittent relationship to Brown University, located as it was on its campus. The Moses Brown School absorbed the University School in 1904. From his own secondary education, as well as later from Brown, Diman received the high-level classical training which he brought to his School. His decision to go to theological school was influenced by his confirmation, in 1885, during his senior year at Brown, in the Protestant Episcopal Church. A trip to Europe, after he had gone to the Berkeley Chapel, enhanced his education and world view.

Qualified as Diman was by his clergyman/educator status to start a school, he began it on the proverbial "shoe-string" and at a most inauspicious period in the American economy.

From 1896 until 1907, St. George's School was a private business. For its first four years it was owned outright by Diman, and from 1900 until 1907, mainly by Diman but also by a few stock-holders. He borrowed $5,000 from his mother, Mrs. Emily Stimson of Providence in 1896 to open his school and another $5,000 in 1897 to move the School to Swann Villa, its second location. While neither of these was an inconsequential sum at the time, neither did they offer the new School anything resembling financial security.*

There is no evidence that Diman paid any attention to the unreliable economics which sent the United States economy into unpredictable

---

*Diman was never required to actually repay these loans as they were deducted from his share of his mother's estate upon her death in 1901.

peaks and valleys from 1890 to 1910, nor that he had sought the counsel of readily available businessmen before setting out to open a school. In 1896 the unemployment rate hit 18%. The nation's move from an agriculturally-centered economy to an industrial one was in full swing. It was not the most prudent time to start a business — and the School was a business, Diman's livelihood.*

Prudent or not, Diman seemed to be illustrating the Biblical Parable of the Loaves and Fishes – as he transformed inadequate cash into amazing returns. And he did this over the entire length of his career as an educator, not just at the beginning. He showed, at the tiny struggling Hunter Avenue location, his incredible ability to stretch dollars so that they had an optimum of purchasing power. This was an ability he was to call upon endlessly. By all the laws of common sense, his School should have collapsed under the "pernicious anemia" of inadequate funding in perilous economic times. It struggled and was hard put at times, but it did not collapse — Diman saw to that, utilizing his skills of management and control with brilliant effectiveness.

Diman made no attempt to explain why he wanted to start his School. Newport had been for years the setting of many private schools. As he began St. George's, Diman seemed to ignore the presence of Cloyne House. Begun in 1895 by Oliver Whipple Huntington, Ph.D., and Leslie Green, M.A., Cloyne occupied a fine estate overlooking the Navy Base and Coaster's Island. Dr. Huntington was a popular Newport figure and was what came to be described later as a "progressive educator."** Cloyne House sought to be somewhat like Eton. It was affiliated with the Protestant Episcopal Church, and demonstrated its affection for Eton with its required attire of high collars and top hats.

If Diman could offer nothing of the patrician accommodations of Cloyne, he offered something else: his visible, self-confident style of

---

*Economist, Dr. A. Gary Shilling, father of Geoffrey Shilling '84, has documented how vulnerable Diman's position was in the first years of the School.

**As in the educational turmoil the word "progressive" became synonymous with 'permissive," so it seemed with Dr. Huntington. He appeared to believe, far ahead of his time, that students should learn from their mistakes. He allowed the school's magazine to demonstrate this by having it sent out with all the errors of grammar uncorrected.

leadership and a strong classical curriculum. As it proved, St. George's and Cloyne were never competitors apart from the athletic field. Cloyne lasted only twenty-two years. In 1917 its property was requisitioned by the Navy and a rift between the two founders remained unsettled. It closed. Maud Howe Elliott, a Newport historian of the social scene,* wrote:

> "Cloyne was short-lived; there was not room for two
> boys' schools in Newport."

Cloyne's misfortunes were to clear the way for St. George's unobstructed monopoly as a college preparatory school in Newport.

The School's first year had overtones of the first winter of Diman's Pilgrim ancestors (descent from John Alden on his mother's side), a close brush with disaster. He knew that he had to find quarters which would both be more livable and permit expansion. They had also to be within his constricted means.

Newport had, around the time of Diman's birth (1863), shown signs of becoming a summer colony for intellectuals and writers, as well as people from the South seeking respite from that area's heat. Those colonists built sizable summer houses, mainly of wood, commodious but nothing like the stone and marble "cottages" of the later 1890's.

Diman found one of those older homes in Swann Villa located on Seaview Avenue, overlooking Cliff Walk, near First Beach. It was the former summer home of Governor Swann of Maryland. Using the second $5,000 loan from his mother, he rented it for occupancy in the Fall of 1897. Thus began the Swann Villa Days.

The School's second location, at Swann Villa, was to become the subject of mixed reviews, in terms of the house. Diman described it with appreciation for its possibilities:

> "It had a very large dining room, a large ballroom,
> which was immediately converted into a schoolroom,
> and an equally large bedroom upstairs which served at
> different times the purposes of a laboratory and of a
> dormitory for five boys and a master."

---

*Mrs. Elliott, daughter of Julia Ward Howe, author of *The Battle Hymn of the Republic,* was among the many who supported Diman life-long.

SWANN VILLA — 1897 - 1901
Sketch by Richard Grosvenor

He conceded that a good deal of ingenuity was required to extract every inch of space for the School's needs. He wryly recalled:

> "To give an idea of the straits to which a school is reduced during the years in which it has to live in a hired house, I might narrate that at one time we used the bath tub adjoining [the large upstairs bedroom] for a lily pond and an aquarium . . . During the last year or two of our occupancy of this house we were crowded to a point which almost passed the powers of forbearance. The landing on the stairs was regularly a recitation room. Mr. Sturtevant's bedroom was another one, and the bathroom adjoining it was invaded by the whole football and baseball teams for their very vigorous and very noisy ablutions."

Notwithstanding these drawbacks, Diman appreciated the house's good points:

> "The eastern piazza was exceptionally pleasant, and in front of it there was a wide lawn sweeping down to the Cliffs. The boys used to coast over this lawn in winter, and it is one of the things for which we have had most reason to be thankful that none of them was precipitated into the sea."

Leonard Bacon '05 was a student in the Swann Villa Days. (He was to become a recognized poet and book critic, winning the Pulitzer Prize for Poetry in 1940.) Forty-one years after graduating from St. George's (at the Fiftieth Anniversary in 1946) Bacon recalled the Villa with something of the satire for which he had become famous:

> "Swann Villa was of a sort to make an indelible if equivocal impression on any mind, for it belonged to an obviously vanishing Newport, which in turn belonged in a novel by Edith Wharton . . .
>
> ". . . a boom was getting underway which would shortly swamp the little summer city with the sort of plutocrats who gave elaborate dinners in honor of pet monkeys and had filet mignons served to lap dogs by butlers in green and gold liveries. The town was not always like that. And I am sure that Swann Villa antedated such antics as it antedated the palaces on the

Cliffs or on Bellevue Avenue. But, architecturally speaking, the house wasn't much handsomer than the manners and customs of the expanding plutocracy. At first glance it seemed to consist entirely of attics and verandas."*

With all its jig-saw-like contortions, such as might appear in a Charles Addams *New Yorker* cartoon a hundred years later, Swann Villa served Diman's needs durably. He used it with maximum efficiency, if not comfort. The tower doubled as a dormitory and his bedroom. Plays were rehearsed in the basement and performed in the schoolroom (ballroom). These incipient efforts, of what was to become a strong tradition of dramatics at St. George's, came in for critical reviews from the Headmaster. Diman clearly favored heavier fare than the light comedies produced, complaining that the latter "lacked literary merit."

The house seemed to lend itself to a brief flirtation with what resembled a college fraternity. A group calling itself Delta Sigma went in for ornate robes, ceremonies and banquets. It died an early death, a somewhat awkward intrusion on the simple life at St. George's.

The move enabled the School to begin an athletic program. Diman favored athletics, although not in the form of the intense competition that sports took on before his days were over. "Muscular Christianity" had been imported from Britain into the American boarding schools with clergy headmasters. Introduced by the famous Dr. Thomas Arnold of Rugby School in the early nineteenth century, developing strong bodies through athletics and equally strong minds and spirits by a response to Christianity were widely sought as an ideal. There is ample evidence that Diman clung to close approximations of that ideal throughout his forty years as a Headmaster.

He was committed to what was called "physical education," with an accent on "education." "Hard play and hard work" went together for him – in sports or studies. Academics had the highest priority, and "gentlemanliness" in sports he considered unarguable.

It was a "make-do" situation for athletics, however. The sloping lawn down to Cliff Walk was good for coasting but not for baseball. As one student later complained:

---

*In 1986, Swann Villa still stands but without its tower and ballroom wing. It is known as Cliffside Inn and is handsomely restored to its Victorian decor.

> "Great difficulty was found in playing baseball because
> the sun shone in the batters' eyes, and the boys contin-
> ually went into the water for foul tips."

A nearby field, known as Gammell Field, became available and proved a boon in developing outdoor sports. Diman described it as:

> "Almost perfectly level and [we felt] that we were
> admirably equipped [to play baseball and football]."

Cloyne House was St. George's chief rival. Later, Rogers High School of Newport and other nearby public schools were added. The small beginnings of athletics, if somewhat short on ideal facilities, were long on school spirit.

The earliest suggestion of boating and crew, two activities to become popular in the future, came during the Swann Villa Days. The new School newspaper/magazine, *The Dragon,* offered the rationale that colleges had crews and were eager to have students from schools with experience in rowing.

Interest in college and university sports was high. Trips were made to watch the Harvard-Yale games. In the *alma maters* of Masters, Harvard was cheered on hands down: Diman, Galbraith, Gregg all had Harvard degrees.

Edward Sturtevant took the boys on long and leisurely bicycle rides to Ocean Drive and elsewhere.

It was common at the time (and up until the mid-1900's) for masters to join the boys in sports, especially football and baseball. The eventual ruling out of this practice had as much to do with masters "taking over" games as anything else.

What is communicated by those who experienced the Swann Villa Days is a *camaraderie* among boys and masters, the like of which was imprisioned in the years 1897-1901. Leonard Bacon, '05 has recalled that "the tiny School was conducted with an informality and ease later impossible."

There were occasional exciting interruptions to the life of Swann Villa. A near-by fire got written up in *The Dragon* in minute detail. A wreck on First Beach Bay occurred, with the boys watching with incredulity as the life-guards pushed through ten-foot waves to rescue the sailors. As reading aloud was in vogue, the boys gathered to hear stories read or, if original, told. Diman's reading of *The Wreck of the Grosvenor* so gripped the boys that it became an annual ritual.

The female presence was apparent at St. George's. Mrs. Edward W. Bacon was the Housekeeper from 1897-1901. Miss Jane Stormont-Lewis taught French and German. Miss Anna Hunter became something of a patroness of the School, hostessing the boys for her famous Welsh rarebit treats. Mrs. Dring, whose house at 45 Dresser Street housed Sixth Formers, liked to entertain the boys at tea time. Miss Emily Diman, to become so vital a part of the School later, was able only to visit occasionally at Swann Villa because she was needed to care for her mother in Providence. It was not, by any means, a totally male preserve at the School.

John Byron Diman wisely surrounded himself with capable people who complemented and enlarged his vision for St. George's. However much he dominated the School – and he did – the boys had access to men and women who brought a contrast to his strong presence.

The high quality of Masters which Diman attracted from the earliest days of the school was evident. Henry Black stayed until 1898 to be replaced by Edward Sturtevant, who remained until 1939. Arthur F. Griffiths (1899 1902) became President of the Oahu College in Hawaii. E. Blake Barton taught for only one year. It was he, however, who introduced dramatics and who was the butt of Diman's criticism for the light touch he brought to the plays presented. John S. Galbraith taught Greek and Latin, for three years (1899-1902). (The School's *Catalogue* lists no courses being taught by Diman; he actually taught Sacred Studies.)

From the earliest days, Diman demonstrated an administrative genius exceeding that of his ability as a teacher. Leonard Bacon '05 has reflected upon Diman the teacher, as he knew him both at Swann Villa and later on the Hilltop:

> "I am sure [Diman] never thought of himself as a teacher of talent and if he had he would have been mistaken, if by a teacher is meant one especially skilled in clarifying the peculiar difficulties of a subject. But he had something more important than that noble but not uncommon gift. I don't know how it was done, but his mere presence in a room heightened interest in whatever was on the program — work or play or conversa-

tion at the dinner table. The world grew positive and affirmative when he was around. And he was always around, even when he wasn't there."*

Beginning at Swann Villa, surrounded by an expanding circle of colleagues, Diman was able to concentrate more adequately on the duties so incumbent upon a headmaster. Here, too, Bacon has spoken for many, for years yet to come, in assessing Diman the Headmaster:

> "Anyone with intellectual equipment equal or superior to an amoeba's could see in him the great natural schoolmaster, in whom justice and humor, which are slightly different isotopes of the same radioactive element, are perfectly mingled." (The modern references are because Bacon offered this in 1946.)

It was visible that, whether on Hunter Avenue, at Swann Villa, or the Hilltop, John B. Diman loomed larger than the roles he had, by function, to fulfill. Not as teacher but as Headmaster, he revealed a chronic restlessness impelling him to build his School to new dimensions of quality and size.

Diman's encouragement was behind the founding of the first publication of St. George's School, *The Dragon,* in the Swann Villa Days of 1899. The first issue came out in March and F.E. Howland '00 was Editor-in-Chief. It was probably Howland who editorialized the purpose of the magazine, meant to appear monthly:

> "This magazine has been started with the object of keeping the boys, their parents and friends, informed in all things concerning the school, both in athletics and other matters. It also aims to foster the school-spirit, and to advance the school's interests as much as it can. We intend to have the work done by the boys; so we hope you will excuse our mistakes."

The earliest generation of future St. George's businessmen were aware

---

*Col. Theodore G. Holcombe '16, has made a related observation about Diman as a teacher. Having had Diman for Sacred Studies, Holcombe remembered little of the content of the course, but has never forgotten the commanding presence of Diman, the man, teaching it.

that their venture had to be run on a business-like basis. They proved this in the first issue, which had as many pages of advertising as of news, stories and comments.

The Dragon became a responsible source of information concerning life in the Swann Villa Days, indeed, the only printed source thus far found. Fledgling authors and poets tested their skills on its pages with the inevitable varying results of promise and less than promise.

From an historical point of view what was possibly most valuable of all, the new publication presented student perspectives. While its earliest issues contained no great amount of criticism of the school *per se,* contributors to *The Dragon* offered critiques on athletics, the behavior of boys, anything that seemed to detract from "school-spirit" and even the jokes submitted. It was a veritable "cheer leading squad" for lifting the School's morale when it was down, or guiding it to desired new heights.

The second issue, April 1899, found a student editor noting the joys of Spring with its "boating, baseball, bicycle riding and, in June, bathing . . ." But, on a serious note, he adds:

> "Let us buckle down to work, both in the schoolroom
> and out of it, with the feeling that there is no school
> like St. George's, and that we must do all in our power
> to build up a name for it among American schools."

There is no reason to doubt the sincerity of this kind of appeal. It was a part of the unusual *zeitgeist* created at Swann Villa. What did it matter if it repeated, perhaps verbatim, a pep talk by Diman or a Master. The important thing was that a remarkable sense of responsibility on the part of students was communicated. The Headmaster had an inimitable capacity to instill such positive responses in students. He was quick to recognize and acknowledge the many times that student responsibilities were fulfilled, even beyond his high expectations.

A surprising breadth of interest is found in the contributions that boys made to the early issues of *The Dragon.* There were serious articles – "Birds of Rhode Island," "Anne Hutchinson," "A Few of Our Winter Land Birds," and a report on owning and maintaining an aquarium. Flights of fantasy gripped fiction writers. "A Ghost in an English Castle" was signed by J.C.B. in the first issue. Stories about trains, the Wild West, and warfare were popular – and even one about the Nihilists of Russia. News abounded about School life – boys taken ill, who had visited School, social life, reviews (largely favorable) of dramatic productions.

There were occasional competitors to the School's magazine (one, called *Cream Cheese,* struggled through three issues), but *The Dragon* was destined to survive them all. Perhaps unintentionally, it became the only written history of St. George's for years to come. It is, for example, the only known source stating that Sunday services were not required in Swann Villa days. A student writer, in the January 1900 *Dragon,* deplored the failure of students to attend services:

> "In former years most of the boys attended the Berkeley Chapel on Sundays. But now, in spite of the fact that Mr. Diman has charge of it,* few go. It would seem that the boys are getting lazy."

From 1896 to 1900 John B. Diman owned St. George's School as its single proprietor. He kept defeating the perils of an unstable United States economy in incredible ways. Charles Dickens' opening lines of *A Tale Of Two Cities* summarize the economics of those days: "It was the best of times, it was the worst of times." Diman knew the School lacked a sound financial base.

With the uncanny foresight for which he was to become justifiably famous, Diman realized that, whatever the problems of the economy, he had to broaden his financial base. The development of the School was threatened by Swann Villa's inadequate facilities (even after he rented two nearby cottages as well as Swann Villa). The growing demand for admission surpassed the space to accommodate students.

Diman was not able to immediately solve this vexing problem by moving to a larger location as he had by leaving Hunter Avenue for Swann Villa. He took another tack, one which had its risks, but which eventually paid off.

He decided in 1900 that the School should become an incorporated private business, with stock-holders investing beyond his limited capital. The 1900 Charter resulted, granted by the General Assembly of Rhode Island, October 26, 1900. Diman's sole proprietorship of St. George's was forever ended.

---

*The Rev. Mr. Diman served the Berkeley Chapel intermittently, officially and unofficially for many years. Over his time at St. George's he was, in fact if not in name, the Chaplain of the School.

The new charter called for "common stock in the amount of twenty thousand dollars, to be divided into shares at the par value of one hundred ($100) dollars each." There has been no record found as to how many shares of stock were sold, or to whom. It is known that Diman was the largest stock-holder and investors such as Hugh D. Auchincloss, Julien Davies and William Binney invested their money. None of these men had any need to make money from their investment in the School. Their greatest value was in the counsel and influence they brought Diman as the decision-making processes were extended to a broader framework. They were more than content, however, to leave the operation of the School firmly in Diman's hands.

For the boys and Masters, those days were unlike any experienced before or after. There were to be far better days ahead, growth in facilities, enrollment and prestige. Yet, the years 1897-1900 had their irretrievable *elan.*

As is evident from the earliest days of the School and throughout Diman's tenure, he was an enigmatic, complicated human being, whose reticence about his personal affairs ran deep. To describe him as a "closed-mouthed, patrician New England Yankee" is probably accurate. What is learnt about him is that his years at St. George's were his biography. His life and the School were so intrinsically intermingled that the two were inseparable.

The Hunter Avenue and Swann Villa periods were to come to an end as Diman plotted his next (and last) move to a new location. Sitting on the eastern veranda of Swann Villa, boys and Masters could look across First Beach Bay to Easton's Point, Middletown. Diman knew well the top of the hill sloping down to the Point. Its commanding view of Second (Sachuest) Beach and the Atlantic Ocean was among the most promising for miles around. His friend and fellow stock-holder, Julien T. Davies, had a summer house in the vicinity (Pinecroft, later a school dormitory.) Open land, sizeable summer houses and small farms occupied the Hilltop's acres. Diman determined to move the School to the Hilltop, away from the crowded, stifling conditions which were holding St. George's back from any further growth.

A major test of Diman's skill as a persuader lay ahead, a fact revealed years later. His Board of Directors were not convinced that the time was ripe for another move. With the exception of Bishop William McVickar, the Board was composed largely of successful businessmen. They were clearly aware of the Headmaster's desire to build a sizeable Georgian manor house overlooking the ocean and equip it as the kind of boarding school he had wanted all along. They were also aware that this involved not only building a facility but supporting it thereafter. From their vantage point, it was not economically prudent to attempt such a far-reaching move.

Nothing is extant to describe just how Diman came to convince his Board that the move had to be made – which it was in 1901. But in *The Diman Papers** a letter has been preserved from his friend, George Gordon King (Vice President of the Board and generous benefactor) recalling the Directors' opposition. It is dated September 11, 1905:

> "You must realize that the existing establishment on the
> Hill is there, not from any special desire on the part of
> your many friends, but from their great desire to further
> your plans."

These men had solid ground upon which to resist Diman's plans. There was shortly to be a stock-market "crash" (in 1901) which was something of a rehearsal in miniature for the massive one of 1929. The School was, after all, a business, affected by the crazy-quilt pattern of economics clinging to the times. Undoubtedly they were indisputably correct in their resistance to Diman. That they capitulated, giving Diman the go-ahead to move to Middletown and build "Old School," was, as King implies, based solely upon their faith in him and his brilliant record of overcoming strategic odds. The venture succeeded, giving St. George's School one of the choicest pieces of real estate in the country for a campus. In hindsight, Diman's victory over the Board's caution had to be shared with them. After all, they could very well have postponed his plans, even scuttled them, and he would have been somewhat hard put to move ahead. It was not be the last time by any means that Diman convinced boards of trustees, faculties, friends, benefactors and others to join him in risk ventures about which they had reservations.

**The Diman Papers* is the title given a suitcase crammed, with Diman's mementos, clippings and personal references, in the keeping of the Portsmouth Abbey School. A somewhat smaller portion of this material involves his life at St. George's School than his later years at the Abbey.

The year 1901 has loomed large in the developing history of the School. Not only was Old School built and surrounding land acquired, but, intrinsically important to the School, Diman began surrounding himself with colleagues sharing his visions and giving St. George's School its impetus toward a stature far beyond its small beginnings.

ST. GEORGE'S SCHOOL
Sketch of Old School – Catalogue, 1901-02

CHAPTER TWO

Growth and Challenge
1901 - 1907

THE SPRING OF 1901 found St. George's boys and Masters antici-
pating the move to the Hilltop, just under two miles from Swann
Villa. On frequent walks past First Beach, up the hill on Purgatory
Road to Second Beach and Sachuest Point in Middletown, they saw
Old School rising on the Hilltop. In May 1901, a student observed in
The Dragon, in one of its last editions from Swann Villa:
> "As we look out of our school-room windows, the
> walls of our new quarters loom up in the distance. The
> first story is up and the work is well under way."

Old School, the "new quarters," was the first purpose-built facility the
five-year-old St. George's School could claim. The Georgian-styled
manor house was designed by architect, Prescott O. Clarke, a cousin of
Diman. Its exterior offered the presence found at St. George's older sister
schools: St. Paul's, St. Mark's and Groton. Its interior was, for the most
part, much more Spartan. Specifically designed to house a boarding
school community, it was crammed with class rooms, dormitories, the
dining room and kitchen, offices and servants' rooms. The architects,
Clarke, Spaulding and Howe of Providence, had planned well and the
builders had constructed Old School with care.

A splendid spaciousness marked the Hilltop. It was attractive to visu-
alize adjacent rough pasture land converted into playing fields, or the
prospect for more and more buildings as the School grew — as all knew
it would.

Everything that is preserved concerning the move to Middletown's
Hilltop suggests an ebulliency, led by the Rev. John Byron Diman and
contagiously caught by the boys. The *leitmotif* was rehearsed and
communicated that St. George's had left its infancy and would soon take
its place among the great American schools.

The ebulliency was somewhat tempered among the members of the Board of Trustees.* Diman's persuasive powers had convinced them to make the move, but the School's financial base was far from secure. The newly incorporated Trustees had taken considerable risk in seeking funds from income producing bonds, notes, loans, and mortgages. Old School had cost $35,000, with land acquisitions and options on other badly needed property adding another $11,000. Enrollment had advanced modestly, to 40 from the previous year's 34. Tuition and board had gone up a slim $50.00 to $700.00 from 1900's charges. A $25,000 operating budget was expected to see the School through its first year on the Hilltop. Only one other building was acquired in 1901, "The Cottage" (which occupied a lot where the north tennis courts are located in 1986); it was moved to a location west of Old School. The Cottage became a dormitory for older boys and a Master; a chemistry laboratory was in its basement for a time. All this to the good, the School was in debt and would remain so for decades to come. Supportive as the Trustees were of the glowing prospects for St. George's, they reflected a note of serious concern over the School's financial condition and chose to proceed with caution.

Diman soon demonstrated that much sought-after ability in headmasters to be both "bricks-and-mortar" men while simultaneously accenting academic quality. He described the curriculum as "not so excessively classical as the one prevailing in most private schools a few years ago. English and not Latin is regarded as the basal language for all school work." This did not eliminate the Classics on the Hilltop. But what was emerging was St. George's interest in a more contemporary curriculum which included Modern Languages among its requirements. Latin and French were required for all six years (if a boy began in the First Form and continued through the Sixth). The choice was given between Greek and German, required for four years. United States, British, Greek and Roman history were required. In mathematics: Arithmetic, Algebra, Geometry and Trigonometry faced the boys. An array of scientific subjects confirmed Diman's awareness of the expanding knowledge from Charles Darwin's influences. Geology, Chemistry, Biology and Physics were taught; Nature Study and Geography had their curriculum roles. Drawing and Manual Training were less prominent; Sacred Studies,

---

*See Appendix B for a list of the School's Trustees, 1900-1986.

taught by Diman, was required but not taught in the usual academic manner.

Any greatness that St. George's could hope to achieve depended upon a first-rate faculty. On the Hilltop there was assembled a group to become the vital "Senior Faculty" over years to come.

Edward Sturtevant, a Massachusetts Institute of Technology graduate, began teaching Mathematics and Science in 1898 and remained with the School until 1939. Uniquely, as a Faculty member, he served on the Board of Trustees as Secretary/Treasurer from 1910-1939. His clear record-keeping served to convey the emerging life of St. George's in a vital fashion. In the early years, he was among the minority of married Masters, having married Miss Theodora Van Horne at the Berkeley Chapel in 1902.

Stephen P. Cabot came in 1901 to teach French and German. Educated at Harvard and on the Continent, he represented the type of well-to-do-young man drawn to boarding school life. He possessed the ability to teach a foreign language to the most inept of boys. In 1946 Leonard Bacon '05 remembered:

> "... with infinite courtesy and patience [Cabot] rubbed
> one's nose in a French verb till the effect of a subjunc-
> tive dawned on aboriginal darkness."

As will be explored in greater depth, Cabot was to play a prominent role in the School's life. He served as acting Headmaster on occasion and finally Headmaster, 1917-1926.

Russell H. Nevins, a Yale graduate, arrived in 1902 to teach Latin and Mathematics. An independently wealthy man, Nevins built his own house on upper Kane Avenue around 1912, which eventually became Haffner House, a dormitory. He, too, served as Headmaster (between 1926 and 1928) at a period when the School needed time to search for a permanent leader. He left St. George's in 1936, returning to his native Connecticut.

Brown graduate, Alan R. Wheeler, also came in 1902. A History teacher, he was said to be "obsessed with history" and conveyed to the boys the vitality of that discipline. He put into place Physical Education, where he was to be notably successful in grounding the School's athletic program on a firm basis. Wheeler's adeptness at gardening brought his touch to adorning the barren Hilltop with flowers, shrubs and trees, long before more professional landscaping efforts were undertaken. He married Miss Florence Williamson in 1905 to further enhance the status of married Masters. His 45 years at the school was the longest tenure in St. George's first 90 years.*

Greek was prominent in the Classical tradition and Arthur S. Roberts, a Dartmouth man, arrived to teach it in 1903. His 43 years at the School added strength to a growing roster of skilled Masters. His marriage, in 1907, to Helene Szelnar, in Budapest, Hungary, brought an international flavor to the Faculty. Their daughter, Ilonka, born in 1908, was the first (and through 1986, the only) child to be born in a St. George's Master's residence, Arden Hall.**

These Masters established the solid academic quality St. George's offered on the Hilltop. They had varying personalities and teaching styles. What they held in common was the ability to be multi-faceted men, serving over many years the ever-changing demands of a boarding school. It was upon them that Diman depended to reinforce the School's development into greater maturity.

One of the best happenings on the Hilltop in its earliest years was the return of Miss Emily Diman in 1904.*** (She had been at the School in 1896-1897 and was a frequent visitor.) Her return to live at St. George's for the next twenty-four years brought an effervescent female presence amidst the sea of pre-adolescent, adolescent and adult masculinity. Her role was essentially that of a surrogate headmaster's wife to her bachelor-headmaster brother. Admired by all, she specialized in nurturing, defending and supporting the needs of younger boys. Boys came to

---

*The Wheeler's son, George Williamson Wheeler '27, served the second longest tenure, 44 years, 1931-1975. The Wheeler Memorial Close, a garden area dedicated in 1958, in the quadrangle — enclosed by the Chapel, the Sacristy, the Cloisters to King Hall and the Student Center, honors Alan Wheeler for his many contributions to the life of the School.

**Ilonka Roberts married Paul T. Rogers, a faculty member in 1925-1926. Their son, W. S. R. Rogers '44, became a Faculty member 1956-1961, 1974-   . (The interruption was to become founding Headmaster of the Pingree School, South Hamilton, Massachusetts.)

***Miss Mirah M. Logan served as School "housemother" from 1901 until 1904, a lady of refinement and greatly interested in the welfare of the boys.

Student's sketch of what became known as Sixth Form House.
The Dragon, October 1903

St. George's as young as 12 (while some of the Sixth Formers were 18 and 19). There was a quiet poise and dignity in the way Emily Diman lent significance to reading to the boys, listening to their woes, serving them tea, and standing beside her brother greeting them morning after morning. She was remembered, however, as no "push-over," as she adroitly discerned the attempts to use her good offices as escapes from responsibilities or punishments. Her niche in the life of St. George's has been given permanency with the carving of her name among those of the Headmasters in the Chapel. Her brother often said, "My sister and I started a small School in Newport." It was his unmistakable way of giving just credit to Emily Diman for her impressive place in the School's life.*

Miss Julia Sheldon served the longest tenure of any woman at St. George's – Secretary to Mr. Diman, 1901-1910 and Registrar of the School, 1910-1940, each vital positions.

What was emerging over those early years was St. George's slowly but solidly gaining facilities, personnel and prestige. To Old School and The Cottage there was added in 1903 a gymnasium and a building at first known as the "New House" and later as "Sixth Form House." The Gymnasium was attached to the east side of the New House extending well into the (1986) Dragon Courtyard, and was also connected to Old School with a passageway. It had a bona-fide stage — a much-welcomed addition. The New House was multi-purpose in design, containing a Study Hall, class rooms, dormitories and Masters' quarters, a darkroom for photography, and a carpenter's shop.

The boys waxed eloquent about the presence of the new Gymnasium, "long-needed and an essential part of every school." Diman and the Trustees saw the new additions as essential to the School's advancement. School spirit got caught up with boys proclaiming, ". . . let us strive to put St. George's among the foremost schools in the country."

---

*Emily Diman's importance to the School was further evidenced, as will be detailed later, in that she was asked to remain after her brother's resignation in 1916. She did remain, under Headmasters Cabot and Nevins. Ten years younger than her brother (born in 1873), she returned to the family home in Providence after leaving St. George's in 1928. Surviving her brother by a scant two months, she died on 12 May 1949.

"School spirit" was a favorite topic at the time. It absorbed the attention of both Headmaster and Masters in chapel talks and in communications of various kinds with the boys:

> ". . . if we then show our school spirit in as many ways
> as possible and pass it on each year to succeeding forms,
> we may feel that we are helping toward the aim of the
> School — to produce boys with the highest standards
> of honor and ability."

The Rev. John Byron Diman's stature among headmasters was growing along with that of the School. In 1903, his *alma mater,* Brown University, gave him an honorary Master of Arts degree. He was cited, in the quaint terminology of the time, for his contributions "to desk and pulpit," translatable as "School and Church." The honor subtly recognized his astonishing abilities as an entrepreneur as well. In founding St. George's he had not acquired a wealthy man's country home, as the Rev. Henry Augustus Coit had most fortunately done in founding St. Paul's School. His considerable and restless energies were the driving force behind the development of the Hilltop, with the growing support of Trustees, Faculty, parents, and the larger public.

The benefactors aided the school not only financially but in other material ways. They gave books to the inadequate library, flags, boats, pianos; they entertained the boys for supper, parties and dances in nearby homes. Dr. Wolcott Gibbs, Professor of Science, *emeritus,* of Harvard, had returned to Newport and took a great interest in equipping the science laboratory with materials enhancing scientific study.

The boys who came to St. George's in the earliest years were mainly from New England. In a surprisingly short time the network of relative to relative, friend to friend, graduate to acquaintances, and parents to parents encouraged boys to attend the School. Diman was especially conscientious about inviting the recent graduates to return for frequent visits, and certain rooms were reserved for them. Common at the time was the practice of enrolling sons at birth in boarding schools – Cornelius Lee, the first recorded graduate, 1899, enrolled his son – Cornelius S. Lee '23 – in 1904. Diman, who served as what would later be called Director of Admissions, was always courteous in acknowledging this type of pre-registration but never promised future admission. By 1906, enrollment had gradually expanded up and down the East Coast and to the mid-West. Boys from New England, however, provided the largest segment of students.

Diman also served as Dean of Students, dealing constantly with misbehaving boys (of whom the records show St. George's had its appropriate share.) "Vandalism", in the form of broken windows and furniture, was decried by him, a note taken up by Masters and boys as well. Boys were frequently reminded that misbehavior was not only unacceptable but also a sign of a low sense of morality and bad school spirit. His Headmaster's letters to parents were masterpieces of tact with firmness. At times he was dealing with wealthy parents who wanted exceptions made for their sons. The most familiar of these came in their wanting sons released early from school to go abroad. Diman was firm and unyielding on keeping boys through the end of term, noting that otherwise havoc was wrought upon the morale of the school, boys' work was incomplete and the entire tenor of school life affected. He wrote firm letters to the parents of boys who were among the School's benefactors, insisting on better school performance for their sons, making a clear distinction between this theme and the next letters asking for money or other assistance.*

There were early attempts to follow the British boarding school model of prefects — older boys taking generous responsibilities for the governance of the boys. The school experimented with Rugby's, Dr. Thomas Arnold's, system of the entire Sixth Form being Prefects and leading the School onward and upward. The experiment was short-lived and Diman turned only to boys who exhibited the leadership skills and, of course, school spirit, required to manage school life. Beginning in 1908, the Prefect System became a permanent part of St. George's. (See Appendix E for list of Senior Prefects)

Prefects were permitted to "rough-up" boys if they deemed this kind

---

*Diman seemed more communicative in letters than in verbal expression. He openly lamented the amount of time and effort poured into letters, but they revealed him at his best communicative skill.

of punishment advisable.* Boys were also encouraged to settle disputes in boxing matches, "the ring" comprised of partisan friends. These proved Pyrrhic victories, if, as sometimes happened, younger boys defeated older ones. The ascendancy of older boys was deeply entrenched. Diman's major concern was over prefect ineffectiveness (a problem at the time), not roughing-up. He was also at a loss to understand why Masters could not control behavior as he did – with a mere look or his presence.

The pranks executed in boys' boarding schools are largely contained in oral tradition. They sometimes surface, years later, at times embellished, and with the perpetrators' identities finally disclosed. Boys' reputations were made — or broken — by the success or failure of pranks. One was long recalled from early Hilltop Days. It was at The Cottage, with Arthur S. Roberts the victim. Roberts was in charge of The Cottage, and his rooms were on the first floor directly above the Laboratory in the basement. An excellent chemistry student managed with considerable effort to pipe odoriferous fumes between the walls of The Cottage, occasioning a search on Roberts' part for dead rodents. Because St. George's was a tightly-run school and because boys dreaded having to face Diman, as if it were Judgment Day,** pranks were undertaken with some risk.

What is conveyed from those early days is life programmed to an intensity of study, monitored by Masters and Prefects. Study Hall included Saturdays for younger boys and deficient scholars of all Forms. The primacy of academic performance determined not only how much time was spent under directed Study Hall hours, but privileges as well. The time-honored discussions in Faculty meetings about "troubled students" went on. In a small school, there was no escaping the over-riding academic purpose for being at St. George's. Boys were being prepared mainly for Harvard, Yale, Princeton and Brown, with an occasional scientifically-oriented student going to one of the Institutes of Technology. The number of admissions to these colleges and universities was

---

*Physical punishment in American boarding schools never had the approval it did in Britain. Its acceptance there is seen in a *bas relief* from a choir stall in Sherborne Abbey depicting a master at the Sherborne School, Dorset, caning a pupil.

**In all fairness, it bears repetition that boys were often surprised to discover in Diman the kind of forgiveness which they never expected. His major interest was in having boys learn from their misdeeds and the consequent punishments.

high and the School's academic reputation steadily increasing.

Life on the Hilltop was not by any means totally programmed. In the early 1900's, boys were expected and encouraged to be self-motivated, to find innovative ways of using their spare time. Boys became interested in gardening and also in the wealth of small animals on the outskirts of the Hilltop. The farms bordering the school were replete with muskrats, rabbits and other small creatures. These were trapped and raised as pets in cast-off crates. Raising chickens was popular and was an accepted form of spare-time activity. Invention and innovation were meant for more than to consume time; also involved was the philosophy, so often reiterated by Diman, of being a part of the well-rounded development of young men.

The younger boys' rooms were small cubicles, partitioned in Old School by red and blue curtains (and later in Arden by green ones). This gave rise to the designations, Red, Blue and Green Dorms. Dormitory life was central in the life of the School, to be long remembered.

There were occasional expressions of discontent with boarding school life. In 1901 some younger boys, in a student debate, sought to prove a grievous error in the boarding school structure. They argued that there had to be something wrong with a system which,

> "...makes you go to bed when you want to stay up,
>
> and get up when you want to stay in bed."

Their forensic efforts, however well-argued, did not change the regime, so long established. (Others in later years would claim, *nor has it ever changed.*)

A St. George's institution, beginning in 1902 and continuing into the 1930's, was "The Pie House." It was located in Mrs. Clara Whitman's home on Paradise Avenue, not far from Second Beach, and the boys were permitted to trek there on Wednesday and Saturday afternoons after three o'clock. The Pie House represented a touch with the outside world. Candy, cocoa, milk, cake and, of course pie, were sold. Mrs. Whitman's special delicacy was her poached eggs with cinnamon toast. The walk back to the Hilltop, whether by road or through the fields, allowed the boys to build up their appetites for one of Nellie Brown's culinary treats in King Hall.

For many years (actually until St. George's became coeducational in 1972) there was no social occasion to match The Dance. *The Dragon's* reporters reviewed each Dance with consummate care. The obvious attraction was the gentle invasion of girls. The first Dance, in 1902, found 4 debutantes coming down from Providence and 2 from Boston, joining others from Newport. The United States Naval Training Station orchestra was commended for its superb playing. Over the years the Dance took on ever-increasing importance and was accompanied by suppers, games, and efforts to transform the event into a rehearsal for later social life in college and beyond. By 1904 the Dance could be held in the Gymnasium and may have been the occasion to re-institute dancing classes, as they had earlier been held at Swann Villa. For boys less gifted in the terpsichorean arts, staying up to the unconscionable hour of 1:00 A.M. and Saturday morning's games were highlights. While The Dance hardly rated a role in Newport's "Gilded Age", and while Diman certainly had no desire to encourage any aspects of *jeunesse doree* among the boys, there remained a social grace to The Dance of significance for many years. Its unique role was unmistakable.

While not officially an Episcopal Church School until 1907, St. George's had many of the aspects of that school league. Required attendance at Sunday Chapel was begun on the Hilltop, the "Chapel" being the Berkeley Memorial (St. Columba's) in Middletown. The five-mile round trip to that charming little edifice was an exercise both in religion and physical education. Its benefits were, however, not always appreciated. An anonymous reviewer in *The Dragon* was subtle but clear:

> "The road to church is very beautiful, but too much
> beauty is wearing. There is entirely too much road to
> church."

Daily services were held at the School, and Miss Diman played hymns for the boys to sing on Sunday afternoons. The second Diman sister, Louise, in 1905 wrote a School Hymn, "O Lord of Truth," which quickly became popular with all and has remained the official School Hymn ever since.* (See Appendix F)

---

*Louise Diman, 1869-1954, was not as active in the life of St. George's as Emily Diman. She founded the Animal Rescue League in Providence and was prominent in the affairs of the Congregational Church. As family historian, Louise Diman chronicled the generations of the Diman-Stimson families for posterity.

Drama had its allure for St. George's boys and, especially after the availability of a stage in the Gymnasium, it took on greater dimensions. Each year a major production was staged, productions which ranged from Richard Brinsley Sheridan's *The Rivals,* to comedies written and produced by the boys themselves (often with Masters also appearing.) Boys played both male and female roles for many years, and each play was subjected to the critical eye of *The Dragon's* reviewers. The art of reviewing was serious business, and care was taken to mention how well (or badly) the boys playing female roles had done. "The Red Dorm Theatre" offered a "school-grown" production which lured attendance by offering free candy. The reviewer praised the candy and dismissed the play as not worth attending.

Vocal and instrumental music was incorporated into life on the Hilltop. Francis J. McCloskey taught violin and led orchestras at St. George's from 1896 until 1928, a pioneer in what was to become an avid interest in music by students. Mr. Cabot enjoyed playing the piano and gave impromptu concerts. Accomplished musicians came to give concerts, including Mrs. Edward McDowell (sister of Russell H. Nevins and wife of the renowned American composer.)

The boys who attended St. George's were mostly from well-to-do-families. They set aside the comforts of home to live in simply-furnished dormitories, a part of Diman's conviction that boys were not to be pampered or coddled by too much comfort. He simply did not believe in making much of anyone's social position or wealth. "Hard work and hard play," together with treating everyone without social distinctions, became a rule of life on the Hilltop. Boys' allowances were strictly regulated; $2.12 a month was considered sufficient for boys in those early days. Some families tied allowances to academic performance, a practice which left the less-than-scholarly hard put for spending money.

However eager Diman was to keep boys from being over-indulged, a corps of servants still cared for the needs of the boys – cleaned their rooms, waited table and cared for the School's buildings and grounds. The servants were treated with respect, but were always servants. Many of them lived in small rooms in Old School, a situation corrected with more ample quarters in 1907.

As at Swann Villa, good fellowship among the boys was common, both because of St. George's small size and the "Club System." By 1903 the Sakonnet and Sachuest Clubs were formed.* Every student belonged to one or the other of them. Around the Clubs pivoted much of the intra-school activity in athletics, debates, and other forms of rivalry. Inevitably, a certain amount of rough-housing went on in the dormitories. *The Dragon* of April 1903 reported that the Blue Dormitory had been given six weeks of "bounds and forty marks" for taking advantage of Mr. Diman's being away and of experimenting with unrestrained behavior.

Until the Civil War, athletics were virtually nil in boarding schools. Headmasters had resisted any undue emphasis on athletics and it was, in fact, the students who instigated them after the Civil War.** The renewal of the Modern Olympics in 1896 propelled amateur athletics into new prominence, especially in schools and colleges. Over Diman's tenure (1896-1916) sports grew to be a sizeable part of every boarding school's life, but more slowly at St. George's than in many other schools.

At St. George's there was an on-going tension between the Headmaster and students over the role of competitive athletics. The Rev. John Byron Diman was a strongly-built man who looked like an athlete but was not one. He could contribute a run or two in Faculty-Boys baseball games but otherwise held some strong convictions about athletics directed toward their being integrated into the academic priorities of the school. He monitored games with an eye to "fair play" and "gentlemanly conduct" and games were played strictly by the rules and with every sign that boys knew how to win or lose with dignity. If a boy slipped too far academically, he was removed from a team, regardless of his importance, until he improved his classroom performance. In 1906, after a winning season of sports, Diman banned outside-the-school competition for a year on the grounds that "the tail is wagging the dog." When he felt the boys had caught the message and re-arranged their priorities for academics better, competitive sports were restored.

---

*These Indian names were appropriated from, Sakonnet, the river providing the eastern boundary of Aquidneck Island, upon which Newport, Middletown and Portsmouth are located, and Sachuest, the point of land east of Second Beach, below the Hilltop.

**James McLachlan's, *American Boarding Schools,* Charles Scribners, New York, 1970, explores this phenomenon.

Understanding boys as Diman did and committed to Physical Education as he was, he was by no means "anti-athletics." To the contrary, he worked towards the Hilltop's having the sports facilities the School had earlier lacked. Tennis courts were constructed in 1901, pasture land transformed into playing fields, and the Gymnasium in 1903 opened up indoor sports, especially playing the new (1891) game of basketball, Dr. James Naismith's invention.

Athletic competition continued with Rogers High School, the United States Naval Training Station, and Cloyne School, as well as the University School, Providence and other nearby high schools, as it had at Swann Villa. In 1902, St. George's began playing football with a school founded the year before, the Middlesex School, Concord, Massachusetts. The first game resulted in a 28-0 victory for St. George's. Gradually, Milton Academy in Milton, Massachusetts and the Noble and Greenough School in Dedham, Massachusetts were added to the list of sister boarding schools played in sports. Progress was impeded in mounting an extensive athletic program because "away" games involved over-night train rides and sometimes hotel accommodations. Alumni have joked about Diman's pecuniary propensity for finding the cheapest hotels in which to lodge teams. Within-the-school athletics flourished, which was heartily approved by the Headmaster. (Athletics took on a greater emphasis in later years when transportation was a less formidable obstacle and under Headmasters with a greater interest in its competitive aspects than Diman had.)

There was no question that the Hilltop and its environs was a choice location for a boarding school. This was obvious in the grandeur of the moors, beaches, islands and ocean readily seen from the hill. Middletown was considered "out in the country" in the early 1900's, a description Diman capitalized upon. It was for Diman a "perfect country setting." Parents in large cities such as Boston, New York and Philadelphia, wanted their sons to be educated away from the glitter and temptations of big city life. (Most of the major New England boarding schools were either in small towns or in rural settings.) Diman's chapel sermons made much of Nature "...with all her delights [and] inviting us to share her life with her, and boys living in the country ought to know how to accept this invitation." The sermonic note was clear:

> "I trust that in many a boy's heart the desire is born
> here to live worthily and to act manfully, and to strive

for truth and honor as long as his days shall last."

The presence of the Rev. John Byron Diman as Headmaster, the Faculty as Masters, and the staff of servants was visible to the boys. Behind the scenes, however, was a crucially significant group – the Board of Trustees – whom the boys saw or knew little. Upon these men fell much of the business operation of the school under the 1900 Charter which had made St. George's an educational business. That year the first Board had been formed. The Rt. Rev. William N. McVickar, Bishop of the Diocese of Rhode Island of the Protestant Episcopal Church, was named President; George Gordon King, Vice-President; Thomas G. Brown, Treasurer; Edward Sturtevant, Secretary; and Julien T. Davies the remaining member. In 1904, Hugh D. Auchincloss joined the Board. It was a group of businessmen and an attorney (Davies) as well as a Bishop.*

All the records of the time indicate that the Trustees preferred to be major decision-makers and leave the operation of the school in Diman's demonstrably capable hands. (There is also indication that Diman wanted it that way.) As few meetings as possible were held, the Trustees' acumen in business affairs sought; their influence was a hidden, but strategic, force.

In 1905, very much behind the scenes, a potential crisis was met, demonstrating the role of an active trustee. Diman was, in the terminology of the time "called" to take a position at St. Paul's School, Concord, New Hampshire, then headed by J. H. Coit. (The precise position offered Diman has been lost to both St. Paul's and St. George's histories, but indications suggest that his brilliant entrepreneurship as a schoolman would have been welcomed at St. Paul's.) It is clear that Diman did take the offer seriously and consulted Trustee, George Gordon King, a long-time friend and solid supporter.

A letter, dated 11 September 1905, from King to Diman, outlines King's urging that Diman turn down the offer. He reminds the Headmaster that:

---

*Bishop McVickar's presence on the Trustees did not make St. George's an Episcopal Church School. It did, however, serve as an indicator of the growing relationship to the church, to be officially recognized in 1907.

> "The existing establishment on the Hill is there, not
> from any special desire on the part of your many
> friends, but from their great desire to further your plans.
> It is this true affection for you which has made Greater
> St. George's; has brought it so prominently before the
> public, and will bring it more and more if existing con-
> ditions continue."

This letter provides some interesting insights into the School at the time and into Diman. King recognized Diman's genius and applauded it. But he had the foresight to see the "Greater St. George's," the School growing more prominent on a larger base than one man, even Diman, intrinsically important as he was to the school. The thrust of the letter conveyed that Diman was needed, he should not leave until the School was out of debt (no one wanted him ever to leave, King notes), and a friendly counsel for patience on the Headmaster's part as to the slow growth of the School.

Diman chafed under slow growth; he was restless to move and to grow, carrying the School along with him. St. George's had not grown at the pace he desired, but King's letter* was reassuring at that point:

> "There is no reason why, in a few years, St. George's
> should not be as large as you desire, and it would then
> give you much added responsibility...Consider the
> reasons; how many there are [for Diman to stay at St.
> George's], and every one most forcible."

Diman stayed at St. George's, but the restlessness, which appeared as an undercurrent in connection with his St. Paul's "call," was increasingly evident.

Diman began sounding out the Trustees in 1905 concerning sabbatical leaves for the Faculty. He was aware both of the endless demands upon them in regard to teaching, dormitory life, coaching, tutoring and com-

---

*The letter-writer, George Gordon King, divided his time between New York and New-port and was known as a generous benefactor to educational institutions. His nephew, Frederic Rhinelander King '04, a New York City architect, became one of the first graduates to serve as a Trustee. His grandnephew, the Rev. Jonathan LeRoy King, graduated in 1947, an example of a family's extended interest in St. George's School.

mittee work and the restrictions placed upon their personal lives. The desirability of a year away from the School, "without loss of compensation or detriment in any way to (a Master's) position in the School," he saw as a growing need. He was especially eager that Masters get into environments different from the Hilltop – go abroad, get into large cities – and improve their skills and perspectives. The Trustees were sympathetic, but it was 1908 before sabbatical leaves were eventually instituted.

There was little doubt that Diman had hoped for more facilities beyond those built in 1903. In the Trustees' Annual Report of 1905, this was acknowledged by that body:

> "It is the desire of the Head Master that in course of
> time the school shall be further enlarged. The Trustees
> are in accord with this wish; but before launching out
> on further expense it is the hope that all the large debt
> incurred shall be materially reduced."

Thus it was that the problem of overcrowded dormitories continued to haunt the School not only in the early 1900's but for years afterwards. In 1906 the enrollment was 88 boys with only two of them day boys. The reach beyond New England had brought a few from North Carolina and Ohio, together with one English student. Boys could no longer conveniently be sent home to Providence, Fall River or Boston upon an outbreak of chicken pox, measles or scarlet fever, but had to be returned to crowded dormitories as soon as possible. Diman's advocacy for expansion was unrelenting, his patience tested, his Trustees sympathetic but cautious.

A part of the problem was that no single benefactor had ever given a sizable amount of money to St. George's to build a facility. In 1906 signs that this was to change loomed large. Negotiations began for the gifts which resulted, in 1907, in a new dormitory (Arden Hall) and a dining hall (King Hall). Indeed, 1907 went down in St. George's history as a benchmark year, for it also found the School re-chartered as a private, non-profit educational institution.

King Hall

The Rev. John Byron Diman's Last Years
1907 - 1917

S T. GEORGE'S FOUNDING HEADMASTER spoke constantly of the School's becoming large. How large was never precisely identified, but certainly greater than the enrollment of 88 boys attained in 1906. Actually, achieving this size was a major gain, considering St. George's humble origins and constantly overcrowded facilities. Diman's visions were always large-scaled, embracing the School's growing to national prominence. Endicott Peabody had founded Groton in 1884 with the financial backing of his father's partner, J.P. Morgan, and an outright gift of sizeable acres of land. Groton, more than any other school, had come to serve as the model of the successful American boarding school. Diman gave no indication that he wanted St. George's to be a Groton "clone", but rather that it should grow in its own way and directions.

The year 1907 saw his hopes given impetus by three significant events: the building of Arden Hall as a dormitory, King Hall (with attached Kitchen/Servants' Wing) as the dining hall,* and the re-chartering of St. George's as a non-profit educational institution affiliated with the Protestant Episcopal Church Schools. In that one year more progress was made than at any previous time. It was for Diman, in particular, an exhausting year. In Dimanesque-style he juggled the unending duties of Headmaster with those of representing the Trustees in the often minute details of managing construction and brokering the new Charter. Despite all this, he managed to get to Europe in the Summer of 1907 to attend Arthur Roberts' marriage to Hélène Szelnar in Budapest. Upon returning in September he was stricken with typhoid fever and laid low until December. Yet, Diman and the whole School were buoyed up by the

---

*The original dining hall was in Old School, in what is now the Common Room (and had served in between as the library), with the present faculty room as the kitchen.

progress made in 1907.

The building of Arden Hall became a story of strategy, negotiations and success completely new in St. George's history. It involved a man outside the immediate and small circumference of the School's constituency. William M. Wood had sent his son, also William, to St. George's — he graduated in 1911 — and a second son, Cornelius came later — graduating in 1913. Wood and his wife became very interested in the School and contacted Diman about "expressing that interest in some substantial way." From that overture emerged a proposed gift of $75,000 which Diman suggested be used for a badly needed dormitory. The negotiations were barely underway when a snag was encountered. Wood registered distress over something he said he had not realized — that St. George's was a stock-holder-operated business (as provided for in the 1900 Charter) rather than a non-profit educational institution. He made his point crystal clear:

> "It was a great disappointment to me to learn of the commercial aspect of your most delightful school. I was under the impression that like Groton it was in the hands of Trustees and could receive benefactions in a way satisfactory to the beneficiaries . . . This commercial feature . . . was an unlooked for barrier."

Wood also had some reservations about the sizable indebtedness St. George's had incurred upon moving to the Hilltop. A highly successful business executive, President of the American Woolen Company of Boston, Wood attached to his interest in the School his personal views of fiscal management.

It fell to Diman to deal with Wood on behalf of the Trustees. He went to great lengths to explain everything Wood wanted to know about the School. The "profit-making" aspect of St. George's, he pointed out, was more of a convenience than an attempt by any stockholders to make money off the School. He identified himself as the largest stockholder with the others either his close friends or friends of the School. Diman made no pretense to having magic solutions to offer that would clear up the indebtedness. He proved successful in allaying the new donor's fears, and Wood agreed to give his donation towards the new dormitory. He specified two important conditions: that the building be forever debt-free and that the land upon which it was built also be free of any liens or encumbrances. The name "Arden" was chosen because

Mr. and Mrs. Wood's estate in Andover, Massachusetts bore that name.

The intense and highly detailed negotiations between Diman and Wood revealed much about both men. The two obviously respected one another, as was apparent in the way they handled the frank discussions of agreement and disagreement. Wood's style, and insistence of "crossing every 't' and dotting every 'i'," was the reverse of Diman's penchant to move in quickly, nail something down and leave the details for later on. Wood's more "prudent" approach served as a healthy counter-balance to Diman's. The experience proved a valuable trial run for dealing with benefactors removed from the heart-center of School life. The Arden Episode was one known all too well by headmasters — walking a tight-rope between a no-nonsense benefactor and a sizable gift, urgently needed. In this case, both men won, and the School profited from their individual approaches.

In building King Hall in 1907, the situation was quite the reverse from Arden Hall. George Gordon King, a Trustee, and his sister, Mrs. Louis McCagg, offered a gift of $50,000 towards constructing a dining facility, to be given in memory of their parents, Edward and Mary LeRoy King.* The result was the gracious "Great-Hall-styled" building, to rank as one of St. George's most attractive buildings. The negotiations were "in-house" and minimal, requiring only an additional $25,000, added to the original gift, to complete the Kitchen/Servants' Wing. Cloisters were also given by the Kings to link Old School and King Hall.

William M. Wood's objections to the "commercial aspect" of St. George's precipitated the move for it to become a non-profit educational institution. There was general support for this change. It necessitated selling the School's stock back to the stockholders at a fair price, and re-chartering St. George's. No problems were encountered selling the stock (Diman was the largest shareholder), but it took time to "broker" the new Charter through attorneys and politicians in the General Assem-

---

*The King Family gave many benefactions to the City of Newport, including their estate (an Italian-styled villa by Richard Upjohn, overlooking Spring Street) to house Newport's public library – and much later to become a major Senior Citizen's center.

bly of the State of Rhode Island and Providence Plantations. Diman was the basic person involved on the part of the School. With amazing patience, he worked on the innumerable details for several months.

An important by-product of having to go through the new Charter process was explaining to an outside world what St. George's was and wanted to do. One Rhode Island legislator who proved helpful was Theodore F. Green (later United States senator). In March 1907 Diman communicated to Green what was tantamount to the founding Headmaster's own charter for the School, but one never written into the official Charter. He felt called upon to explain with care that he did not want St. George's to be one for rich boys only:

> "It is my earnest hope and desire that the school may
> not only be a large one, but that it may throw open its
> doors to boys who are not the sons of rich parents and
> that such boys may eventually constitute a considerable
> part of its membership."

Diman was not "politicking" for passage of the Charter in expressing this desire; it was a wish he always had during his entire career, for the Portsmouth Priory School as well as St. George's.* He realized that a lack of endowment was the major impediment to becoming a cosmopolitan School for all – it took every bit of income, plus some borrowing, to manage current expenses and develop buildings and facilities. That Diman was able to do what he did, in the light of sizable debts, remained a tribute to the man's entrepreneurial abilities.**

The 1907 Charter made St. George's not only a non-profit educational

---

*In his eightieth year, semi-retired as headmaster of the Portsmouth Priory School, Diman wrote regretfully in 1943:

> ". . . the greatest disappointment of my school career has been that
> the schools with which I have been most closely connected have
> always been classed [truly so, unfortunately] as 'expensive schools.' I
> have never ceased to hope that they might become schools for the
> rank and file of our people with a fair sprinkling of the definitely
> rich and the definitely poor on either side of this general average."

It was small comfort to Diman that this idealistic hope, as old as the earliest British public schools, was rarely achieved either in Britain or America.

**In a later era, the Astor Fellowships, given in the name of Diman's former student and close friend, Vincent Astor '10, have provided, along with other funding, substantial scholarship help for students at St. George's.

institution but linked it to the Protestant Episcopal Church Schools. In founding his School in 1896, Diman had no intention of affiliating with any denomination.* The 1900 Charter had not made St. George's a Church School, even though Rhode Island's Bishop William N. McVickar became President of the Board and Episcopal Deacon Diman, Chairman of the Board. (It was uncommon for even the intentional Episcopal Church Schools to have a Bishop in such an influential position. It was also unusual to have the Headmaster as Chairman of the Board, a position to be held by no other St. George's Headmaster. This created a clergy dominance which would later provide problems for St. George's.) Just why Diman changed his mind and wanted a church connection remains undocumented and thus unclear. The 1907 Charter specified the School as "being in conformity with the doctrines of the Protestant Episcopal Church", an ambiguity in terms of the actual operation of the School. The provisions for implementing that relationship remained unspecified.

The result was that St. George's continued, *de facto* rather than *de jure,* some familiar practices of Episcopal Schools. They included: required Chapel attendance and required courses in Religious Studies under the general guidelines of Episcopalianism. The new Charter did not include anything specifying that the Headmaster had to be an Episcopalian priest, or even an Episcopalian layman, contrary to those of some sister schools. (The latter issue would arise in 1917 in conjunction with the appointment of Stephen P. Cabot as Headmaster, who was neither a priest nor an Episcopalian.) St. George's reputation as an *inde-*

---

*In a brochure Diman put out in June 1896, he noted:
> "Religious training and instruction will be positive, systematic and
> regular, but the School will not be a denominational one. Unless it
> is otherwise desired by parents, boys will attend the services of the
> Episcopal Church." (They did, first at Trinity Church, Newport and
> later at St. Columba's, Middletown.)

Diman's "Purposes for the School" (also 1896) is couched in secular language but reveals his religious intentions:
> "To teach a reverent attitude toward life, even to the so-called
> common-place things, respect for all members of the human family,
> just and fair dealings with others, truthfulness that is deeper than
> mere outward expression, the dignity of simple living, respect for
> hard play and hard work, and the value of persistent effort in over-
> coming difficulties."

pendent Episcopal School was a reputation rooted in part in what appears to be a deliberately ambiguous second Charter.

In 1907, there was a sense of the School's having finally arrived in league with Groton, St. Paul's, St. Mark's and other better known Episcopal Schools.

The year 1907 was possibly Diman's greatest in terms of the progress made by St. George's. It was a benchmark year, a coming of age as it were, a time of singular significance.

The School Year, 1907-1908, opened later than scheduled, awaiting the completion of Arden Hall and due to Diman's illness. He had contracted typhoid fever and had to convalesce until December. Because he was residing in Old School and could not be moved until October (when school finally opened), the building had first to be fumigated against the then seriously contagious disease. King Hall was completed in time for the opening of the Winter Term in January 1908. Tuition, board and fees advanced from 1906's $730.00 to $912.00; the Faculty increased by one full-time master to fourteen, including three part-time. Enrollment went up twenty-five boys to 112, with only 3 day boys.

Another St. George's faculty stalwart, Paul T. Christie, arrived in 1907, to give thirty-six years to the School. A highly regarded teacher of French with a degree from Harvard, he also made his mark coaching gymnastics and (after 1925) swimming. Christie completed the Faculty sextette of Sturtevant, Cabot, Nevins, A.R. Wheeler and Roberts: these men would bring the School a needed continuity for many years to come. Herbert F. Preston, a Harvard graduate and studies abroad, came to teach Latin, German and History in 1910, remaining until 1947. Preston's interest in the medieval, prompted him to introduce the Yule Feast, which became the Christmas Festival, an annual institution at St. George's through to the present. For many years he was Chairman of the Disciplinary Committee, a demanding task. William H. Drury, an Art master with his background from the Rhode Island School of Design and the Museum School in Boston, came in 1915 to remain thirty-eight years. Harold Noel Arrowsmith '04, became the first alumnus to return to teach at St. George's, teaching French and German from 1909 until 1912. The Faculty numbered never more than 14 between 1907 and 1916, and the enrollment ranged from 111 to 138 in the same period. The School was set up to accommodate 125 boarders. (The number of day boys was never more than 5; the emphasis was on St. George's as a boarding school.)

As Senior Faculty stayed on, the need for sabbaticals became apparent. It was common for Masters to tutor boys over the summer, some even going to Europe with families. Extended time off was a luxury for some. The unceasing twenty-four-hours-a-day regimen of teaching, dormitory duty, coaching and committee work, left little time for the Masters to enrich themselves academically or in any other way. (Headmasters, like Dr. Samuel Drury at St. Paul's, worried about men becoming stagnated in a world dominated by "seething youth." Headmasters sought ways to give teachers sabbaticals within the constraints of tight budgets.) This was formalized in 1908 at St. George's with Sabbatical Years offered to those with six continuous years of service to the School. No financial or other loss was to be incurred because of a sabbatical. The program was welcomed and constructively used.

The more solidly St. George's became accepted as a major boarding school, the more it had to face the mixed motivations of parents who sent their boys away to school — an issue of universal and timeless proportions still. In the early 1900's, the desire for social prestige was openly attached to a boarding school education. Headmasters became exercised to the point of irritation at the notion that boarding schools were "finishing schools" for the rich. They fought hard against the residue of attachment to "polite learning" which had been accepted by many in the 19th century. Polite learning proposed that young gentlemen were being polished with a minimum of intellectualized disciplining as a part of the rite of passage to upward social mobility. Among some of the wealthy parents of boys attending boarding schools, the disdain of disciplined study was undisguised. They plagued headmasters and masters with objections to their sons' being required to meet academic standards. Others, caught up in a fashion of the time, expressed fear that too much studying would drive boys insane. This kind of expression made life for the schools difficult in striving for academic excellence.

The Rev. John Byron Diman found it a matter of integrity as well as educational policy to unrelentingly promote academic excellence at St. George's School. He was an idealist. He established idealistic goals for himself and for the School. His Headmaster's letters to parents reflected the hard row the School had to hoe to keep academic integrity alive.

With adroitness and tact but with an ever-present honesty, Diman commended or chastised as he felt needed. Yes, James was adjusting well to life at the School; no, William was not measuring up to St. George's standards. A letter sent at the close of the 1909-1910 year is an example:

> "We have carefully gone through [unnamed's] examinations for our Third Form. He passed well in Geography and, with some indulgence, his paper in English may be considered as passed, but he is a little deficient in Latin and Mathematics. In fact, in Latin he has no knowledge of the very elements, and in that subject he should have a very thorough drill beginning at the very beginning of an elementary book. The same remarks would apply, though with not quite so much force, to his Mathematics. He evidently is rusty in his Arithmetic and should review that subject in its elements."

There remained in this boy's case some question that he would go on to the Fourth Form, and Diman wanted to give fair warning of the student's deficiencies. There seemed no limit to what he wanted to do to help students. In a December 1912 letter, he offered to have Masters "send home a daily report" of a day student's work. For Diman to write, "I am sorry to say that we are not permitted . . . to make departures from the rule," conveyed to parents that their sons would neither be academically nor socially indulged. Tutoring was proposed both for those needing remedial help and those needing to settle down because they were "lazy" – an oft-used word – or unmotivated, or both.

There was a problem with the quality of preparation some boys brought to St. George's. The answer Diman had was not to yield on the standards but to double the efforts to help boys succeed. This elicited letters from boys to parents plaintive in their expressions of academic challenge. A boy of the Class of 1915, who later became a nationally recognized industrialist, wrote his parents:

> ". . . I am working so hard and obtain such poor results that my mental powers are quite discouraged. But I shall never give up."

And in a later letter, having seen his English grade rise to a 75 after "special voluntary work till 3:30 every afternoon," he wrote to his father:

> "I am now working very hard at my tasks and I am

giving but little thought to anything but lessons."

In the 1910's there was an emphasis on "Formlessness" — boys placed in a Form (class) neither by virtue of age nor parental request, but by merit. This was done not only to help the boy achieve maturity academically but also personally and socially. Boys were under constant threat of having privileges denied, of being returned to Study Hall (from which they may have recently escaped), or denied coveted athletic and extra-curricular participation. In 1913, the entire Fifth Form was threatened with Saturday Night Study Hall — held regularly only for First through Fourth Forms — unless they showed mass improvement.

On the positive side, Masters were expected to spend extra time tutoring boys. Somehow, even with the multiplicity of duties, they managed to devote amazing amounts of time remedying boys' deficiencies. This was to be noted by graduates in later years (if not at the time) as yeoman service and appreciated.

Despite all the effort expended on the part of the Faculty, there were periods of abysmally weak academic achievement in the second decade of the 20th century at St. George's. At one point, seven-eighths of the boys failed at least one subject, and the School's scholarship average fell to slightly over 60%. The situation was eventually turned around, attributable in no small measure to a refusal to lower standards and incredible amounts of time spent by the Faculty in remedial work with students. The number of boys successfully prepared for Harvard, Yale, Princeton and other first-rate colleges underscored the success of the attack on academic mediocrity.

The relatively simple life of St. George's earliest days changed into a more complicated one of multiple activities. This required the development of more sophisticated forms of student government. While boys' lives remained largely regimented by the Headmaster and the Masters, incipient forms of student governance came into being. The four hundred year history of school prefects in the British public schools was used as the basic model. Prefects were meant to be models of constructive behavior, supporters of strong School spirit, monitors of the behavior of other students, and a link between the Headmaster, Faculty and the student body. The earliest efforts were, to Diman's disappointment, less than successful. There was a reluctance on the part of Prefects to accept

-Jacob Bates Abbott '13

The Dragon, December 1911

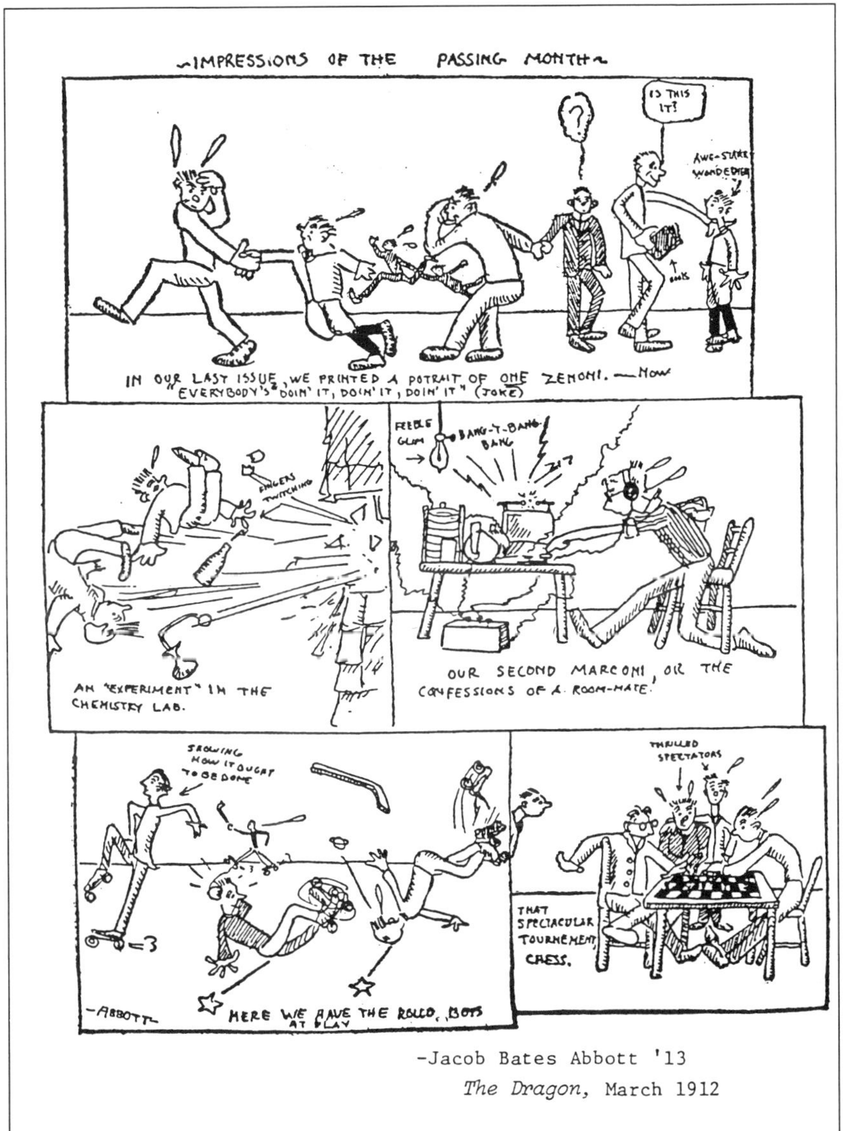

-Jacob Bates Abbott '13

The Dragon, March 1912

responsibilities which brought them into clashes with their peers. At one point, Dr. Thomas Arnold's prefect plan at Rugby School was tried — the whole Sixth Form as prefects. This was abandoned because it became plain that many St. George's boys were simply not equipped to be leaders (as the plan was found wanting elsewhere.) It took time, but eventually the prefect system got rooted and student governance established. Laurance David Redway '08 was the first Senior Prefect. Prescott Sheldon Bush, Senior Prefect, 1912-1913, brought his considerable leadership skills to usefulness and later became United States senator from Connecticut.*

The Lance, the School's yearbook, began in 1908. At first published biennially, it became an annual in 1912. Successive years of staffs sought to preserve as many aspects of School life as possible through the printed word and photography. It became a major source of preserving the School's history. "The Review of the Year" was a chronicle of major events. An emphasis upon the graduating VIth Formers sought to lift up their life at St. George's.

The School's oldest publication, *The Dragon,* continued month by month to give boys the experience of writing and editing a literary magazine. Through it the increasingly broad spectrum of boys' interests was communicated – e.g. trips abroad and the developing airplane. Occasionally a clever artist or cartoonist appeared. Jacob Bates Abbot '13 whimsically caricatured School life. As a 13 year-old Second Former, the later benefactor John Nicholas Brown '18, wrote an excellent article, "The Great Swamp Fight," about King Philip's War in Rhode Island. Boys had a lot of fun with the magazine, making up jokes and reporting on the minor eccentricities of classmates. John G. Wright '10 was the centerpiece of a February 1908 joke:

"Mr. Wheeler: 'What was the Peace of Paris?'

Wright, J: 'There were several pieces of Paris.' "

They would not have made *Life,* but jokes did leaven the life of St. George's boys and Masters.

Poetry was popular, with most of it in a serious vein. In November

---

*His son, George Bush, became Vice-President of the United States under President Ronald W. Reagan.

1913, Fifth Former Ronald W. Hoskier '14 contributed a poem, "Unto Death."

> "The shades of night fell swiftly
>   The moon large and red,
> It shone on the bloody bayonets,
>   It shone on the heaps of dead,
> It shone on a great roan charger
>   That stood by his master's side —
> Who tossed his arms and fought for breath
>   Till at the last he died."

The grim note Hoskier sounded was tragically fulfilled in his own life. On 21 April 1917, as a volunteer in the French Lafayette Escadrille, he was killed when his two-seater Morane Parasol plane crashed.

Both *The Lance* and *The Dragon* kept careful tabs on St. George's athletic progress. Baseball averages were recorded — Senior Prefect Bush had a .403 and Mr. Russell Nevins a .000 in the Spring of 1913. Beating Middlesex in football 6-0 in 1912 brought a victory celebration to the Hilltop. Moses Brown, Pomfret and Roxbury Latin were added as rivals

athletics were in full force. The need for a proper athletic field had been the subject of editorials in *The Dragon* persistently. The need was met in 1913 when Charles T. Crocker gave funds for a purpose-built field in the names of his sons, Bigelow '13 and Charles T. III '15, and his nephew Weyman '14. It was appropriately named Crocker Field.

The vitality of athletics was further evidenced in a ground-swell for a gymnasium larger than the 1903 one attached to Sixth Form House.*

In 1914 Mrs. John Nicholas Brown Sr. gave two squash courts and an enclosed playground for the younger boys. Hockey was played on nearby ponds, something of a problem with the erratic New England

---

*A genealogy of gymnasiums looks like an intricate family tree:

1903 – first gymnasium, attached to Sixth Form House, converted in 1911 into a Schoolroom; eventually torn down in 1922 and its timbers used to construct the Boat House at Third Beach.

1911 – Auchincloss Gymnasium's foundation was poured but funds ran out which kept it from being completed until 1914.

1911 – A temporary wooden gymnasium was constructed just north of the Auchincloss foundation. It was designed so that it could be later remodeled into a dormitory. It was used until 1914 as a gymnasium and in 1918 moved across to upper Kane Avenue to become Twenty House.

coastal weather. Boating, sailing and crew found the nearby waters of the Sakonnet River and Second Beach a natural habitat. Tennis continued as popular as ever, as did soccer and gymnastics. Boyish enthusiasm proclaimed successions of annual individual sports' heroes as *Victor Ludorum* – Conqueror of the Games. It appeared that Diman had relented somewhat on tying games so strictly to Physical Education; they had their own growing role in School life.

The completion, in 1914, of the solid, handsome brick Auchincloss Gymnasium brought St. George's athletic facilities in league with older boarding schools. Auchincloss became, as well, the gathering center for large School meetings: Sunday Services in inclement weather, lectures, and Prize Days on occasion. Named for Hugh D. Auchincloss, a trustee from 1904 until his death in 1913, he and Mrs. Auchincloss had provided the major gift making the building possible. In 1912, however, alumni were solicited for the first time to help complete the facility – which they did.

St. George's was in an anomalous situation for a newly related church school – it had no Chapel. Seeing no way to have a Chapel large enough to accommodate the entire School, Diman personally gave the funds to build The Little Chapel, completed in 1911. It seated about forty, and was used for Services of Holy Communion, Bible Study, Form meetings, and other small group occasions. Sunday services continued at St. Columba's but were for a time not required of Fifth and Sixth Formers.

In 1910 Diman was on sabbatical. In Germany he came in contact with a form of education which intrigued him. *The Real Gymnasium* schools offered a carefully synchronized form of work and education for lower income families. Given the benefits of both formal education and the opportunity to work in alternative periods, the scheme was pondered by Diman after his return home. Blocked from fulfilling his dream of helping less fortunate students to attend St. George's, he proposed a vocational school to the School Board of Fall River, Massachusetts, through its Superintendent, Everett B. Durfee. In 1912, he gave $2,500 towards the purchase of equipment to teach mechanical, electrical and woodworking skills to boys who would go to school a week and work a week, without loss of pay. The School Board provided a room in the basement of the John J. McDonough School and Diman gave another $1800 for the salary of the teacher. He was instrumental in gaining the cooperation of the mill and factory owners in the venture.

The school was successful from the start. Diman kept up his share of the funding for three years. In 1964 a new $3,500,000 facility attested to the continuing importance of vocational education, and was given the name, The Diman Regional Vocational Technical High School.

Diman's initiation of the Fall River school received national attention. It expressed his constant concern for children caught in cycles of child labor, unable to get a basic education and gave impetus to Vocational Education on the Secondary School level in this country.* In his obituary in *The New York Herald Tribune,* 19 March 1949, it was stated that Diman had begun the vocational school:

> ". . . as a sort of compensation for the atmosphere of
> wealth that came to surround St. George's."

This was undeniably true. It was clear all along that Diman took pardonable pride in his contributions to vocational education.**

Fifteen days after Prize Day, 28 June 1914, the assassination of Archduke Francis Ferdinand, heir presumptive to the throne of Austria-Hungary, took place in Sarajevo, capital of Bosnia Province. There was little indication on that Prize Day of how significantly this event would affect the life of St. George's School. Three years were to pass before, on 6 April 1917, the United States declared war on Germany. The School however, became involved in the War Effort in the Winter of 1914 through the formation of a Battalion of Infantry — one of the first in any private school. From 1914 until 1919, the Battalion continued, led by various officers available from the military services in Newport and environs. In time, all physically able St. George's boys participated in what came to be called "Military Drill."

---

*Diman wanted St. George's students to be able to use their hands in practical skills. He pushed the development of Manual Training and, eventually, shop work in machines and electricity as well.

**Diman Vocational became coeducational in the 1940's. Later in life, while visiting the Fall River School and seeing both boys and girls at the School, Diman was said to have observed: "I wouldn't have done it this way, but it's all right; yes, all right."

Herbert French Preston of the Faculty, edited a book, *St. George's In The War.* It pays tribute both to those who died in the war and those who served in it. Preston expressed the passion for the Great War, the one "to end all wars":

> "The Great War has furnished an opportunity not given in ordinary times for the youth of this country to show their true mettle. The response to the call to serve will ever remain one of the glorious pages of American history."

Before World War I ended, 287 men connected with St. George's (80% of the Alumni) were in some form of war service. Sixteen gave their lives, including one Faculty member, Norman J. Merrill. Some of the older boys were eager to leave school and enlist in either the military or ambulance services. Before the United States entered the War, a number had gone into the Canadian Force's or in France's Lafayette Escadrille.

As early as the Fall term of 1914, St. George's students were rolling bandages for the American Red Cross. In the later years of the War, some stayed through the summer to tend the lawns of the School which had been turned into potato, corn and bean fields. Boys were discouraged from spending their allowances in such self-indulgence as Mrs. Whitman's Pie House and were encouraged instead to give to various War Causes. A St. George's ambulance, costing $750.00, was sent to France from funds raised by the boys. In time, a summer military training camp became popular. The boys' imaginations were stirred to write war stories, brimming with military action. Alumni serving in France sent back diaries and accounts of battles, further stimulating the support of the War by the boys and Masters.

The heavy head of steam built up for the War Effort was not always that easy to sustain. There were some boys for whom Military Drill was tedious, seven o'clock in the morning exercises disruptive; still others simply refused to take the Drill seriously. These "slackers," as they were labelled, were duly chastised by their peers as well as the Masters. Their behavior was held up as unpatriotic. "Let patriotism rule over all!" urged writers in *The Dragon,* as a rallying cry.

The Class of 1914 contributed the largest number to military service – thirty-two. From the 1911 and 1913 classes, six gave their lives, three from each class. Of those who died, eight were killed in action and eight while on duty but not in action (this included Norman Jesse Merrill of the Faculty.) Two brothers were lost, Galbraith Ward '11 and Marquand Ward '12.

A visible and fitting memorial to those dying in World War I was the Memorial Schoolhouse, completed in 1922.* Remembering those lost, through a building in which all are instructed, seemed a particularly appropriate expression of appreciation. The names of those who died were carved in oak wainscoting, in a design by Frederick Rhinelander King '04, on the walls of the foyer.** Leonard Bacon '05 contributed the verse inscribed above the names:

> "You who are passing by, a moment halt!
> These for their country perished. They are gone.
> If you have faith in courage without fault,
> Consider, and march on!"

St. George's involvement in World War I paralleled that of the nation – an intrinsic commitment to what was believed to be a "just war." The fervor had overtones of a Christian Crusade, one extolled from pulpit and classroom alike.

In the midst of the Great War, in 1916, the Rev. John Byron Diman resigned from the School he had founded and to which he had given twenty years of his life. He was fifty-two and at the peak of his career. The expectation that he would remain at St. George's into retirement in old age was shattered. *The Red & White,* seven years before, had engaged in some light-hearted "crystal-ball gazing" into the School's future. The student author had set 1945, when Diman would be seventy-eight, as the time when, "Mr. Diman resigned and Miss Diman left with him." Not meant to be taken seriously, the prediction that the Founder would "resign" proved surprisingly accurate. (Miss Diman did not, however, leave until 1928.)

At some point in the early Winter of 1916, Diman verbally informed Bishop James DeWolfe Perry, Jr., Bishop of Rhode Island and President

---

*The funds were given by alumni, masters and friends of the School.
**The names of those dying in World War II, the Korean War and the Vietnam War were inscribed later. (See Appendix D for names)

of the Board of Trustees, of his intention to resign as Headmaster.* Still convalescing from an emergency appendectomy, on 15 December 1915 in Chicago, Diman's activity at the School was considerably curtailed. As correspondence later revealed, Bishop Perry was understandably shocked at the prospect of Diman's departure; he urged him to reconsider. By April, however, it became clear to the Bishop that the Headmaster's decision was, if anything, even more deeply rooted. Diman's intentions were shared with two inner groups of the School: the Trustees, who would have not only to deal with the resignation but also the finding of a successor, and the Senior Masters. No official action was taken at this time.

In June, the Trustees reluctantly accepted Diman's resignation, but their action was not made public.** The Board members went on their various holidays over the Summer of 1916, the search for a successor begun, but no public notice of Diman's leaving was announced. Diman had stated that he wanted to leave "no later than September 1917," so there seemed to be adequate time to handle the situation.

As it happened, there was a possible successor on the horizon – the Rev. Remsen Brinckerhoff Ogilby, Headmaster of the Baguio School for American Boys, an Episcopal School in the Philippines. He appeared to be the ideal man to further everything Diman had done. Ogilby was not only an experienced schoolman, but also a fully-ordained Episcopal priest. He had taught at Groton and held bachelor and master degrees from Harvard. Ogilby was in the United States but was preparing to return to the Philippines in September. Diman was actively involved as an agent of the Trustees (he was, of course, Chairman of the Board) in the Headmaster search. All hopes were dashed by Fall, however, when Ogilby declined, his commitments to the Baguio School and Bishop Brent of the Philippines overriding any possibility of his serving St.

---

*Bishop Perry had a long and honored ecclesiastical career as Bishop of Rhode Island from 1911 on and from 1930 to 1937 as Presiding Bishop of the Protestant Episcopal Church. He served as President of the Trustees from 1911 until 1947, a consistently strong supporter of St. George's School.

**Col. Theodore G. Holcombe '16 has recalled (nearly seventy years later) his complete surprise when the news of Diman's resignation reached him the next fall when he was a Freshman at Harvard. There had been no indication the previous June that the Headmaster's resignation was impending.

George's.*

By October, Diman became very uneasy because his resignation was becoming known, questions asked, and no official answers forthcoming. He was exercised enough to track down Bishop Perry at the General Convention of the Episcopal Church in St. Louis, urging him to have the Trustees make public his decision to resign. Diman claimed that he had wanted the decision made known when he first spoke to the Bishop in the Winter, "so that before the opening of this School Year (1916-1917) fully eight months' notice would have been given to parents, graduates, boys and all friends of the School."

Another factor entered into the Trustees' search: Diman decided that he wanted to leave sooner, at the end of the Winter Term of 1916. Their hope for plenty of time to find a successor was thus ended. It was understandable why Diman wanted the earlier departure date. It remained a mystery how he had been able to pick up the heavy responsibilities he had assumed over the Summer, after his near-fatal operation of a few months before. Moving expeditiously, the Trustees decided to reach into the Faculty and appointed Stephen P. Cabot as Acting Headmaster, to be effective 1 January 1917. This was done in September, but they still did not make any official announcement of Diman's resignation or Cabot's appointment.**

On 15 November 1916, the Board finally announced, formally and officially in a printed letter, the Founding Headmaster's resignation:

> "It is with profound regret that the Trustees of St. George's School announce that the Rev. John B. Diman, founder of the School, has tendered his resignation as Head Master. The resignation, which has been accepted, is to take effect on January 1st 1917."

The Trustees went on to pay the kind of oblique tribute to Diman he

---

*Ogilby's long career in education was completed as President of Trinity College, Hartford, Connecticut, beginning in 1920.

**There is confusion about the long delay in announcing the resignation. Both Diman and the Trustees appear responsible for the procrastination – Diman in hedging on the timing, the Trustees in putting off any substantial action until pressured by Diman.

preferred.* It was one which linked him not only to the past but to St. George's future:

> "The Trustees take this opportunity to announce that the policies, standards, and ideals for the School of the future will be maintained as in the past, and the spirit infused by the Founder will be fostered and preserved."** And there was the futuristic aspect: "[The Trustees] look for a larger School in accordance with Mr. Diman's oft-repeated suggestion."

They specified "the completion of Arden Hall" (which actually became Diman Hall) in 1926, the gift of Vincent Astor; and the construction of "a new Schoolhouse" (completed in its exterior in 1921, but not occupied until 1922, when funds were eventually available to complete the interior).

The Trustees were openly concerned to accentuate the positive and eliminate undue concern that St. George's would be irreparably damaged by Diman's leaving. Ideally, the announcement would have been accompanied by the appointment of a permanent successor. The presence of Cabot, well-seasoned as a Master and Acting Headmaster, was one of most positive factors in the entire situation.

St. George's students were apprised of their Headmaster's resignation after the November announcements. A student editor in *The Dragon,* wrote:

> "It is with deep regret that we learned that Mr. Diman has resigned his position as headmaster of this school and will leave at the end of the term. We have always looked up to Mr. Diman as the life, the spirit, every impulse of which makes St. George's what it is."

Few tributes could have more cogently summarized the feeling that all had for Diman. The boys looked upon him as the model of the

---

*It was widely known that both Diman and Cabot possessed the "Yankee" trait of being uncomfortable with praise or compliments given to them (or to others.) An old saying applied to them:

"A compliment to the face is out of place."

**As will be seen, this was easier said than done. The perpetuation of the Diman Legacy did occur, especially through the legacy of Cabot and Nevins as Headmasters, the senior Faculty, and the Trustees. It did, however, prove a stumbling block in both 1916 and 1926 in the search for headmasters.

Christian Gentleman. They were fully aware that he had given the School its dynamism and had propelled it from obscurity into prominence. The boys would – and did – miss him.

A basic problem in attempting to understand Diman's leaving St. George's has always been his deep-seated reticence to divulge much about himself. There was nothing clear-cut about his reasons for resigning. Inklings began to slowly filter through, and some came many years afterwards.

Diman had asked himself if his "best work can be done in the same position [as a school Headmaster] in the future." His resignation suggested a negative response to that vital inquiry. He appeared somewhat overwhelmed by it all, as he communicated in October 1916 to the Trustees:

> "The Head Master must in the near future take up the problems connected with providing for more boys, the construction of new buildings, and raising money for these purposes...In spite of my sorrow, when thinking of laying down the work, I do not feel like continuing to give my time wholly and entirely to these needs...
> In recent years I have become increasingly interested in many subjects — educational and others* — for which I wish to have opportunity for study, perhaps some writing, and at any rate for more freedom in the use of my own time."

Beyond St. George's was a tight fellowship of Episcopal and Independent School Headmasters, among whom Diman was prominent. He apparently had not confided in them concerning his resignation. When the news became known, one of the most distinguished of them, the Rev. Dr. Samuel S. Drury, Rector of St. Paul's School, Concord, New Hampshire, and one of Diman's closest friends, wrote of the group's sense of loss:

> "It has been a shock to all of us school folk to know of your leaving St. George's. The loss to the corps of headmasters will be deep, if you plan permanently to withdraw. And yet, I have said often to myself while

---

*Diman did not appear ready to disclose that central to "others" was his long struggle with his religious faith — a discussion of which follows.

> thinking of you: 'He knows best; he's been at it a long time; he has built up a great School out of a handful of boys in a hired house. If he craves rest, he deserves it.'"

Drury did his own conjecturing as to the unexplained resignation of his friend:

> "Perhaps the constant dealings with the ultra-prosperous has got a trifle on your nerves!* Perhaps you insist on that mental expansion that is so hard to achieve in a crowd of seething youth...I honor your character so highly, that I know that you must be doing right —that absolute right which 'the world' can neither perceive nor really cares for."

The belief that Diman must have been doing "the right" — whatever it was — seemed to prevail. Among those who knew Diman best it became plain that his mind was indeed "unalterably" set upon leaving. Hindsight proposes that he experienced what came to be called "burn-out" in later years. He really did not want to face yet further rounds of fund-raising and administrative tasks needed to accomplish the continued advancement of St. George's. He wanted, and needed, a freedom denied him for twenty years as a headmaster. He found it by cutting himself free from the School he would never cease to love.

In December 1917, a year after leaving St. George's, the Rev. John Byron Diman took the most drastic personal step he was ever to take – he converted to the Roman Catholic faith. He described his conversion as "a long voyage." It was not a St. Paul-on-the-road-to-Damascus-instantaneous one. He had moved to Catholicism slowly, away from his family's Congregational-Unitarian-Episcopalian affiliations. Significantly, he later traced his interest in Catholicism to "soon after giving up my active ministerial work." That would make it around 1892, four years before he founded St. George's School, and after he had served as Deacon-in-Charge of the Berkeley Chapel (St. Columba's) in Middle-town. Effective and popular though he was in parish life, he did not take

---

*Drury's observation is particularly illuminating, coming as it did from the Head of what was probably the most socially prestigious school at the time.

to it as something he wanted to do permanently.* His religious certainties had been shaken by the important findings of Darwin, Huxley, Tyndall and other nineteenth century scientists. Their new and revolutionary theories cut across orthodox Episcopalian Christianity's tenets. Diman was interested in Science and committed to teaching it in his School. Buffeted about by the Science/Religion controversies growing around him he admitted that he did little to pursue his doubts. He lacked the penetrating intellectual curiosity and daring of his father, Prof. J. Lewis Diman, and he showed no taste for controversy *per se*. He acknowledged that he found an accommodation to his doubts — absorption in the growing Protestant emphasis on humanitarian service, a movement he liked as both optimistic and filled with good works. He described himself as interested for a time in what came to be called "Christian Socialism"; it resembled the Christian Social Action of the later 20th Century. The residual effect of this accommodation brought to him a life-long interest and commitment to social service and efforts to involve his schools in it.

As the sole instructor of Sacred Studies at St. George's, Diman appcarcd ablc to kccp his doubts out of his teaching   at least overtly. In company with many Church School teachers of the time, he rejected intellectualizing Religion and avoided anything resembling the new findings in Biblical Criticism which were electrifying the age. He concentrated on Bible stories, a bit of Church History and a lot of *The Book of Common Prayer*. It was a somewhat sophisticated form of evangelizing youth for Episcopalianism, and it went largely unquestioned.

Sometime around 1905, Diman paid a visit to a young friend, John LaFarge, studying for the Jesuit priesthood at St. Andrew-on-Hudson, Poughkeepsie, New York. He later counted the visit a vital one to his "religious voyage." LaFarge has recalled:

> "I don't know exactly why he came to St. Andrew to
> see me, except that he had always been sympathetic and
> was interested in the Catholic Church and had made

---

*Diman's friend and younger contemporary, Father John LaFarge, S.J., says in his book, *The Manner Is Ordinary* (1954), that Diman had talked with the young priest's mother about his uncertainty regarding what he wanted to do with his ministry. Mrs. LaFarge suggested that he start a school. The LaFarge's were prominent Newport Roman Catholics, the senior John LaFarge being the famous artist.

many inquiries about it."

In 1949, shortly before Diman's death, LaFarge had a talk with him at the Portsmouth Priory. Diman remembered the earlier visit as a turning point in his conversion.*

Diman's sympathy for Catholicism was known. This was clear to The Twenty Club, a group of some of New England's best known Episcopal clergymen and headmasters (with a bishop or two thrown in for good measure.) Diman had joined in 1909 but resigned from the Club in 1913.

In February 1909, he presented a paper, "The Right and Wrong Methods of Controversy." He centered upon the controversies surrounding Protestants and Roman Catholics, past and present, mounting a strong critique against the popular anti-Catholicism of the time. The Twenty Club minutes reported the controversy which Diman's paper fueled:

> "We were all alarmed at the Romanish influences of
> the essayist, who thought that most of the historic and
> traditional attacks upon Rome [Roman Catholicism]
> were useless and false. He went so far in sympathy that
> we beheld him charmed by the glamor of halos and
> altar lights."

In defending Roman Catholicism, Diman was not only expressing his own interest in that faith (although obliquely), but was also in company with his father's defenses forty and more years earlier. As an outspoken religious liberal, the Rev. (and Prof.) J. Lewis Diman, was impatient with the late 19th century religious intolerance. He used disciplined scholarship and a brilliant speaking ability to promote an understanding of Roman Catholics and Unitarians – two groups treated intolerantly. His efforts brought him the criticism of many and the appreciation of others. Diman, facing The Twenty Club, could hardly have forgotten his father's example. He was not, however, the scholar nor the spell-binding orator his father was. He retreated from such public defenses and mulled over his personal religious quandaries in private.

---

*Another LaFarge, John's sister Margaret, was a close friend of Diman's. They were, in fact, matrimonially linked by the Newport social set, to their mutual amusement. It was suggested that Diman "had turned Catholic to marry Margaret LaFarge." To this Diman wryly responded, "I hadn't seen her for two years. That didn't make me a very good suitor, now did it?" (This quote was found, in Diman's handwriting, in papers he had saved over the years.)

The long and circuitous voyage of Diman's conversion took on greater certainty after his near-brush with death on 15 December 1915 (his emergency appendectomy in Chicago, while on a trip to Colorado.) His sister, Louise, was with him and was, in Diman's words, "dumbfounded" when he called for the ministrations of a Roman Catholic priest, not a fellow Episcopalian. After his return to St. George's, he began visiting the Rev. Edward A. Higney, Pastor of St. Joseph's Roman Catholic Church, Newport, to discuss religious matters.*

The most conclusive published account of Diman's conversion came in 1942. The now Father Hugh Diman, Benedictine monk/Headmaster, wrote an article in the widely-circulated Roman Catholic newpaper, *Our Sunday Visitor.* A long, rambling piece entitled "From Episcopal Deacon to Benedictine Monk," it was immensely revealing of his conversion. He wrote, for instance, of the day, nearly thirty-two years earlier, when he was received into Roman Catholicism as a layman:

> "[It] was a Sunday morning, December 16, 1917. After High Mass, I . . . asked for the pastor, and when he appeared, I asked at once to be received into the Church. Father Higney reflected for a moment, and then said, 'Come right over to the church and we'll get it done now.' Once inside the church, I read with unwavering conviction my profession of faith, received conditional baptism [I had practically no doubt that I had received valid baptism in infancy], and made my confession. In a few minutes the whole thing was done. My long voyage was over. I found myself at last a full-fledged member of the Catholic Church."

Two days later he made his First Communion as a Roman Catholic. This, too, was recalled with intense clarity:

> "It was a cold December morning. The church was cold, or so it seemed to me. A coffin was up at the head of the middle aisle, and a funeral was going on. As I walked up to receive the Body of Our Lord, my reason and my conscience were at ease and satisfied;

---

*Father Higney was for some half a century Pastor of St. Joseph's. He and Diman had much in common, in that they were activists and builders, Father Higney building St. Joseph's Church and Parish into prominence.

but as for any emotional reaction, I didn't seem to have
any at all...In my rational nature, I was glad."

The effects of Diman's conversion upon St. George's were (and remain) not easily assessed. After all, just ten years before he had led the School into a relationship with the Protestant Episcopal Schools. As was to be learned later, this occurred while his interest in Roman Catholicism was mounting. Diman was not positively committed to the institutional side of Episcopalianism – his perpetual diaconal relationship with it confirmed that time and time again. Yet, there could be little doubt that the Protestant Episcopal Church lost a vital clergy/headmaster in losing Diman. He was far from being an insensitive person; he could hardly be unaware of the surprise, incredulity and pain his conversion brought to others. Above it all, one thing became clear: his long, lonely, struggle-filled "voyage" to Catholicism brought an eventual self-discovery of vital meaning to him. He found structure and discipline, facets his life needed. In a curious, almost mystical way, he found freedom within the seemingly monitored freedom of a religious order.

Frederick Rhinelander King '04 had known Diman almost all his life – first as a St. George's student, then as a Trustee. He was one of the younger Trustees who had to deal with both Diman's resignation and conversion. He reflected, in 1966, on the extreme difficulty he had had in understanding the conversion:

> "[Diman] suffered from doubt which led him to The Church of Rome where he found the authority he sought and peace of soul. To us he was a lost leader and we resented what we felt was a desertion, but we never faltered in our devotion and gratitude for the influence he had on our lives...I have never in my long life known any man I admired and loved more and whose memory I more cherish."*

There was bitterness and there was anger, both within St. George's and beyond it. The years have left uncontested that some wanted Diman's name expunged from St. George's forever. That this never occurred was due to cooler heads dominating the decision-making processes of the School.

Over the years, it was clear that Diman changed. He lost some of the

---

*In a letter to the Rev. William A. Buell, 18 December 1966.

austerity (though not all) which had marked him at St. George's. Pictures of him as an aged monk surrounded by boys, reveal a smile, absent from earlier portraits and photographs. He liked to tell of a Newport Roman Catholic lady who claimed, "Father Diman wasn't half so stiff after he became Irish."

Following his 1917 reception into the Roman Catholic Church as a layman, Diman became a priest in 1921. In 1924, he joined the Benedictine Order as a monk, founding the Portsmouth Priory (later Abbey) School in 1926. His return to school life, at age sixty-three, was not of his own choosing.* At Portsmouth, Diman headed a School intrinsically tied to the Roman Catholic Church. He found, to his satisfaction, the backing of one of the most durable and successful of Orders, the Benedictine. He once again brought into being a School of strength and prestige.

When he died, on St. Patrick's Day 1949, the loss was reflected in obituaries in major newspapers up and down the East Coast. He died with the hurt and resentment of his perplexing conversion diminished and largely forgiven. His simple monk's grave on the Portsmouth Abbey grounds bespeaks the kind of peace and tranquility he craved – and finally found.

Diman Hall at St. George's, the dormitory given in 1925 by his friend, Vincent Astor '10, pays tribute to his memory, while Miss Diman's Room, a reception room in Old School, remembers his sister, Emily.** In the permanency of a stone-carved plaque, among those honoring the School's deceased Headmasters, his has its own understated dignity (as he would have wished):

"John Byron Diman, Founding Headmaster."

The lack of "The Reverend" or of "Father" seems not to be an oversight. It is rather a mute testimony to the way that many at St. George's want to remember him – John Byron Diman, the brilliant, self-giving, Founding Headmaster.

---

*It is well-documented among the Benedictines that Father Hugh was troubled about returning to Rhode Island to start a school so close to St. George's. He did so in obedience to his vows and as the most logical candidate at the time to meet the need.

**Portraits of both Dimans hang in the School. See Appendix F for a complete listing of portraits.

On the Chapel's Cornerstone

Ad Dei Honorem
Hic Lapis in Angulo Ecclesiae
Sancti Georgii Die XIII Mensis Iunii
Anno Scholae Sancti Georgii XXVIII
Dominique Nostri MDCCCCXXIIII
Positus Est.

(To the Glory of God
This Stone has been placed in
The Corner of the Church of
Saint George on the thirteenth
Day of the Month of June in
the Twenty-Eighth Year of the
School of Saint George and in
the year of our Lord nineteen
hundred and twenty-four.)

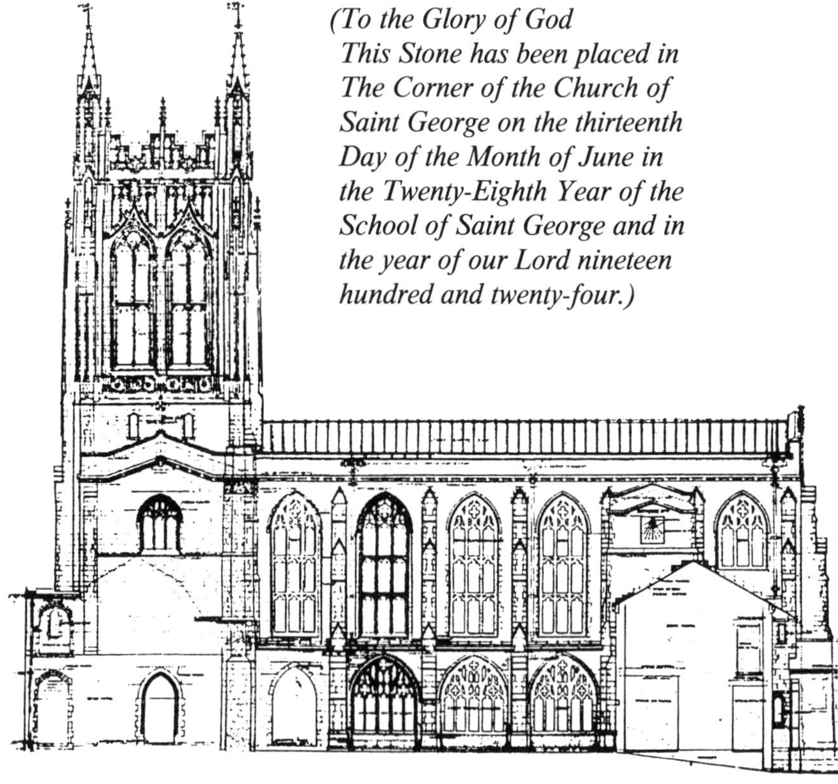

From Architectural Drawings
of the Chapel
Ralph Adams Cram, Architect

CHAPTER FOUR

A Halcyon Era
1917 - 1928

THE Rev. John Byron Diman left St. George's on 1 January 1917. For the boys of the School, there was no immediate change in the School's life. The dire predictions that St. George's would diminish and dissolve were found to be happily in error. To the contrary, the years 1917-1928 proved to be a Halcyon Era, one of the calmest and most productive in the first ninety years of the School's history.

It was a commonly held expectation that St. George's second Headmaster would be an Episcopal priest. This would more clearly define the School as an Episcopal School. The Board of Trustees evidenced every intention of moving in that direction. They even knew the priest they wanted: the Rev. Remsen B. Ogilby, Headmaster of the Baguio School for American Boys, in the Philippines. After extensive negotiations, Ogilby proved unavailable, feeling called to remain in the Philippines. There were other clergy on the Headmaster Search list, from both educational institutions and parishes, yet what was anticipated as a relatively easy venture turned into a challenging one. The search dragged on for a variety of reasons. The clergy/headmaster candidates were either not wanted or declined to accept the position. A good "fit" did not seem to show up.

In the midst of the search, an Episcopal layman/headmaster had surfaced as a viable candidate – Mr. Archibald Hoxton was Principal of the Episcopal High School, Alexandria, Virginia, one of the oldest (1839) of the Church's schools. He was an especially attractive prospect in that he was a thoroughly experienced schoolman. The Senior Masters in particular had expressed the need for a seasoned, mature man, as they were concerned about the scholastic standing of the School. Arthur S. Roberts explained this in a letter to Trustee George Gordon King, 31 July 1916:

"A man who is keenly interested in the academic

standard of the School [is needed], a man who is abreast
of the best education programs and determined that the
boys who go from St. George's to college shall challenge the highest standards set anywhere."

Hoxton, while unfortunately not a cleric, seemed to meet this kind of
hope. He was wooed with the Headmaster's salary increased to $5,000
($1,000 more than Diman had received) and the promise to remodel
Julien T. Davies' "Pinecroft," at the edge of the Hilltop, as a Headmaster's House for him and his family. Once again, the negotiations proved
futile; Hoxton chose to remain at the Episcopal High School.

The proposal of a layman/headmaster had raised the question as to
whether the School, with its 1907 Charter affiliating it with the Protestant Episcopal Church, was required to have a clergy/headmaster. This
question took root when a new Trustee, Samuel P. Bush (who had
come on the Board in 1913) proposed that Acting Headmaster, Stephen
P. Cabot, be made full Headmaster. As Acting Headmaster, he was
already functioning as a resourceful and competent leader.

The valuable counsel of Trustee (and attorney) Julien T. Davies was
sought. Davies advised that nothing in the 1907 Charter prevented
either a layman or a non-Episcopalian from heading St. George's
School. He proposed a "division of functions" separating the roles of
Headmaster and School Chaplain, giving the Headmaster oversight of
the School, but placing the Chaplain "in full charge" of the School's
religious life. Both of these were accepted and, as will unfold, became
primary Trustee practices over the years. This did not mean, however,
that all agreed with these practices. Thus began in 1917 a division
within the School between those favoring a clergy/headmaster as against
those favoring a layman/headmaster. This division arose again and
again in various contexts.

Armed with the legal right to appoint Cabot, a Unitarian layman, as
the School's second Headmaster, the Trustees felt assured that he would
stay the course Diman had set. Cabot had worked closely with Diman
from 1901 on, and they shared the similar personality traits of being
reserved, closed-mouthed "Yankees." Both men were knowledgable
about the educational philosophies needed to sustain a boys' college
preparatory school, and both offered a no-nonsense type of administration. Stephen P. Cabot and John Byron Diman remained fast friends
long after both had left St. George's.

A factor in Cabot's make-up, which helped provide calmness and understanding, was that he knew when to leave things alone and when to initiate change. There was no cause for alarm in terms of St. George's as an Episcopal School led by a Unitarian; Cabot clearly supported this definition. With the appointment of the first official School Chaplain,* the division of functions went well, confirming Davies' wisdom in administrative affairs. Cabot delegated to the Faculty more responsibilities than Diman had (although some younger members still believed Cabot a bit domineering.) The boys found him acceptably reserved, the prototype of the British public school headmaster, impeccably attired, tough but fair, and enjoyed watching him play hockey. In that sport, Cabot was energetic but less-than-skilled. The word was, "God help the boy who got in his way." In due course (1954), the Cabot Rink of the School paid tribute to the pleasure he found in playing ice-hockey.**

The gradual, but significant, changes which the new Headmaster led in instituting came in a deepening of the academic quality of St. George's. Cabot was that valuable combination of a natural scholar and gifted teacher. He was sympathetic with the strenuous curriculum Diman had mounted but also aware of the diminution of academic standards during Diman's latter days. An unabashed academic elitist, he had studied widely the development of educational theory and practice in both the United States and Europe. He recognized the need to enlarge the scope of Science in the curriculum in the light of the rush of early 20th Century developments. Few men were better equipped to be an academically-oriented headmaster than Cabot.

There was a Faculty collegiality during Cabot's tenure which reflected that he had been one of its members over the years. Few roles are more difficult than being placed in charge of one's peers. Cabot's success in this was that he remained essentially unchanged in personality, while functioning indisputably as *Head* master. He was remembered as a non-smoker and non-drinker, which set him somewhat apart from the con-

---

*The Rev. Israel Harding Hughes, appointed in 1917 and remaining until 1921, was the first of twenty-seven Chaplains and Assistant, and/or Associate Chaplains, to be appointed in the first ninety years of the School. Chaplains' tenures tended to be brief, most remaining for only one to three years.

**Records of the time refer to Cabot's "delicate health, but not to what his health problems were. Both he and Diman lived to be 83, remaining active into their oldest years.

viviality which these brought to Faculty occasions. It was with considerable skill that he chose when, and when not, to assert his authority.

An incident remains in the memories of some involving The Rev. Arthur Peaslee and Cabot.* Peaslee was famous for his quick-temper and strong sense of independence. A physically small man, he was intellectually keen and known to spend his spare time reading Dante and translating *The Inferno* and *Paradisio* as a hobby. He approved of intellectual prowess among the students and rewarded it, extravagantly at times, Cabot believed. Peaslee once gave the brilliant William S. Sims '29 a grade of 100 for a year's work. In Faculty Meeting, Cabot challenged the grade as "unrealistic." Peaslee responded that Sims had received a grade of 100 for everything he had done over the year — papers, quizzes, tests, mid-year and final examinations. "What grade would you give him?" he asked Cabot. The Headmaster dropped the issue forthrightly.

Cabot's calm, firm hand on the affairs of the School was praised during the remaining days of World War I, 1917-1918. It was said that he gave the School its "uninterrupted pattern" during this period. His leadership included taking St. George's beyond its immediate academic life, into Red Cross work, and with the continued activity of the School Battalion. In everything, he sought as normal a pattern of School life as was possible.

Armistice Day, 11 November 1918 was celebrated at St. George's in the Auchincloss Gymnasium with a Service of Remembrance and Thanksgiving. The American, British and French flags, together with the national anthems, were featured, and the boys joined in a national day of joy and relief — the Great War was over. Interestingly enough, at the close of the Service, the School turned out in battalion formation to husk the corn growing on 10 acres of former lawns-converted-into gardens. St. George's Masters and boys had frequently traveled the Continent,** but now the war had brought internationalism home to them in vivid and often tragic ways. An Across-the-Atlantic outreach of uniqueness came in 1918, when "A Friendly Alliance" was established with a coeducational boarding school, St. George's, Harpenden, Here-

---

*Peaslee taught Mathematics from 1902 - 1924.

**Both boys and Masters gave lengthy reports of their travels in the pages of *The Dragon* and in talks to the School.

fordshire, England. This was said to have been the first such alliance of an English *public* school with an American private school.

In 1918, still caught up in the patriotism of World War I, it was proposed that the School should have a War Memorial, one fitting to recognize those who had fought and died in the military. Plans were announced in February 1919 and $150,000 set as the goal to build a much-needed Schoolhouse as that Memorial. The hope was to have the Schoolhouse ready for dedication at St. George's Twenty-fifth Anniversary in 1921. No one at the time anticipated the problems that would arise in escalating costs and in raising funds. It took until June 1921 before the cornerstone was laid and work begun.* By March 1922, funds were exhausted and work ceased, leaving a completed exterior but an incomplete interior. The project actually dragged on for four years. The Schoolhouse was finally dedicated on 13 January 1923.

This disappointing experience was out of step with the positive progress St. George's was making. It has remained a mystery why this worthy and much-needed Memorial proved so problematical. About 260 contributors gave toward the $290,000 cost of the building, but of this amount, $109,000 came from one donor, the ever-generous Vincent Astor '10. There was no disguising the fact that the fund-raising effort had left much to be desired.

The clearest explanation was that the strong emotional motivation, while the war was in progress, dwindled under the delay encountered in the construction of the Schoolhouse. Very much missed on the scene was the entrepreneurship of the Rev. John Byron Diman, fund-raiser extraordinary. It was some years later before any attempt was made to undertake another project involving a general subscription; the School continued to depend upon large individual gifts for major capital funding.

An example of the return to a single donor was the School Chapel. On Prize Day 1922, an announcement electrified everyone – a School Chapel was being given by an anonymous donor. For the boys, the news boded well to halt the five-mile-round-trip to St. Columba's on Sundays. For those who wanted the School more religiously-centered, it

---

*Among the items placed in a bronze casket in the Cornerstone were: copies of *The Alumni Bulletin, The Dragon, The St. George's School Catalogue,* together with a list of the names of those contributing to the construction of the Schoolhouse.

offered tangible hope that this might occur. The need for a Chapel to accommodate the entire School had long been felt.

When an artist's depiction of the Chapel was published, the magnificence of the stone Gothic edifice was virtually overwhelming. A wooden model further imprinted its carefully crafted symmetry. It was truly a small cathedral planned for St. George's School. The Chapel and the Schoolhouse attached to one another expressed the symbolization of Religion and Education in the life of the School.

In due course, the Chapel's donor was revealed — John Nicholas Brown '18, not long out of Harvard — vitally interested in architecture and a strongly-committed "Anglo-Catholic" Episcopalian.* Brown's gift found him intricately involved in its architecture and construction. When the Chapel was completed and consecrated, Sixth Former, Samuel Powel '28, said it well when he called it "the crystalization of John Nicholas Brown's vision."

The Groundbreaking was on St. George's Day, 23 April 1924. It was especially moving for the boys as they stood shoulder to shoulder forming a human delineation of the Chapel's foundation. Into the foundation were placed representative artifacts of St. George's.**

Under Brown's inspiration and the detailed plans of the Architect, Ralph Adams Cram, the Chapel took shape. One model for it was St. Stephen's Church, Rochester Row, Westminster, London, near the Westminster Cathedral (the Roman Catholic cathedral). The Chapel became a visualization of iconography of the first order. Joseph Coletti, Brown's friend and Harvard classmate, sculpted statues, cornices and other works of the saints (St. George being the most prominent), of Christ, the Virgin Mary, and contemporary figures, such as the heads of the Donor, the Architect, and the Headmaster, Russell H. Nevins. In time, tapestries and paintings were to further adorn the already rich symbolism of the Chapel, and also plaques, carved in stone, to honor deceased Headmasters, Trustees and Masters, and, significantly, Emily Diman — the only woman to be so honored.

---

*Some would use "High-Church" here; the choice of terms is open to considerable subjectivity, having ritualistic and doctrinal connotations broadly interpreted.

**Included were: copies of the School's publications, selected plans of the Chapel, the Deed of the Gift, photographs, a list of the faculty and boys in the School at the time, the Order for the Laying of the Foundation Stone, and copies of *The Book Of Common Prayer* and *St. George's In The War.*

At the mid-point of the Chapel's construction, in 1926, Stephen P. Cabot shocked the St. George's constituency by announcing his resignation. Unlike Diman, who had left his 1916 resignation cloaked in secrecy, Cabot explained that, as a Unitarian, he could not conscientiously support the Anglo-Catholic worship desired for the new Chapel by its donor and others. The Trustees reacted by refusing to accept his resignation. Cabot, however, like Diman earlier, had "unalterably" decided that he must leave; with great reluctance, his resignation was accepted.*

The need to find a new Headmaster revived the clergy *vs.* layman Headmaster issue, in hiatus since 1917. With the new Chapel underway it appeared that new impetus had been given to its proponents. Bishop James DeWolfe Perry, Jr., always a force to be reckoned with, had found a strong ally in Brown. This was evident in a strongly-worded letter the young Chapel donor sent to Edward Sturtevant in April 1926:

> "We have never in the history of the School had a Head Master who could fill all the requirements. When the School, assembled together as one, came to the religious service in order corporately to worship Almighty God, the Head Master had to step aside and allow an inferior in rank to perform what was in reality his own duty. The School now has the chance to remedy this defect by calling as Head Master a clergyman.
>
> "Consequently, the Head of the School should be able to represent the School as a whole in Divine Worship. The opening of the new Chapel will open inevitably a new chapter, and one which I hope will prove to be glorious in the School's history, but I am convinced that in order for the School to attain its full measure of success, the new Head Master must be Master in the Chapel as well as in the School Room."

Few could have stated more clearly the model of a church school

---

*It has remained enigmatic in the history of St. George's that its first two Headmasters resigned with religious reasons as a part of their leaving — Diman's Catholicism and Cabot's Unitarianism.

which Brown and others desired St. George's to follow. The most prominent example of this model was St. Paul's School, Concord, New Hampshire, a Chapel-centered school with a clergy/headmaster and with School and Religion inextricably intertwined. This model was not followed for St. George's, either in 1917 when the "division of functions" separated those of Headmaster and Chaplain or thereafter.

Trustee Vincent Astor was in favor of St. George's continuing as an independent Episcopal School, free to select its Headmaster, whether cleric or layman, and with education the primary focus. Using nothing of Brown's polished expression, he bluntly communicated his opposition to the prevailing practice of appointing Parish Rectors as heads of boarding schools; he was emphatic in his call for an experienced educator to lead St. George's. He was joined by increasing numbers of Alumni and others favoring a "Low-Church" position and a layman Headmaster.

A highly-recommended clergy candidate was approached – Alexander G. Zabriskie, a Professor at the Protestant (later Virginia) Episcopal Seminary, Alexandria, Virginia. In January 1927 strong efforts were made to convince him to leave Seminary teaching and head the School. Zabriskie declined, saying that he preferred to have an influence on future priests rather than head a boys' school.*

Cabot, in the main, kept out of the search. He did, however, fuel the *pro*-layman side by communicating a viewpoint of which he was thoroughly convinced. It was stated in a letter to Bishop Perry:

> "The School has established a policy of liberalism and
> tolerance on both its educational and religious sides that
> is worthy of the best traditions of this state."**

What had emerged from the previous efforts (in 1916) to find St. George's second Headmaster, was that the School did not become the orthodox model of a church school which Perry, Brown and others wanted it to be. It remained a School exercising a strong sense of autonomy in all matters of its life. Men like Brown and Astor, on opposing

---

*In a lengthy appendix to his letter declining the position, Zabriskie offered some frank assessments of St. George's. He found it in no way the strict church school he thought it should be; it had interested few boys in the priesthood and was anything but an example of "aggressive Christianity."

**Cabot referred to the historic precedents for religious and social freedom established in the founding of Rhode Island.

sides, accepted their wins, losses and draws in this issue with dignity, putting the needs of St. George's ahead of all else.

Stephen P. Cabot reluctantly* left St. George's in 1926, honored for the strength he had contributed to the School. Something of his "Boston Brahmin" breeding and urbanity had permeated School-life, as well as his more obvious skills as a Master and Headmaster. His formal manners, impeccable attire, reserved demeanor, were not lost upon the boys or anyone else.** The School was far the better for the twenty-five years he gave it, especially his nine as Headmaster.

He was fifty-eight when he left the School, with twenty-five years of life ahead. In 1927, he served as Regent of Avon Old Farms School, Avon, Connecticut, advising in the founding of that school. Upon returning to Boston, he continued his interest in education, especially Progressive Education. His frequent travels to the Continent found him studying that often controversial field. His lectures at the Harvard Graduate School of Education were published in 1930, under the title, *Secondary Education in France, Germany, England and Denmark.*

It was his return to Social Service work which seemed to be Cabot's greatest interest. As a Harvard undergraduate and graduate student he had done much volunteer social work. He picked it up again giving leadership to the Judge Baker Guidance Center and to Family Services agencies in Boston. He died in Boston in 1952.***

As in 1916, the *pro*-cleric advocates failed in their efforts to have a clergyman appointed to head St. George's. Once more the Trustees reached within the Faculty and appointed Russell H. Nevins as Acting Headmaster. This done, they proceeded to take their time to search for Cabot's replacement.

In appointing Nevins, the Trustees had a man far from eager to assume

---

*Upon Cabot's resignation, Diman had written him saying that Cabot must be happy to leave. In a poignant reply he wrote "I am not glad to get out. I would far rather stay on for another period of years." (28 January 1926)

**Students remembered Cabot's unusual ability to carve a roast with one hand, standing at table in King Hall, straight as a Prussian soldier.

***An article, in the nationally-circulated *American Weekly,* hailed Cabot's social service work. For whatever reason, only a single line was devoted to the fact that he had "once taught at St. George's School."

this exacting position. In fact, records show that none of the Senior Masters desired to be Headmaster. Nevins finally agreed but only after candidly expressing that he felt ill-equipped for the job. He accepted as of 1 August 1926, for a year only and with the provision that he was willing to return to the Faculty upon the finding of a permanent man. Because he remained for two years, it made it feasible to recognize Nevins as a Headmaster in his own right.

Like Cabot, Nevins was an independently wealthy man. Not required to teach for a living, he did so out of a love for school life. He had built his own house* on the Hilltop in 1912. It became a center for Nevins to entertain frequently and with sophistication, aided by a cook-house-keeper and butler.

> Wheaton B. Byers '11 remembered Nevins in 1946:
> "Though he was a disciplinarian, he had an astonish-
> ingly tender and generous side. He became known,
> much against his will, for infinite quiet kindness to
> people who really needed help. Kindness was his deep-
> est trait. It warred with a deeply ingrained modesty
> which sometimes made him seem excessively shy."

He played football at Union College and was the first St. George's Headmaster to have been a varsity athlete. During the years boys and Masters played varsity football and baseball together (up to 1911), Nevins was a fine football player. It was claimed that he also taught Latin with an athletic zeal:

> "[Nevins] rammed the distinction between the Latin
> gerund and gerundive into our minds as earnestly as he
> rammed his shoulder into the midriff of Mr. Fred Win-
> sor** in the Middlesex [football] games, when Winsor
> tried to break up our long gaining end-run play."

Nevins did not have an easy two years as Headmaster; it was essentially a "holding" period for him and for the School. There was a rapid turn-over of Faculty, a situation quite constant for the School over most of its years. In Nevins' time, however, several Masters came who served

---

*In 1986, Nevins' house is Haffner House (the name acknowledging it as the gift of Gen. Charles C. Haffner, Jr. '14), a dormitory and Faculty Residence. From 1936, when Nevins left, until 1968, it was in the hands of private individuals.

**Winsor was Middlesex School's first Headmaster.

long and durable tenures. Ashley T. Day came in 1927 to teach English, remaining until 1941; Edmund P. Coe, Mathematics, staying until 1941; and one of St. George's most beloved men, William P. Elliott, a teacher of Science, an admirable coach, an exemplary family man and counselor of boys, a vital presence until 1952. These men brought a greater diversification to the Faculty, a second layer between the Senior Masters and the rapid turn-over of younger men. They were a valuable asset.

Periodically, a restlessness developed in the Faculty over St. George's academic standards. Nevins appointed a "Committee of Five" in 1927, responding to dissatisfaction with academic life. Alan R. Wheeler, Arthur S. Roberts, Paul T. Christie – all Senior Masters, together with newer Masters, Cyril B. Judge and Bernard A. Hoban,* served on the Committee.

The Committee minced no words in its report, saying among other things:

> "Not one member of the Faculty is satisfied with present
> or past results. Not only has there been a signal lack of
> success in the results of the College Board exams, but
> also there is constant anxiety over the failure of boys in
> the lower forms to measure up to our requirements. We
> are also disturbed by the failure of many of our boys in
> college to do better work."

It is difficult to assess whether having two colleagues as Headmasters contributed to the blistering frankness of the report; it sounds like peers dealing with peers. It is known that the Committee made some pragmatic proposals to remedy the situation. They proposed that the Headmaster be alert in keeping in touch with the preparatory schools "feeding" St. George's.** Poor scholars were to be dropped to a lower form to see if that would help them catch up. (Nevins was quick to drop boys who were poor risks scholastically.) The Faculty was advised to spend

---

*Judge taught Mathematics and English, 1910-1927; Hoban was Director of Athletics, 1912-1914 and 1920-1934. It is interesting to find athletics involved in a review of academic standards.

**Far more responsibility for Admissions was placed upon the Headmaster in those days than in later years.

less time on "the dull boy in the classroom" and give tutoring outside the classroom setting.

Viewed in retrospect, it was this kind of response, to what was deemed unsatisfactory academic standards and performance, which kept St. George's a lively scholastic School. Positive values resulted; remedies would work for a time, only to have to later be challenged and new answers found.

The social stratification of the School into a "rich boys'" boarding school was a concern which took root among the growing Alumni body. In Nevins' time, Alumni considered setting up a fund to offer admission to financially disadvantaged, but academically promising, boys. The actual implementation of this idea on any large scale had to be delayed for some years. What was important was that the concern was kept alive until given a measure of answer, first in reduced tuitions, then in endowment funds marked for scholarship aid.

The Diman Legacy was diminishing, although it was bound to remain with many Alumni and Senior Masters. Emily Diman's departure in 1928 was a benchmark of that decline. She had wanted to leave in 1926 but had been persuaded to stay. Over a quarter of a century she had seen the School through innumerable experiences. No written record has surfaced of how her brother's resignation from the School and eventual conversion to Roman Catholicism affected her – they must have been deep intrusions into her life. Her formality and poise were not always to the liking of some boys, but as Oliver Prescott '16 pointed out:

> "...many, many more of us found her good to look
> upon, good to listen to, and someone boys were to
> remember and admire."

Miss Diman returned to 300 Angell Street, Providence, to the Stimson-Diman Family home, to live with her sister, Louise. Emily Diman died in 1949, just two months after her brother.

With Nevins heading the School, the Trustees were slow to deal with the exacting task of finding a permanent Headmaster. Only two Trustees remained who had been on the Board during the 1916-1917 search:

Bishop Perry and Edward Sturtevant.* The presence of four alumni brought into play a dual dimension — their awareness of the School they had known as students and the one they had come to serve as adults and Trustees. They made known their views, and their involvement was significant in influencing decisions from newer perspectives. A sizable list of candidates was in hand for the Trustees to work through. It included well-known** and lesser known Parish Rectors, as well as clergy and laymen from other schools.

In 1928 no one welcomed the appointment of J. Vaughan Merrick, III, as St. George's fourth Headmaster more than Russell H. Nevins. He promptly asked for a Term Sabbatical to recover from the exhausting duties of the job he had never really wanted, but which he had helpfully fulfilled. He then returned to the Faculty, remaining until 1936.

During the tenures of Cabot and Nevins, life for the students showed slow but perceptible changes. Discipline remained firm but fair; the Senior Masters continued to exert their visible power; and an increasing parade of younger Masters kept life in a state of flux.

The boys were intrigued by the growing architectural splendor of the new Chapel, were happy to have Twenty House, the new Swimming Pool, and even the commodious accommodations of the Schoolhouse.

The trek to St. Columba's Church for Chapel offered the opportunity to be briefly off the Hilltop. The St. George's Choir sang and the boys provided the largest share of the congregation. For a select set of boys, pumping the organ at St. Columba's was a much-sought after assignment. T. C. T. Buckley '28 has reminisced:

> "The chief advantage was that during the sermon the
> organ pumpers disported themselves outside among the
> tombstones [in the church yard]. Sometimes it was a
> pretty close call whether we got air into the bellows in
> time after [the sermon] had wound up and Mr. Kellett,

----

*The 1926-1927 Trustees also had: Stephen P. Cabot (replaced by Russell H. Nevins in 1927); RAdm. William S. Sims, U.S.N., Mark A. DeWolfe Howe, Marion Eppley, M. M. vanBeuren; and from the Alumni, Frederick R. King and Harford W. H. Powel (both from the Class of 1904), Vincent Astor '10, and Thomas P. Hazard '11.

**The Rev. Arthur Lee Kinsolving, Rector of Grace Episcopal Church, Amherst, Massachusetts, was elected Headmaster in May 1927, but declined the appointment. He was also active in the religious life at Amherst College and had been a Rhodes Scholar at Oxford.

the Choirmaster, was frantically attempting to make
some music."

The bitter Winter of 1919-1920 has been long remembered. St. George's boys were pressed into shoveling Purgatory Road down to Easton's Beach to make contact with Newport, and the School's fifteen coal-fired furnaces went full blast all winter. The boys took advantage of excellent skating and sledding and expressed no anguish when Sunday Services had to be held in Auchincloss for all but one service during the Winter Term.

The threat of a fire at one of the Hilltop's buildings occupied the minds of Masters – the Newport Fire Department was distant – and a Fire Brigade was formed with its own limited equipment. It passed one of the few tests of its competency when, in February 1917, it contained a fire on the roof of Old School, to the satisfaction of all.

An absorbing interest in motion pictures took hold in the 1920's, with films shown regularly at the School. The "Jazz Age" captured the musical tastes of large numbers of boys. The School's Jazz Orchestra began to give visiting musical groups a run for their money. The School Dance remained *the* social event of the year, taking on growing sophistication.

The proliferation of extra-curricular activities included forming the Wireless Club in 1921. A banner day for that Club was in 1925 when St. George's Station I-AOA, was heard in Portland, Oregon. The Tuck Shop also began in 1921, dispensing light refreshments. Boys interested in shooting found great satisfaction in the Gun Club, started in 1923. Others organized the School Bank whose purpose was unmistakable:
"To teach boys accuracy and how a check book is kept
and not simply receive and pay out money."*

There was more than a philosophical interest in boys being able to use their hands in woodworking and mechanical repairs. Edward B. Blakely, a civil engineer, came on the faculty in 1924 (to remain until 1928) to teach an optional course in Applied Mechanics. Behind the swimming pool, he led the boys and two carpenters in constructing a

---

*Over the years, business and industry attracted a lot of St. George's graduates. The School Bank was influential, even if not immediately – given the notorious ability of boarding school students to spend more than their checkbooks provide. On another economic note: the boys found it impressive that, in 1924, seven Masters "are so luxurious as to have cars."

frame building to be devoted to the new course. The boys worked on automobiles and small mechanical devices, finding these especially attractive.

Athletics became more diversified between 1917 and 1928. Football remained "King of the Hilltop" with varying degrees of successful seasons. Baseball continued to be popular, as did basketball. The irregularities of Rhode Island's seacoast weather plagued winter sports, but the swimming pool, the gift of Mr. and Mrs. Ernest Behrend, went into operation in 1925. Ice hockey gained in favor, as did wrestling and boxing. In season, boating and crew found their devotees, both enhanced by the Boat House built at Third Beach in 1923.* Increased availability of transportation afforded the opportunity for more competition with other boarding schools. All boys participated in sports, and the "Club System" of Sakonnet and Sachuest Clubs continued to be a great success, especially in making non-varsity participation available.**

As for scholastic extra-curricular activities, strides were taken which built them solidly within the School's life. The Civics Club rose to a prestige and popularity which required, by 1925, a Senior and a Junior Civics Club. Speakers from within and beyond the School were sponsored by the Club, and its debates ranged widely across school, social and political lines. The amount of speaking in the School raised the need for attention to Public Speaking as a part of the curriculum. Whether the first inter-school debate helped precipitate the call for better training in speaking has been lost, but well it might have. The debate, in 1923, with Rogers High School, Newport, ended up in a loss for St. George's. Headmaster Cabot wryly noted that the presence of two articulate girls on the Rogers' team did the St. George's boys in.

In the 1920's, the Civics Club was prone to urge boys to consider becoming an "American presence" in political life. This was in answer to the tendency of boarding school graduates to eschew public service in

---

*Most of the timber used in the Boat House was from the old Gymnasium-Schoolhouse, torn down with the advent of the Memorial Schoolhouse.

**The Club System was, indeed, well-liked. It left the varsity teams intact while providing the values of team sports for those less skilled.

favor of more lucrative business careers.* Leadership skills for both were being honed in a much-improved Prefect System. By 1924, Fifth Formers were chosen as "honorary members" with the prospect of being appointed full Prefects as Sixth Formers, if found worthy.

The 1917-1928 era seemed to reveal less concern, so intense earlier, for quantitative growth at St. George's. Concentration tended to be placed on qualitative progress as evidenced by efforts for scholastic success, the diversification of athletics and extra-curricular activities, and an enrollment pretty much matching the School's capacities. Notwithstanding, the School continued to acquire sizable tracts of adjoining land. Deals seemed to go on *ad infinitum* – by gift, swapping or outright purchase. The major goal of these acquisitions was the protection of St. George's from the encroachment of unwelcome abutters. At one point, there were rumors of developing Second Beach into a "Coney-Island-style" Amusement Park. This precipitated for the School the purchase of nearly 280 acres of Sachuest Point land with the financial assistance of erstwhile supporters — John Nicholas Brown, Vincent Astor, Thomas P. Hazard and Michael M. vanBeuren. Also the west end of Second Beach was protected with the purchase of 3 acres of Purgatory Shore from E.I. Ashurst and a gift of adjacent land to the south from Trustee Marion Eppley.

When Cabot assumed the Headmastership in 1917, there were 140 boys and 16 Faculty, with tuition and fees at $1,050. After a dip in 1918 to 134 boys, by 1922 there were 171 boys and tuition and fees had risen to $1,325. Upon Cabot's leaving in 1926, 180 boys and 24 Faculty were present, while charges were $1,475. Enrollment slacked off between 1926 and 1928 to 170 boys and 20 Faculty, with charges of $1,485.

---

*An Alumni Questionnaire in 1923, to which 310 graduates responded, found only 3 Alumni in professional governmental service. The boys of the Civics Club, in their call for an "American Presence" in political life, could hardly have been unaware of the growing bias against first and second generation immigrants being successfully elected to office, nor of the Immigration Quota Laws enacted to stem the tide of immigration into the United States.

Alongside the era of struggle preceding it, and the turbulent one to follow, 1917-1928 was indeed a Halcyon Era. In a manner to be nostalgically looked back upon, St. George's had enjoyed some of the calmest, happiest years it would have in its first ninety years. The soaring, majestic Chapel, well-dressed boys entering Ivy League colleges, expanding property – these bespoke a St. George's of stature. However disappointing it had been to not readily raise the funds for the Schoolhouse, that facility *was* built. The issue of St. George's as an Episcopal School, that of clergy *vs.* layman Headmaster, had been settled, at least for the time being.

Ahead were a new Headmaster and challenges brought by the Stock Market Crash, the Depression, World War II, and the post-War years. The Halcyon Era would soon become a pleasant memory as the School faced testing and trying days of unforeseen intensity.

Sketch by Charles A. Richards, III '59

George and Margery Wheeler
To whom this book is dedicated.

Founding Headmaster
The Rev. John Byron Diman
Tenure 1896-1916

*"My sister and I started a
small school in Newport."*

Miss Emily Diman

Headmasters

Stephen P. Cabot
Tenure 1917-1926

Russell H. Nevins
Tenure 1926-1928

J. Vaughan Merrick, III
Tenure 1926-1943

Willet L. Eccles
Tenure 1943-1951

Headmasters

The Rev. William A. Buell
Tenure 1951-1961

Archer Harman, Jr.
Tenure 1961-1972

Anthony M. Zane
Tenure 1972-1984

The Rev. George E. Andrews, II
Tenure 1984-

Headmaster's Wives

Beatrice Merrick

Dorothy Eccles

Lois Buell

Mari Harman

Eusie Zane

Lil Andrews

Hunter Avenue Houses
1896-1897

The School, 1899

Foreground: building of the Memorial Schoolhouse
Background: first gymnasium, which later became the schoolroom

Interior, the schoolroom

Early Hilltop Tennis Courts

School Battalion, 1919

The Little Chapel,
1911

Diman Hall
Cubicles

Drama, 1905

Drama, 1985

Faculty, 1936

Faculty, 1986

Study Hall, 1951

Viking Ship, 1983

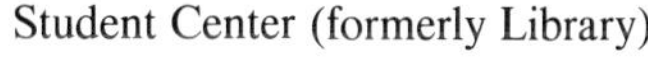

Girls, Astor Hall

Student Center (formerly Library)

Chapel, interior

Chapel, exterior

The Christmas Festival

The Dragon

Frostbite Picnic

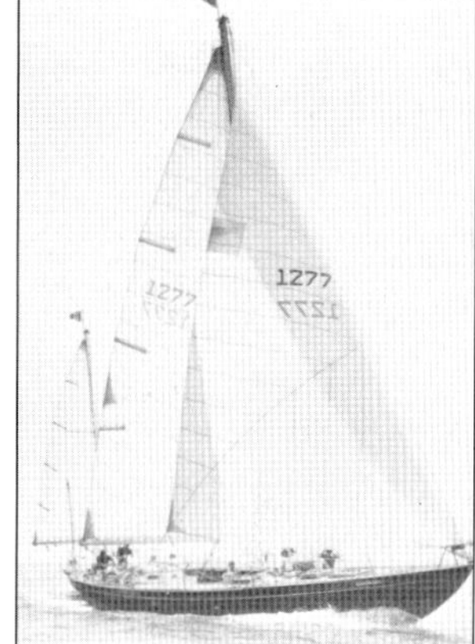

Research Vessel
"Geronimo"

Coeducation

Parents

Prize Day

Alumni Dinner

Crew

Basketball

Hockey (before rink was covered)

Football

Girls'
Field Hockey

Baseball

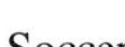

Cross Country

Soccer

CHAPTER FIVE

The Crucible of
The Great Depression
1928 - 1943

THE SPRING OF 1928 was a time filled with great enthusiasm. The centerpiece was the Consecration of the Church of St. George* as the School Chapel on St. George's Day, 23 April. The pageantry and ceremony found Archbishop Barsaum of the Syrian Church, Bishop Booth of Vermont and Bishop Perry of Rhode Island (President of the Trustees) accompanied by chaplains, candle bearers, a crucifer, leading a procession into the new edifice. The elaborate service has been preserved in a bound volume. Sixth Former, Samuel Powel, sought to convey the historic occasion in *The Dragon* of that June:

> "To describe minutely all the details of the long and magnificent service would only confuse the reader, for mere print cannot convey the spirit of perfection of each rite... It seems but fitting that such a service should consecrate forever the crystalization of John Brown's vision. May our Chapel inspire others who shall come to this hill top long after we, who saw his dream realized, have passed away and are forgotten."

With the new Chapel, the long walk to St. Columba's was past, and the anomaly of an Episcopal School without an adequate chapel corrected. The Anglo-Catholic predisposition of both the architect, Ralph Adams Cram, and the donor, John Nicholas Brown, found expression in the Consecration Service as well as in the impressive array of symbolism

---

*This is the official name of the Chapel as found in both Latin and English on the cornerstone: "This Stone has been placed in The Corner of the Church of St. George on the thirteenth Day of the Month of June in the Twenty-Eighth Year of the School of Saint George and in the year of our Lord nineteen hundred and twenty-four."

contained throughout the Chapel. The building was meant to be a bold statement of St. George's full-fledged maturity in the Episcopal School league. Interestingly, during the Summer of 1928 some 2500 people came to view the edifice, further communicating its fame beyond the Hilltop.

Together with the triumph of the new Chapel, the School had finally found a new Headmaster and, significantly, a Headmaster's wife. J. Vaughan Merrick, III and his new bride of June, Beatrice (Jones), came in September. They were both warmly welcomed, Vaughan Merrick because he brought impeccable, tried and true credentials as a Vice-Rector of St. Paul's School, and Beatrice because she was not only the first wife of a St. George's Headmaster but a charming, witty, enduring person in her own right. There was every evidence that the Halcyon Days of the 1920's would continue under the leadership of the Merricks.

Vaughan Merrick drew upon a strong academic background to assert the priority of academics from the beginning of his tenure.* A powerfully built man (he had been captain of the Crew at the University of Pennsylvania), he embodied the essence of the Christian Gentleman. He was the first St. George's Headmaster to have a B.S. rather than a B.A. He also had an M.A. from Pennsylvania. For those favoring a priest/headmaster, the disappointment, once more incurred in having another layman/headmaster, was assuaged by Merrick's considerable experience in that "most churchly" of Episcopal Schools, St. Paul's. He had demonstrated, there, immense skill in dealing with Dr. Samuel S. Drury, who ruled St. Paul's with a strong hand for twenty-seven years (1911-1938). Drury once left Merrick in charge and then returned to question a decision the Vice-Rector had made. Merrick stood his ground informing Drury that he could question the decision, but not Merrick's right to make it as the man left in charge. Drury admitted he was wrong, an admission rare enough to become history at St. Paul's. At St. George's, Merrick's good judgment was apparent from the first and, as it was to

---

*The seriousness of Merrick is still remembered by those who, during his early tenure in particular, did not receive a full St. George's diploma because of academic deficiencies. Some of them, after "prepping" through tutoring or in other schools, did go on to Ivy League colleges and considered St. George's their *alma mater.*

turn out, imperative for the School's life in the future.

Vaughan and Beatrice Merrick's arrival was especially gratifying to the boys. Older boys were into their third Headmaster (Cabot, Nevins and finally Merrick). This was especially unsettling, as students like Alan T. Schumacher '29 recalled more than a half-century later. Merrick had his own type of "no-nonsense" relationship with the boys which reflected his knowledge of them and the kind of open relationship he wanted to establish.

Over the 1930's St. George's athletic program became more competitive with other schools; varsity sports came into their own, while "Club" sports faded. This was to help bring the demise of the Sachuest and Sakonnet Clubs in 1933. Their role in providing essentially intramural sports was diminished, and it was felt that they had served their purpose. With this change the success or failure of varsity teams became more completely the barometer of school spirit than ever before. With football most notably, the win-loss record could mean elation or depression. The Middlesex rivalry was lop-sided in favor of Middlesex, and the occasional win (as in 1937 football 7-0) by a determined and successful team, refreshing and a tonic to School spirit. Crew survived the loss of its boathouse during the 1938 Hurricane, and St. George's went on to row schools such as Brooks, South Kent, St. Mark's and also college freshman crews. Strong swimming and soccer teams began to reveal the increased role of athletics on the Hilltop.

Extra-curricular activities also flourished. The Civics Club (uncontested leader of Clubs), the Junior Civics Club, Chapel Council, Library Association and Red Key offered boys the investment of their time, energies and abilities. Camp Ramleh,* opened in 1926 on Lake Yawgoo Kingston, Rhode Island, brought boys during the summer in contact with needy youngsters in a camping setting. The Prefect System continued, not without occasional controversy as to how well or evenly Prefects meted out punishment. The School's publications, *The Red and White, The Dragon* and the *Lance* were active. The senior of all, was *The Dragon,*

---

*Named "Ramleh" after the spot in ancient Syria where Richard the Lion-Hearted (1159-1199) first heard of St. George. He vowed that if he returned safely to his throne, he would name St. George patron saint of England.

and it assumed a more "literary and artistic" format with *The Red and White* assuming increased responsibilities to convey the news of St. George's on-going life. *The Lance* favored increased photographic coverage of the School Year going, in 1938, from its long-time 10" x 8" size to an 11" x 8" one.

William A. Buell helped bring Dramatics to a fruitful sophistication during the 1930's. Whereas earlier, Mr. Diman had despaired of the largely comedic fare offered, there appeared such productions as George Bernard Shaw's *The Devil's Disciple* and, in 1939, bringing attention to the School, a revival of Mathew Gregory Lewis' *The Castle Spectre.* This 18th Century Gothic melodrama had not been produced in the United States for something over a century. The plays demanded much from the boys, including the ability to enact girls' roles with some degree of communicability. Buell's interpretation of Dickens' *A Christmas Carol* added dramatic flavor to the already stimulating Christmas Festival.

School holidays were invariably a welcome break from the routines of School life. One came in 1928 with boys visiting the aircraft carrier *Lexington* anchored off Newport's Naval Training Station.*

Graduates of the 1930's would remember: "The Great Pinkeye Epidemic of 1930," which meant some boys missed two weeks of classes; the devastating hurricane of 1938; the debates over paddling and the eventual curbing of it to some extent; the growing rage over popular music and the admonition, "Turn down the gramaphone!"; "Snowballing" boys against an Auchincloss wall; "Walking off demerits"; the shock of the death of Alexander "Husky" Neilson '24 in 1938, by then a popular Master and coach; good times in faculty homes with the Roberts, the Alan and George Wheelers, the Vermillions, the Elliotts and other families; Alan Wheeler's habit of twirling his watch chain while making history come alive in the classroom; Edward Sturtevant's greeting to the Pinecroft boys on a foggy day, "Tricky morning, boys."**

The 1930's were very good years for the boys at St. George's. This was reflected in later years:

"After [1931] the School settled down to enjoy a period

---

*John R. Wadleigh '33, who became a Rear Admiral in the Navy, has vivid recollections of this visit.

**1929-1930 was the last year of the First Form (Seventh Grade), a victim of the Depression and a lack of desire by parents to send their sons away at a young age.

of ten years of leisurely life, unmarked by any notable
events."　　　　　　　　　　　　　　　*The Lance, 1946*

"Mr. Merrick ran the School so smoothly that one
alumnus wished for a fountain of youth so he could
return to those untroubled, good old days."
　　　　　　　　　　　　　　　　The Lance, 1969

What the boys were largely unaware of was that St. George's was
undergoing some of the most serious problems it would meet in its first
ninety years.* The Depression Years nearly destroyed the School, a closely-
kept secret. Behind the scenes, a coalition of Trustees, the Headmaster
and Faculty were placed in a crucible of problems which exacted from
them the investment of enormous and detailed attention. It is a mainly
untold story that needs relating.

St. George's School was relatively unaffected by "Black Thursday",
24 October 1929, and the Stock Market Crash. The School had little
endowment, and hence, few invested funds to lose in that economic
debacle. What happened, however, was that the Depression which followed was like a slow, disintegrating disease, revealing itself but being
unheeded by the patient. As among human beings facing up to a disease
can be painfully difficult and postponed as long as possible, so it was
with the School.

During the Depression, there was a collaborative effort, on the part of
those leading St. George's, to maintain the School's hard-won lifestyle.
That lifestyle included an exceptional, seaside campus, with acres of
lawns, hedges and playing fields to be maintained, all of which befitted
the image of a prestigious boarding school. Hardly more than forty years
old, the School still needed buildings and facilities to keep in league with
Groton, St. Paul's, St. Mark's and other leading schools. The physical
plant alone, designed for an enrollment of one hundred seventy-five, was
expensive to maintain, but maintaining it was the goal, of the Trustees in
particular. They led the growingly intense battle of the 1930's and early
1940's to hold St. George's high in the estimation of others.

---

*Conversations in the mid-1980's, with graduates of the 1930's, about how close St.
George's came to disaster in those years, revealed complete surprise on their part.

Even after the Depression hit, new facilities continued to be added to the School, usually the gifts of generous individuals. Vincent Astor '10 gave a Master's House at the north end of Diman Hall in 1929 and the Astor Infirmary in 1931; Sachuest Point was purchased in 1935;* the Chivalry Window added to the Ante-Chapel in 1938; and Mrs. Edith DeLong gave a new pipe organ in 1940, in memory of her grandson, Richard L. Perry.**

There was a concerted effort to protect the boys from the realities of the Depression and to maintain life on the Hilltop the way it had always been.

The desire to maintain St. George's in a lifestyle it had worked so hard to achieve was but one reason for, in the phrase of a later generation, "failing to bite the bullet" of fiscal solvency. Another was a sense of responsibility to those who worked for the School — faculty and staff. The Trustees were loathe to turn any School people into the unemployment lines. They were also keenly aware of those faithful people who had come to retirement age without the School's having funded a reliable pension system. The Trustees gave priority to arranging pensions for such people as Nellie Brown and "Old Sam" Ross, and a Master such as Paul T. Christie.

As early as 1932 the Trustees were having to face the fact that they had a problem with the finances of the School. Borrowing $20,000 to $50,000 annually became routine; between 1928 and 1943 nearly $700,000 had been sought from that source. At one point, in a confessional mood, the Trustees acknowledged:

> "Expenses [have] increased since 1922 in greater proportion than income, [because] expenditures for capital improvements in land and facilities have gone beyond

---

*The purchase of Sachuest Point came at a time of mounting indebtedness. The purchase price of $91,000 was staggering, but deemed necessary, to offset a possible Coney Island-style amusement park on the Point. Two-thirds of the cost was taken care of with gifts and one-third with borrowing. (Later, in 1942, portions of the land were sold to the Army and Navy for military purposes.)

**Richard L. Perry entered St. George's at the age of 12 in 1919. He was an enthusiastic athlete and popular boy. His death came in 1929 while he was piloting an experimental plane, and the Richard L. Perry Memorial Trust was established in his name.

the capacity of the School to fund."

What suffered from procrastination was coming to grips with the endless borrowing which had itself become a part of St. George's lifestyle. It became necessary to cut salaries. Vaughan Merrick set the example by cutting his own salary in a larger proportion than that of faculty and staff. New faculty members were guaranteed only one-year tenures, benefits in housing were curbed or eliminated, but still the fiscal crunch grew.

A restiveness grew among the Trustees themselves over the unsolved problems. Newer trustees believed that the School had too long depended upon a few generous benefactors, not only for capital improvements, but increasingly to "bail out" the budget. The truth of this conviction came at the wrong time. The School was in no position to forego this traditional form of support. What the newer Trustees wanted, a healthy balance between large givers and a broader support base, would not become a reality for many years.

Another "Catch-22" faced the School: the unresolved dilemma of tuition and fees. At a time when higher fees were needed, the ability of parents to pay them plummeted. St. George's had, even in Diman's time, sought to give scholarships to students deemed worthy of the education offered. The Trustees had long been as generous as funds would permit in allowing the Headmaster much discretion over the distribution of tuition reductions. As the Depression ground on, it pulverized the finances of families who had never needed such assistance and now found it imperative. A St. George's education was high on the list of priorities for these families.

To say the least, it was the most trying time yet to be a Trustee or Headmaster of the School. The Board had implicit trust in Merrick, so much so that it began to over-load him with problems usually settled within the Trustees.*

Realizing the need for professional business management, the Trustees appointed William Palmer as the first Business Manager. He served from 1934 to 1936, to be succeeded by James Hawke from 1936-1947. This was a much-needed, valuable and permanent addition affording clear, accurate reports and a professional monitoring of the budget.

---

*The inability of Trustees to attend meetings, caught as they were in other responsibilities, became a growing problem. Bishop Perry, as Board President, was absent 13 out of 28 meetings between 1936 and 1942, with Merrick asked to preside.

In retrospect, it seems strange that the School's imperiled financial state was not more visible beyond the Trustee's, Headmaster and Faculty. The signs were there throughout the 1930's: e.g. the Red and Blue Dorms were closed in 1936 for lack of enrollment; Alan R. Wheeler assumed supervision of the Buildings and Grounds for a three-year period, beyond his normal duties. The Alumni began to respond as best they could but many of them were personally caught in the Depression's hold. They showed special interest in attempting to raise scholarship funds to enable boys to both come and remain at the School.

Over the late 1930's the erosion of enrollment helped raise questions in the minds of some parents about the undeniably expensive education of boarding schools. The School could house 175 boys, but 1931-1932 was the last year for enrollment to show an increase (183). By 1936-1937, it was 150 and by 1941-1942 it had fallen to 130. In 1940 even parents were asking:

> "Whether schools [like St. George's] are an adequate
> answer to modern conditions and social trends."

The expensive boarding schools were beginning to look like anachronistic islands of luxury in a sea of national and international fiscal problems.

The Trustees began to look for alternatives to keep the School afloat. They were visibly shackled with not being able to charge anywhere near what was needed to maintain the facilities adequately, to say nothing of keeping up the academic goals so vital to the School's reputation.

In their search for answers, in January 1941 the Trustees took another tack; they sought the advice of experts outside the School. The John Price Jones Corporation of New York City was authorized to evaluate the School as a whole.

With surprising alacrity by March 1941 the Jones Educational Survey was in hand. Viewed against the backdrop of later, more sophisticated efforts, it appears to have been done hurriedly. The Trustees selected four aspects which they chose to act upon:

> That the Headmaster be asked to nominate an Assistant
> to the Headmaster to relieve the extraordinary (one
> could say, inhuman) overload under which Merrick
> and his predecessors had worked. They recommended

that he be from outside the Faculty. (An alumnus, Jay
B.L. Reeves '29, was appointed to fill the post, staying
for one year, 1941-1942.)
That an "all-around athletic coach, one particularly
versed in football be found." (Jeremiah Ford II, freshman football coach at the University of Pennsylvania,
came and remained until 1952.)
That "an outstanding scholar in Science" be found;
(Anthony Q. Keasbey was brought on, staying until
1943.)
Finding the School "under-promoted," the survey advised that it be better promoted in its "feeder schools"
and through improved public relations materials in bro-
chures and catalogues. (A different catalogue format
was instituted.)

Although widely disseminated (the Report appeared as a whole in
The Alumni Bulletin) there is little indication that it really struck at the
basic financial-enrollment problems. An enrollment of 130 boys in
1941-1942 brought with it a deficit of $51,161. And the prospect for
1942-1943 was further drastic reduction to only 99 boys.

Alarmed, the Trustees asked Merrick to mount a program which
would embrace:

"As great a savings as possible. . . even if certain customs
of the School have to be given up, and the budget must
be balanced for 1942-1943."

Merrick was one of the best Headmasters St. George's has had in its
first ninety years; he was not, however, a miracle worker. He had inherited many of the fiscal problems, and the Depression prevented him
from finding ready solutions. There seemed to be no way the Trustees'
strong request could be met. $100,000 was borrowed to see the School
through the 1941-1942 Year.

The die had been cast, however, and the procrastination of years
came to a halt. Employees were let go and the School's belt tightened.
The beginnings of a program of "Self-help" involved the boys in taking
greater responsibilities for what employees had previously done. It was
necessary, nonetheless, in October 1942 for Merrick to prepare the most
difficult Headmaster's Report of his career for a Trustees meeting at the
Hope Club in Providence. He was candid and reported that he could not:

> "...see any way of continuing the School in operation
> after this year [1942-1943] on the present basis."

Merrick made some drastic suggestions:

> That the School be leased to the Military for whatever
> use it might have of it; or
> That the School be changed into a Junior Naval College,
> with a Navy officer in charge; or
> That the School be reduced to a low-tuition, self-help
> institution for 250 to 300 boys.*

It was out of this period that a famous St. George's legend was born: that the Portsmouth Priory School,** headed by Father J. Hugh Diman, sought to buy the beleagured St. George's School. Moreover, the legend states that the black-garbed Benedictine monks arrived in a long black limousine and waited outside the Headmaster's Study during a Trustees meeting to make their offer. Intriguingly, so claims the legend, wealthy Trustees whipped out their checkbooks and "bailed out" the School, preventing a take-over of Episcopal St. George's by the Roman Catholic Benedictines.

The legend is more dramatic than the truth. Monks at the Portsmouth school categorically deny that it has the slightest truth. They report, to the contrary, that the Portsmouth Priory School had its own severe financial troubles and, anyway, Father Diman would never have stood for any such action.

As if reading from the Book of Job and his endless catastrophes,*** in the Spring of 1942, the physical giant of a man, Vaughan Merrick, was stricken with a heart attack and hospitalized for a month. He returned to his duties but by the Winter of 1943 declared himself physically unable to continue heading the School. With Mrs. Merrick, he retired to their Matunuck, Rhode Island home in June 1943. He was able to continue his valuable services to others through his writings, as a Trustee of St.

---

*There was talk during this period of St. George's absorbing St. Michael's, a day school in Newport serving the lower grade levels; they, too, were having financial troubles. This did not come to fruition.

**The Portsmouth Priory School became the Portsmouth Abbey School in 1969.

***Some may prefer "Murphy's Law" which states that if anything can go wrong it will.

George's until 1948, and in community services, especially to the Library, at Matunuck. He died in 1980 and the Memorial Plaque in the Chapel identifies him simply as "Headmaster."

There is in "Headmaster" a wealth of hidden meaning. Merrick's endurance of the crucible of the Depression is a striking story of an endless battle against the heaviest of odds. For the School which he served for fifteen trying years, he stands as the Headmaster who gave the most and was given the least in return of any St. George's leader. The perspective of time heightened his unyielding dedication and commitment, aspects of Merrick which those working closely with him knew about all along.

Unusual burdens were placed upon the Board of Trustees over the years 1928-1943. Bishop James DeWolfe Perry, Jr. was senior in every respect, having come to the Board's presidency in 1911 and remaining until 1946, the longest tenure of any Trustee. Harford W.H. Powel, Jr. '04*, Vincent Astor '10, RAdm. William S. Sims and Mark A. DeWolfe Howe were also veterans. Leading businessmen served during this period: Marion Eppley, M.M. vanBeuren, Barklie Henry '20, Charles S. Cheston '10 and Archbold vanBeuren '23. Kenneth S. Safe '20 and John Nicholas Brown '18 added their strength. Alumni Council Presidents (who serve *ex officio* as Trustees) during the 1930's and 1940's included A. Livingston Kelley '06**, R. Keith Kane '18, Graham B. Blaine '13, Harrison G. Reynolds '13, Weyman S. Crocker '14, H. Gates Lloyd '19, and Ashbel T. Wall '10.

If a School history had been written in 1946 at the time of St. George's Fiftieth Anniversary, it might well have called upon the memories of these men to assess the trying days of the Depression. This was not done.

---

*Harford W.H. Powel, Jr. resigned as a Trustee in 1930 and made bold to urge other Trustees to do likewise (except the President and Secretary-Treasurer). Powel, an articulate progressive, said that he did not want the Board to resemble the United States Supreme Court, a collection of old men making decisions out of a by-gone era.

**In 1939 A. Livingston Kelley succeeded Edward Sturtevant as Secretary-Treasurer of the Trustees, serving until 1946 when it was decided to appoint a Treasurer who would be an Administrative Officer of the School, but not a Trustee.

Their own carefully kept records, however, attest that they came to realize that mistakes had been made (especially in allowing the School to live in indebtedness), but the enduring commitment these men had to keep St. George's going is also revealed. They earn the thanks of those who have followed after them, for they were engulfed in the heaviest flames of the crucible of the Depression Years and the early days of World War II.

It is a painful loss to the School's History that Faculty Meeting Minutes have not surfaced for the vital Depression Years (and for many other years). Thus, written documentation of the intrinsically vital roles the Faculty played is missing.

What is known is that the Faculty was expected to be an accessory to the fact of the Trustees' desire to keep the School's problems from the boys. Also it was obvious that as cuts in salaries, added duties, fewer housing benefits came about, the Faculty became keenly aware of how hard the Depression had injured the School.

Forty-five new Faculty members came in the Merrick years. William A. Buell '14 returned in 1929 (he had also been a Master in 1919 and 1920) to continue until 1961 (from 1951 to 1961 as Headmaster). Others arriving were C.P. Beauchamp Jefferys in 1930, to remain until 1963; George W. Wheeler '27 in 1931 for his long service of forty-five years. The Rev. H. Martin P. Davidson, one of the most beloved of School Chaplains, began his fifteen year tenure in 1936. J. Raymond Fritz brought Manual Arts to the School from 1928 to 1948.

Veteran Masters retired: Russell H. Nevins' thirty-four years (two as Headmaster, 1926-1928) were closed out in 1936; Paul T. Christie, who had come in 1907, retired in 1943.* Frank McCloskey concluded a thirty-two year presence.

The all-male environment of the Hilltop was increasingly influenced by the presence of Faculty wives. They opened their homes to the boys, created a familial setting, and gave care and counsel, mostly to individual

---

*Christie went immediately to work for the Lockheed-Vega Aircraft Company in California. In letters back to the Hilltop, he noted that he had become a member of the Aeronautical Union, A.F. of L. as a machinist. This nudged the student editors of *The Dragon* to dub the retired Master, "our representative to labor."

boys, from their feminine perspectives. The four daughters of the William Drurys were among the girls of Faculty families – Hope, Kate, Sarah ("Sally") and Margaret ("Miggy") and have been long remembered by the boys of the time as attractive additions to the Hilltop. Other Faculty daughters have recalled (in 1986) the uniqueness of growing up in a boys' School setting and the pleasure they found in it – among them, Elizabeth Wheeler, daughter of the Alan R. Wheelers, Joan (Wheeler) Kaufman, daughter of the George Wheelers, Nancy (Jeffrey) Dees and Barbara (Elliott) Fargo.*

In 1939 a potentially disruptive Trustee/Faculty episode occurred with the Trustees moving in on the traditionally sacrosanct domain of the Faculty — academia. The Trustees became upset over reports that recent St. George's graduates were not doing well in the Ivy League colleges. They asked the Headmaster to appoint two Trustees, but no Faculty members, to investigate the situation. As it turned out, the graduates' deficiencies had been distorted. The Trustees returned with the report that Harvard and Princeton were exceptionally well satisfied with the freshmen the School had sent them; Yale and the University of Pennsylvania were less enthusiastic in their findings. While the right of the Trustees to investigate anything and everything in the School was undeniable, (they do, indeed, have full legal responsibility for the School's life), the breaking of the tradition of autonomy within the Faculty for academics was unfortunate. In the light of the disruptive Depression Years, the episode revealed how uneasy everybody became at the time.

In the final analysis in the crucible of the Depression there proved no escape for anyone in facing the taxing problems incurred. Eventually, Trustees, Headmaster, Faculty, Staff, Students, Parents, Alumni — all be-

---

*Elizabeth Wheeler, in 1986, when asked what it was like to be a girl at St. George's replied with a twinkle in her eye, "It was fun!" – a response also given by other girls from Faculty families. Years before, Arthur S. Roberts had expressed the hope that St. George's would become coeducational so that his daughter, Ilonka, could become a full student. As it was, she was the first girl to be taught on the campus. Since she was tutored by Jay Moody in Greek in the early 1920's.

came embroiled in keeping the School going. Of these no one was at greater risk than the Faculty. They were the professionals whose livelihoods depended upon the effective continuance of the School. Theirs was the greatest investment of education, experience, time and abilities, and they were the first to be struck with curtailments. Even before the Trustees "bit the bullet" to curb St. George's expensive lifestyle, the Faculty had salary cuts. Especially jeopardized were the older Faculty. Their "marketability" was dubious; some of them had given entire vocational lifetimes to St. George's. Younger Faculty had a mobility of opportunity (the turn-over was great during the Depression), but not the older ones. The Trustees did not always evidence as complete an understanding of what they were asking of the Headmaster and Faculty under the extraordinary circumstances. It was difficult to be heroic in the setting of the frustrating economic upheavals which dogged the School during those years. The 1930's and 1940's were exhausting years, demanding durability and a stick-to-it-tive-ness that certainly was shown time after time. If there was any one hero, it had to be Vaughan Merrick. With unusual skill he bridged the gap between the multiple constituencies of the School.

Pearl Harbor, 7 December 1941, brought the United States into World War II; it also brought new and further challenging problems. The Depression ended; a new war economy took over. St. George's Alumni, Masters and older boys were drawn into military service. The School did not repeat the intensity of involvement on the Hilltop itself which had marked World War I – there was no School Battalion, no planting vegetables on the lawn. There was, however, Red Cross work, including students in Mr. Fritz's Manual Arts class building a Red Cross Canteen to be mounted on a truck chassis and used in Newport; (a second Canteen was purchased and sent to England for use of troops). Boys listened daily to the radio to follow the progress of the war. They established an abbreviated daily newspaper reporting the events abroad, especially of St. Georgians in combat. Reports were given in *The Dragon* in greater detail. It was *The Alumni Bulletin,* however, which dealt most definitively with Alumni in military and related services around the globe. It became the most vital connector communicating what the war had brought to those formerly on the Hilltop.

Shortly after Pearl Harbor the Chapel's lofty tower became a Spotter Station, monitoring aircraft and shipping on Rhode Island Sound. The Station was operated around the clock, seven days a week until October 1943, and on a partial basis for a time thereafter. Staffed by volunteers led by George W. Wheeler '27, there were boys, Faculty members, Aquidneck Island residents and, somewhat neglected in memory, Faculty wives. Those recalling Tower duty years later remembered it as being far more tedious than dangerous. No record of enemy aircraft or shipping being sighted is known, although at least one crash of an American military plane was sighted and reported.*

The already damaging situation of declining enrollment was exacerbated by the nation's involvement in the war. A fear, of boys being caught up in hostile action if the Torpedo Station at the Newport Naval Base were ever blown up and of the School's presumed vulnerable position to the open Atlantic, grew in intensity. Some parents preferred to send their boys further inland. With 99 boys enrolled in 1942-1943 (and only 89 projected for 1943-1944), the impact of this fear was substantively felt.

On 4 June 1943 as Vaughan and Beatrice Merrick were leaving, Willet and Dorothy Eccles arrived. Dr. Eccles became St. George's fifth Headmaster. He brought some radically new approaches to the School and made his own penetrating impact upon it.

---

*An alumnus has told Anthony M. Zane (Headmaster, 1972-1984) of being in Germany after the war and hearing a former submarine sailor tell of sighting the Chapel's tower through a periscope. The hidden danger was, it would appear, closer than anyone fully realized.

The Studious Dragon

CHAPTER SIX

Collision and Restoration
1943 - 1961

OVER THE YEARS, St. George's had drawn boys mainly from affluent families able to afford the increasingly expensive tuitions charged. All along, there were those, Diman and others, who wanted it otherwise. They preferred a mix of students from a broad spectrum of society, admitted on the basis of intellect and character more than the ability to pay. This high-minded goal eluded the School chiefly due to a lack of endowment to fund the scholarships required. The Depression forced the School to increase its financial aid, but this was expediential, rather than a planned program to acquire a broad mix of students. Hence, the traditions and practices of St. George's had been formed and influenced by its being a rich boys' School.

Dr. Willet L. Eccles, the School's fifth Headmaster sought to change this historic situation. In doing so, he deliberately set out on a collision course with tradition, a course to become growingly controversial as his tenure moved on.

Significantly, however, it was the habitually traditionalist Board of Trustees who first collided with tradition, and they did so in their appointment of Eccles. In choosing every Headmaster since the Rev. John Byron Diman, the Trustees had expended much painstaking effort interviewing many candidates. In 1943, within a few weeks, not months (nor two years, as in securing J. Vaughan Merrick), Eccles had been found and appointed. The sense of urgency was real. Merrick – dogged by ill-health – had to retire, enrollment was down to about half capacity, and the precarious financial situation of many years standing remained unresolved.*

---

*An affirmation, made at the Twenty-fifth Anniversary of the School in 1921, proved premature. It was that "the School is now formidable, able to demand and free to give. The fight for existence is over."

There was relief that the Trustees had so quickly found a man of Eccles' proven administrative stature. At 46, he brought the most impressive of academic credentials (Bachelor, Master and Ph.D. degrees from Columbia University). Having taught chemistry at Phillips Academy, Andover, Massachusetts, he went on to serve as Dean of Students/ Registrar. With his wife, Dorothy, a splendid musician who enhanced the fine arts program over the years, and their children, Eccles arrived on the Hilltop. Beyond the polite, *pro forma* introductions given to new Headmasters, St. George's Trustees expressed their unqualified enthusiasm for Eccles.

He wasted no time getting down to work. It was soon apparent that he was a hard-driving, hard-working, demanding, meticulous and knowledgable administrator. Once he decided what he wanted, he moved toward its fulfillment with speed, precision, assertiveness and vigor. From the beginning it was clear that he both understood the School's problems and intended to solve them as quickly as possible.

Eccles tackled first the serious problem of diminished enrollment. The School, equipped to handle 175 boys, had only 89 in 1943. Tuition money was urgently and immediately needed for cash-flow and on-going operations (quite apart from that needed for capital indebtedness or improvements, the purvue of the Trustees). Operations' income was considerably improved as Eccles was able, by his second year, to lift enrollment to 123 boys.*

To attract increased enrollment the School deliberately lowered its scholastic standards and also accepted boys from lower economic levels than had earlier been found on the Hilltop. This was in collision with the past, with Eccles mainly responsible for it, and at first he was given little opposition. He was the center of a recovering St. George's, driving hard, refusing to take vacations and pressuring everyone in a relentlessly exacting manner. This became the basis for the fact that Eccles had led in "saving the School" from an undetermined fate; whether to close,

---

*Over the next several years increments of about 20 boys each year describe the growth that took place. By 1949-1950 a full capacity enrollment (175) was achieved and the operational budget balanced. However, in 1950-1951, enrollment began to drop again; it was down to 165 in Eccles' last year.

temporarily or permanently, never had to be decided. Eccles did not, of course, accomplish this recovery single-handedly. Nothing is taken away from his brilliant crisis management to recognize that Trustees, Faculty, Alumni, students and friends of the School shared in its recovery. However, in the particularized world of boarding schools, who the headmaster is and what he does usually determine much of the direction of a school.

It proved that Eccles' plan to bring a mixture of students to St. George's was not a temporary, war-time, emergency action. He was, in fact, dedicated to a similiar kind of eclectic breadth of enrollment that Diman had hoped for but never achieved (an admission Diman made later in life). A tough realist, Eccles knew all this was a gamble at St. George's, but he was determined to effect the changes in scholastic and social traditions with some sensible undergirding. The passing years seem to have blunted the fact that Eccles did not simply take boys willy-nilly (or merely "Handovers" – rejects from Andover and other schools); he produced remedial programs designed to support students and bring them up to St. George's standards as a college preparatory school. The Language Training Program he put in place became a permanent asset to the School. The Self-Help Program had boys doing their own chores and helping others beyond the Hilltop. Eccles saw these as a part of an educational philosophy to be permanently implanted in St. George's soil. This sense of permanency seemed to be lost for some as the years went on, especially those who viewed the changes as collisions with long-established and hard-won traditions.

Eccles' administration was marked by another serious collision – the result of his often blunt and sometimes abrasive personality traits. He grew increasingly authoritarian as the years went on. He alienated people (and some felt needlessly) by being amazingly insensitive in the ways he dealt with them. His assertive strength, very much needed in the early crises of his tenure, seemed unneeded as the problems appeared solved. What is clear, from a dispassionately objective review of the Eccles Years, is that the crises were never really over. In the often obtuse way financial management went for the School (an obtuseness the Trustees were eventually to acknowledge), the improved cash-flow and balances in the School's operational budget were not matched by enough improvement in paying off capital indebtedness, getting around to deferred maintenance, and other serious problems. Eccles was fully aware of this (as were the Trustees) and kept up his crisis management to the end. It cost him friends and support eventually (abetted by his abrasiveness) but actually served to make the School's approaches more realistic. It appeared that more credit was given Eccles outside the School than within it.*

The financial problems which faced St. George's had accrued over many years; they certainly were not of Eccles' making, for he helped solve them more than contribute to them (a major achievement). The continuing heart of the financial difficulties was that too much had been spent (mainly borrowed money) on capital outlays. The indebtedness accumulated on buildings and land just never got paid off (a repeat scenario from the 1930's). One interesting indication was that $14,250 was still unpaid on the original (1901) mortgage on Old School. As earlier, there continued the strong motivation to both protect the School and enhance it by buying property in its environs. Amidst crucial indebtedness the Easton Farm was bought in 1946. It lay to the east and northeast of the Hilltop, protecting an openness to Second Beach. This was done on borrowed money (although some of the investment was recovered later in sales of the Easton Farm land deemed not needed). There even came the day, in the Winter of 1949, when a major lending bank in Providence notified the School that it could no longer loan it money without better payments on that already lent. The bank did so, however, upon the intervention of prestigious Alumni who were also School Trustees.

St. George's financial affairs remained a mystery to all but a few, mainly the Trustees. A reluctance to make known the School's true financial state was deeply and historically embedded in that body. In 1949, in yet another collision with tradition, Morton Goodspeed '14, an influential Trustee who proved to be an excellent fund-raiser, urged his colleagues to "level" with the Alumni and divulge the true fiscal situa-

---

*Dr. Lewis Perry, Principal of Phillips Exeter Academy, Exeter, New Hampshire, described St. George's recovery during World War II as unprecedented in the annals of American boarding schools. It was no secret that the Depression and World War II had devastating effects on many schools; the road back was long, demanding and rough.

tion of the School. He believed, and correctly, that more funds would be forthcoming from Alumni if they were adequately advised of the perpetually unresolved money problems. The Trustees agreed, and this became one of the most important moves taken by them. Among the salutary effects was that it laid the groundwork for further successful fund-raising for endowment in the 1960's through a network of willing alumni benefactors. Between 1949 and 1952, under Goodspeed's strong leadership in the Trustees, $100,000 was raised to aid in bringing down the capital indebtedness (running over $200,000). The presence of Henry Schereschewsky (brought by Eccles in 1947 as Treasurer/Business Manager) provided a much needed clarity and sensibility in the School's management.

Throughout any recital of St. George's fiscal affairs in the difficult years 1930 to the mid-1950's, it must be kept in mind that the Trustees worked endlessly hard on the problems. 20/20 hindsight can fault them for accruing an astonishing indebtedness, but it must take into account their high hopes and great expectations that St. George's become recognized, self-sufficient and famous. Their efforts were badly damaged by the Depression, World War II and, as became clear later, from some ineptness in business management, together with expansion beyond the reach of reasonable fiscal prudence. But there was evidence of "Yankee thrift" among them, too. When the destructive 1944 Hurricane wreaked its havoc along the New England coast, St. George's was caught in it. The boathouse on Third Beach, so long a popular center for boating and crew, was irreparably damaged. It had been built in part from the timbers of the 1903 Gymnasium-become-Schoolhouse which was torn down after the 1911 Gymnasium-become-Twenty-House was built. In yet another reincarnation, some of the timbers from the destroyed boathouse went into enlarging the Manual Training Shop on the Hilltop.

The constant villain in the financial drama remained an inability to build up enough endowment to buffer the seismic shocks of enrollment variances or temporary financial reverses. The work begun in the 1940's to correct this lack was valiant, if not thoroughly successful. Eccles' "strong hand on the tiller" helped balance the School's operating budget, but this was continually offset by the imbalances in capital expenditures.*

---

*It was to be the late 1950's before solid advances were made in acquiring endowment, accumulating to over $1,500,000 by 1961.

Whereas in the 1930's there had been a concerted attempt to keep the boys unaware of the School's problems, this was not the case under Eccles. While they were never apprised of the financial difficulties *per se,* the boys were aware that all was not well. The diminished enrollment was evidence, as were the curbs in the previously achieved and traditional life-style. Also, the mix of boys from across economic and social groupings changed the image of life on the Hilltop.

In 1946, about to retire, Senior Master Arthur S. Roberts, with characteristic candor, looked favorably upon that new image. He put it well:

> "The easy fortunes of the 20's brought some boys from families socially ambitious and culturally deficient. A new obligation arose to furnish ideals as well as ideas. Emphasis shifted from culture to character.
>
> "In a way, the financial crash and consequent Depression helped in this shift. Boys who had earlier taken comfortable homes for granted found in them no refuge. With rising income taxes wiping out security, education and not inheritance became insurance against the future."

Roberts had been known for forty-three years as espousing the broadest possible mix of boys. He understood boys, and welcomed them from a variety of intellectual and family backgrounds. It was said of him:

> "[He] cared little for form. He believed in simple living [and] always regretted that more boys whose parents were of the lower class could not have come to St. George's."

The demands upon boys for academic and behavioral discipline and conformity were not really relaxed. St. George's would not then – nor later – meet William James' description of Harvard's:

> "...tolerance of exceptionality and eccentricity...Our undisciplinables are our proudest product. Let us agree in hope that the output of them will never cease."

Schools such as St. George's have traditionally placed a value upon conformity and uniformity. These are carefully defined in terms of everything from dress codes to honor codes, together with detailed prescriptions regulating student behavior, often with rigidity. Critics outside boarding schools complain about a "preppie" intolerance of failure and a lack of compassion for suffering. The tough-minded Eccles revealed considerable tolerance for boys who could not readily succeed. He did not want them to suffer for their failures, but to redeem them with St. George's mounting remedial assistance possibilities. It was more than rhetoric when Eccles spoke of wanting boys well-grounded in knowing how to think, study, research and communicate; these were practical goals. He wanted more freedom for Sixth Formers, that they might be prepared for the larger freedoms of higher education. Anything but "soft" on students, neither did he peremptorily expel them, preferring to work for their continuance, rather than severance, from the opportunities St. George's offered.*

It would be a grave error to chalk up the 1940's and the Eccles Years as filled only with grim-faced people mired down in seemingly insoluble problems. The sub-culture of a boarding school was played out (as it inevitably is) in dormitories, athletics, extracurricular activities. Henry Hager '45 upon graduating from the Hilltop wrote his *Fields Of Play*** in which he makes this abundantly clear. A review of the School's student publications, together with reminiscences shared by Alumni, reveals the 1940's as a unique time to be a St. George's student. Life was indeed different. The long era of maid service largely ended, the boys were expected to do for themselves what had earlier been done for them. The School was smaller than it had been for years, and this helped forge an *esprit de corps* brought about in part by the disjointed times, but also by

---

*In 1986, a former Eccles Years student, who had kept in touch with Eccles, observed that this controversial Headmaster had "given us dummies a chance," and that he had inspired confidence, taught boys how to study, and "tried to get boys back on the track when they strayed." The man had made "a tremendous difference in his and other boys' lives."

**Fields Of Play* is a valuable memoir of Hager's years at St. George's (1941-1945) in an unpublished manuscript of some 280 double-spaced, typewritten pages, written soon after he graduated from the School. (He later became a professional writer.) His descriptions of the times are replete with his keen eye for people and events. As the title conveys, Hager was avidly into athletics, an area he chronicles during an especially trying period for the boys. This history is indebted to Henry Hager for capturing the times with such clarity.

the new mix of varied personalities and backgrounds.

The boys sought to outwit Masters and Prefects (an old game) with escapades – their actual success somewhat uncertain. Hager tells of raids between the Third Formers of Arden's Green Dorm and Twenty House's Fourth Formers. There was the allure of "after lights" expeditions, testing whether or not the Masters were truly alert.

The Dance indeed remained *The* Dance, anticipated with growing excitement and orchestrated along the lines of a mini-Hollywood production. Hager recalls girls housed in Twenty House and boys leaving pictures, notes and various pieces of masculine apparel around, hoping for an exchange of pictures, notes and feminine apparel. The negotiations for dates, the "loves" won, lost and exchanged, continued to make *The* Dance the highlight of the social calendar, with an imprimatur on some boys' memories to remain remarkably clear years later.

Athletics, despite their popularity, were curbed at first during the war, but were renewed afterwards. The football victory of 1944 over Middlesex (21-0, with William Elliott, Head Coach), the first since 1904, elicited a School Holiday.* Crew continued, despite the loss of the boathouse in the 1944 Hurricane. The early post-war years were a time of re-building athletics and were savored, by the boys who played in them, as integral to life on the Hilltop. The significance of athletic victories, held to be a major force in "holding the School together," continued unabated in the 1940's and into the 1950's.

The "perpetual welcome" of students by faculty families in their homes was especially important at the time. The homes were often open as if they had "revolving doors."** Nothing dimmed the popularity of extra-curricular activities such as the Civic Clubs, debating, the St. George's Society, working on the School publications, singing in the Choir and other musical groups, playing games of bridge, "bull sessions" in the dormitories – all apart from, yet woven into, the strenuous academic schedule.

In the "1947 School Review" (a feature in *The Lance*), Jonathan

---

*Jeremiah Ford, II (1941-1952) was also a respected coach who went on to become Director of Athletics at the University of Pennsylvania.

**Barbara (Elliott) Fargo in 1986 told of her good fortune to be a daughter in a Faculty family in those years. She noted it as being a rare and unmatched life. She found one drawback: when girls like her would have most enjoyed the company of boys *(and vice versa),* parents shipped them off to boarding schools.

LeRoy King '47 found it worth recording for posterity that "the Prefect's paddle is no more." In sentiments, recognizable across other years, he observed:

> "The School may have made its mark in our minds educationally, but its greatest contribution has really been in our hearts, for it is the friendships we have made here – with our school-mates and our masters – that will keep us close to St. George's in the years to come."

The "1950 School Review" (unsigned) revealed the good humor with which the profile of an entire class could be communicated:

> "Since the Class of 1950 first came into being, many changes have taken place at St. George's. Masters who were once confirmed bachelors have settled down to domesticity, television aerials have sprouted from the staid rooftops of Old School and Arden Hall, black dogs and small babies have appeared on the campus in ever-increasing numbers, dilapidated faculty automobiles have become a thing of the past."

At Alumni Reunions some forty-years later, it became apparent that the "tough" years of the 1940's had their own mystique. Arguments could still be raised *pro* and *con* regarding Dr. Eccles' collisions with change and tradition, yet underneath it all, there was a recognition that those years had developed for most a unique love for and commitment to St. George's School. The names, Wheeler, Elliott, Roberts, Vermillion, Jefferys, Eccles, Ford, "Padre" Davidson and others were centerpieces for reflection and gratitude.

The Faculty and Trustees were somewhat in flux during the war years and after as men went into the armed forces and related services. The march of time brought veteran Masters to retirement: Arthur S. Roberts in 1946, Herbert F. Preston and Alan R. Wheeler in 1947, with J. Raymond Fritz retiring in 1948. The vital presence of the Rev. H. Martin P. Davidson, School Chaplain and Rector of St. Columba's Church, Middletown, was impressive over the years he served, 1936-1951. Very much the priest, yet thoroughly a human being, "Padre's" presence spoke volumes in the contagiously Christian life he expressed. His was not a "muscular Christianity," but one of quiet persuasiveness. It reached some boys on the periphery of religious interest as well as those with greater awareness and commitment. His leaving, at the same time that Eccles did, was to go into parish work, and he was sorely missed.

Eccles revealed an ability to attract well-educated men to the Faculty. Three Ph.D.'s came: Alexander Rice, to teach Latin (1943-1946); Richard Knowles, Latin (1944-1953); and Norris Hoyt, to remain 29 years teaching English, coaching swimming and crew, and becoming photographer *par excellence* graphically recording School life. Charles G. Thornblade came in 1947, to remain 18 years, establishing his inimitable parties with their formal dress and panache, hard to match ever after. There were also more Faculty with Master's degrees and others taking courses toward that end.*

The most intense years of the participation of the United States in World War II came during Eccles' first two years, 1943-1945. The realities of the war were never far away – the Chapel's Aircraft Spotting Station, Red Cross Blood Drives, the black-outs, reduced food and fuel, the perpetual uneasiness about fathers, brothers and other relatives in war zones.

Between World War I's Class of 1919 and World War II's Class of 1941, some 840 young men graduated from St. George's School. They provided a much larger manpower resource from which to draw than in World War I. Some 660 alumni were eventually engaged in World War II. They served in the United States Army, Navy, Marine Corps and Air Corps and also in the Office of Strategic Services, the Civil Air Patrol, the American Field Service and in civilian related positions allied with the armed forces. Some were in the armed forces of Canada and Great Britain.

Twenty-nine men gave their lives, beginning with George Rathbone Dyer '26 on 5 May 1941 through William Donald Twining '40 on 4 July 1946. (See Appendix D) On 19 May 1949, a Memorial Tablet,

---

*Twenty-four St. George's Faculty members have become headmasters at other schools. Of that number, nine were at the School during Eccles' Years, supporting the fact that its most controversial Headmaster had brought quality Masters aboard. (See Appendix A for names.)

designed by Frederic Rhinelander King '04, was unveiled in their memory in the foyer of the Schoolhouse, across from that of World War I. Within an Italian marble frame the names of the dead were inscribed and the poignant words:

Tell the Republic that by land and sea
These men were valiant as our sons must be.

In a subsequent annual rite, it was the custom to read the names of the war dead and honor their sacrifices. A moving occasion for many students, it could evoke strong emotions. A student, identifying himself only as "Bartleby, early '70's," has recalled George W. Wheeler's participation in the reading of the names, and of his being unable to continue because of the emotions stirred. As a veteran Master, he had known most of those who had died, either in the classroom, on athletic fields, in dormitories, or from having spent virtually a lifetime on the Hilltop. "Bartleby" commented:

> "This gray-haired man, not eight feet in front of me, could tell me about every one of those names, which of them had a good curve ball, or chicken pox his first term, or was a good swimmer down at the beach...We were not a quick witted group, but schoolboys know history when they are shown it."

World War II brought the only mid-year graduation St. George's has ever had. It was the conclusion to the Accelerated Program for students who would reach their eighteenth or nineteenth birthdays within the first half of the School year and hence be subject to being drafted into military service (or be permitted to volunteer). In January 1945 three young men, Oscar L. Gubelman, Henry B. Hager and Alfred R. Hunter, Jr., were graduated in ceremonies held in the Chapel. Hager has recalled the solemnity in the Chapel, together with a sense of separation from St. George's soon to occur; but he also remembered dinner at a Newport hotel, reviewing football movies and farewells to Hilltop friends. This was a very clear signal that the world was at war and that St. George's was involved in it.

The hope had persisted in 1918 that "The Great War" would be one "to end all wars." The restless geopolitical situation after World War II promised no such hope. On 25 June 1950, the Korean War broke out.

United States Forces were a part of those of the United Nations caught in a distant war, in a strangely remote Asian nation, meant to halt the advance of Communism in Asia. By the time an armistice was signed, 27 July 1953, two St. George's alumni had died. (See Appendix D) A third memorial plaque was placed in the Memorial Schoolhouse foyer. The continuing generations of the Hilltop's young men, called to give their lives for their country, were yet again represented.

Bishop James DeWolfe Perry, President of the Board of Trustees from 1911 until 1946, died in 1947, having retired the previous year. His distinguished service to the Church included being not only Bishop of Rhode Island but, from 1930 to 1937, Presiding Bishop of the Episcopal Church. Bishop Perry brought a strong ecclesiastical presence to St. George's; he was its most visible tie with Episcopalianism. He stood most forcibly for what St. George's never became – a church-centered school. The "independent school" identity, older than that of a church affiliation, was a factor which kept intruding upon a church-centeredness, making it what is best described as an independent Episcopal School.* Whatever his disappointments, Bishop Perry never lost his touch of authority as a prelate; he took his wins and losses with consummate grace. His friend and constant ally at St. George's, John Nicholas Brown '18, praised the Bishop's constant concern for the total welfare of the School and as one whose interest in its life "never flagged." Bishop Granville Gaylord Bennett assumed the Board's Presidency in 1946 to serve until 1954.

The School celebrated its Fiftieth Anniversary in 1946. The observance was punctuated with nostalgically recapturing the memories of the past. In the limelight were those, well along in years, whose numbers were rapidly declining. No history of the School had yet been written (something for which Eccles expressed regret), and the major source of its past was wrapped up in the experiences of Trustees, Senior Masters, Alumni, and scattered other people who had known the School from

---

*The continuing affirmation of the independent school aspect of St. George's is a thread
  running throughout its first ninety years.

the beginning.

Much of the flavor of the Anniversary was preserved in issues of *The Alumni Bulletin* in 1946. The years were rolled back in reminiscences. There were reunions of classes, Masters and students which stirred up friendships lapsed after years of separation from the Hilltop. Possibly nothing could have captured the essence of the Fifty Years more brilliantly, however, than a photograph of the five Headmasters. Attention was irretrievably drawn to Father J. Hugh Diman, thirty years gone from the School, and in the garb of a Benedictine monk. He was 83, and the years had softened the sternness found in earlier portraits and photographs of him around St. George's. (Three years later he died, as did his sister, Emily.) Russell H. Nevins is in the photograph, tall of stature but often in ill-health. He died in 1951 at the age of 71. Stephen P. Cabot is there, small and frail, nonetheless to live to 82, dying also in 1951. The towering J. Vaughan Merrick looms over his colleagues; living until 1980, he achieved 86 years of life. Willet L. Eccles completes the picture; the youngest, he died in 1982 at age 85. (The generous lifespan of these St. George's leaders must somehow bespeak their durability through thick and thin.) In this one photograph fifty years of St. George's history is represented with an opportunity to retrieve something of what these men have meant to the School.

The Anniversary found Faculty members recapturing their remembrances with wit, wisdom and appreciation. In a collage effect, these came alongside confessions by former students of pranks and squanderings of time and energy dredged up with boyish glee. The deep affection for Nellie Brown, "Old Sam," "Young Sam," Theo, Maggie Galvin and others who served the School so faithfully, was sincerely expressed.

In a collection of nostalgic remembrances, printed in *The Alumni Bulletin,* Edward Howland led off with a vivid description of the first night in October 1896 of "Mr. Diman's School for Boys" at the two Hunter Avenue houses in Newport. G. Andrews Moriarty '02, Harford W.H. Powel '04, Leonard Bacon '05, revealed near photographic memories of events and people unknown to new generations of students and Masters. The names Peaslee, Moody, Sheldon, Griswold, Barton, Judge, Hoban were catalysts in reminiscences that went on and on. H. H. Powel '10, F. B. Todd '14 and Douglas S. Byers '21 recalled the World War I years, including Diman's startling resignation, and went on to extoll Stephen P. Cabot's schoolmaster's genius. Time was rapidly passing as Wilson Ware '32 encapsulated the more recent Merrick Years, with the new and persuasive Headmaster's wife added to the Hilltop. William Edgar '37 wrote of "The Upswing in Athletics" between 1936 and 1938. D. A. Demarest '42 offered a short piece on "World War II Comes to St. George's," observing "in the gym we writhed in calisthenics under the grim and gimlet eye of Keene Shortell." H. C. Hamilton '44, wrote:

> "[World War II] was a dominant and sobering factor in School life, but never sobering enough to prevent an occasional water battle from breaking out in Sixth Form House."

The famous humorous poet, Ogden Nash '20, dredged up some poignant reminiscences:

IT'S A LONG TIME BETWEEN RESERVOIRS
By Ogden Nash, '20

At Middletown in nineteen twenty
We craved no *spiritus frumenti;*
We'd never heard of jive or rumba
Our hearts belonged to St. Columba.
At Pinecroft in that bouyant year
Our eyes were bright, our heads were clear.

Miss Diman, tranquil as a sonnet,
Led Sachuest to speak Sakonnet.
Not yet, in Red or Blue or Arden,
Had arteries begun to harden.
Cider and cake, dropped eggs on toast,
The apple pie of Whitman boast,
Served but to whet our supper hunger;
Conclusive proof that we were younger.

Those were the days of very giants
From classics up, or down, to science.
See Stephen Cabot at the head,
His evening socks were Harvard red;
On land, an affable Headmaster,
But on ice, hell and disaster.

How shall I sing those other Messrs.,
Our tyrants, helpers and confessors?
Kind Sturtevant of the boyish heart,
Physics his science, boats his art;
And Roberts now, that two-fold menace,
He'd whale you, Tennyson or tennis.
Erasers hurtling from the heavens
Proclaimed the wrath of Russell Nevins;
And who with nostrils can forget
Christie's Lord Salisbury cigarette?

Watch Peaslee's mental acrobatics,
Teaching this quadruped quadratics;
And Preston, shaken to the viscera,
As taurine fullbacks tackle Cicera;
Or Wheeler's patience put to rout
By Latin scholars striking out.

The Old Guard's colors will not fade
Long were they honored, long obeyed —
Perhaps they'll find the jest sublime
To learn we loved them all the time.

Nostalgia ruled, even as Masters laced their signed and unsigned articles with scholastically-inspired Latin quotations. William Buell '14 reviewed the 50 years of athletics, 1896-1946. He helpfully included "Club" sports of the long-departed Sakonnet and Sachuest Clubs, together with boating, crew, swimming, gymnastics, soccer, as well as the crown princes, football, baseball and basketball. (Ice hockey had not achieved its later royal position.)

There was a singular absence of serious reference to the intellectual life of the School, with two exceptions. One was Arthur S. Roberts' paper, "Academic Purpose." This was vintage Roberts – splendidly written and an overview of "Fifty Years of Independent Schools." He had known a professional life-time as a St. George's Master. He had joined with Stephen P. Cabot in serving the larger private school world, Cabot through his "Progressive Education" leadership after leaving St. George's, and Roberts as President of what has since become the National Association of Independent Schools. Eschewing nostalgia entirely, Roberts analyzed how independent schools had remained not fixed, totally predictable institutions, but had changed traditions, social customs and academic expectations over the years. He pictured St. George's as having evolved into a much stiffer academic institution than it was in its earlier days:

> "...the progressive movement [having] done much to ameliorate the smugness of conservative schools with their encrusted form and dull immobility."

Roberts' clear-headedness and his gift of perception had served St. George's long and well.

Willet L. Eccles contributed a second seriously intended paper. In his sensible "What of the Future?" he pursued the need for quality schools and wrote:

> "Not only will St. George's and other schools of its type survive, but they will have a more important function to perform in and for American life than heretofore."

He saw the need to:

> "...[teach students] how to get good results from whatever they undertake, which means to work intelligently and hard; and training them in the principles of living useful, constructive, unselfish, Christian lives.
>
> "Ours is no starry-eyed approach, but rather, a practical one. To achieve our aims will require all our energy and all our skill in dealing with boys. But in due course it will produce men of character and purpose, for we can teach boys by our precept and example."

It was an impressive and important philosophy conveyed to a School with vital years ahead of it.

The Fiftieth Anniversary celebrated, the factor of unrelenting realities faced St. George's. Eccles was not yet under the heaviest fire he would encounter from his collisions with tradition, for opposition against him mounted most heavily in his last two years. In 1949, having been offered another position, he asked for a registration of the Trustees' support of his administration. They gave him their unanimous assurance of that support, but said that they did not wish to stand in the way of his advancement. Eccles stayed, only to be pressured to resign two years later. A key factor in his leaving was said to be that he had turned St.

George's into "an unhappy School."* But there was also a downswing in the enrollment, going from 187 in 1949-1950 to 165 in Eccles' last year, 1950-1951. Discontent was registered, especially by the older Masters; a change of leadership was deemed needed.

All along Willet L. Eccles had been to some extent "a prophet not without honor, except in his own country and among his own people." It was recognized beyond, as well as within St. George's, that few could have done what he did – stay the course amidst enrollment, financial and opposition crises. In 1950, there was a move to honor Eccles' achievements with a building, possibly a library or science hall, given in his name while he was still living. Even the enthusiasm of Harford W. H. Powel '04, did not suffice to make this a reality. Libraries were built and a science building, but not in Eccles' honor.

There is, however, a memorial to Willet L. Eccles in the form of a delightful park-like entrance at the west end of Memorial Schoolhouse. It was given by William Bayne '48, in 1983, in appreciation of the Headmaster who had given him, and others, the chance they might not otherwise have had to attend St. George's School. Bayne remained a close friend of Eccles after the former Headmaster became associated with the Central Intelligence Agency (where he established a distinguished record directing the training of agents) and until Eccles' death in 1982 in Pasadena, California.

Eccles' efforts to move the School in new directions, away from older traditions, had limited success. The desire to restore the School to its pre-Eccles identity and image was strong and became successful over the 1950's. However, his collisions with tradition and his efforts to move the School along, were not, by any means, totally lost upon the School. Increasing numbers of students, chosen by talent and character, beyond the range of their parents' ability to pay, came to St. George's later under the Astor Scholarships.** The emphasis placed upon supportive systems to help students along academically and socially was never dropped. The pragmatism which Eccles incorporated into St. George's administrative life has remained as a valuable contribution.

---

*William A. Buell quotes this (as coming from a Trustee at the time) in his memoirs, *My Life And St. George's School* (1967).

**Begun in 1964 in memory of Vincent Astor '10, these have provided scholarship aid to some 130 students between then and 1986.

Of the Headmasters to serve in the first ninety years of the School, none left a greater impression *pro* and *con* than its fifth, Dr. Willet L. Eccles.

William Ackerman Buell '14 was appointed Headmaster in May 1951. This announcement and that of the resignation of Willet L. Eccles were both made at a School Assembly on 23 May. Buell was the only graduate of the School to become its Headmaster in the first ninety years, but the third to be chosen from within the Faculty. He had spent 22 years as a member of the Faculty. Over the ten years that he led the School (1951-1961) he became one of its most popular and honored leaders.

Buell's appointment came as a surprise to some of his colleagues – he had kept a low-profile among them and his lack of interest in administration was well known. In 1930, Buell had built "Little Rest," a charming Colonial house on the eastern edge of the Hilltop. With his wife, Lois, he entertained there but was somewhat removed from the center of School life in comparison with Masters supervising dormitories. He tended to shun controversy and had kept out of that stirred by Eccles' collision with tradition and change. (This, in a converse manner, had its positive side, demonstrating traits which stood in studied contrast to his predecessor.) His contributions were unique. He had founded and was the guiding spirit of Camp Ramleh, the School's summer camp for disadvantaged children. He had taught English as his major discipline (but also Sacred Studies at times) and had directed drama. In drama, he elevated that art form to dimensions of expertise rarely found in secondary schools. His "Frostbite Picnics" on winter Sundays became famous, held on the rocks at the shore below the School. The Buells were exceptionally skilled as hosts, whether it be having boys in their home (and later in the Headmaster's Apartment), entertaining the Faculty or the many Alumni they had come to know over the years.

As Buell came into the Headmastership, what was unknown was how his low-profiled personality would meet the still crucial needs of the School's administrative side. There had been twenty almost inhumanly demanding years for Merrick and for Eccles. For a short while, the uneasiness surrounding Buell seemed justified. There was a drop rather than an increase in enrollment his first year. Indeed, it did not become stabilized until 1955.* This, in an all too familiar fashion, put a crimp in the School's operating budget.

Buell, however, seemed to have time on his side. He orchestrated a close working relationship with all segments of the School's constituency. He was seen to be a man of abounding faith – faith in God, in the School, in people, in himself. He exuded faith so self-confidently that, whether shared by others or not, they honored him for it. Furthermore, he was the very epitome of what many believed a headmaster should look like. His presence invariably attracted favorable attention.**

One measure of Buell's success, especially over his last five years, was that he left much administrative work to others, particularly the resourceful George W. Wheeler, who became Assistant Headmaster in 1956. (During Buell's first five years, for reasons not clear, he had shown no desire to have a right-hand-man at his side.) The combination of Buell's energetic faith and the practicality exerted upon him by the Trustees and Faculty, turned out to be a valuable one. The Headmaster kept things lively, proposing ideas-without-benefit-of-budgetary-backing; his colleagues and the Trustees held him back until his excellent ideas could be prudently funded. (In this, Buell resembled Diman, whom he had known as his Headmaster, 1910-1914. The Founder's penchant for leaping before cash-in-hand was legendary.) It became clear as the years went on that the Trustees' faith in selecting Buell as the sixth Headmaster was significantly rewarded. As best as can be determined, he had been the only candidate considered to succeed Eccles.

Buell had an interesting background. Upon graduating from St.

---

*165 boys were enrolled in Eccles' last year and only 141 in Buell's first (1951-1952). A further serious drop to 129 occurred his second year (1952-1953). However, enrollment reached a healthy 177 by 1955-1956, and when Buell retired in 1961, he left a strong School of 204 students.

**A St. George's schoolman, who came as a young teacher in Buell's early years, made an interesting observation. He said that the man's charm was so compelling that it made people with him on public occasions proud to be seen in his and Mrs. Buell's presence. Lois Buell was a valuable ally to her husband and the School. As the Headmaster's wife, she involved herself deeply in School affairs. She knew how both to be the perfect hostess or go to the aid of a Faculty family with a sick child with equanimity and quiet competency.

George's in 1914, he went to Princeton, where he received his B.A. degree in 1919 (delayed because of Y.M.C.A. work in Scotland and France during World War I). He met his wife-to-be, Lois Cochran – a Smith College student, in 1919. She was the daughter of a medical missionary in China, and they went out to China in 1924 to be married. After Princeton, he returned to St. George's (and then left twice, in 1919 and 1921; the year between was spent in China.) He taught briefly at the Hill School, Pottstown, Pennsylvania, returned to Princeton to take an M.A., then, in 1925, with Wayne Conner, founded the Indian River School in New Smyrna, Florida. It was back to St. George's for good in 1929, a Master until appointed Headmaster in 1951.*

William Ackerman Buell had long felt drawn to the priesthood. He was an active layman who, at 56, three months after becoming St. George's Headmaster, was ordained a deacon and a year later a priest of the Episcopal Church. He met the ordination requirements by "reading for Holy Orders" under a senior priest. While he did not attend a Divinity School, or hold a theological degree, he was a full priest of the Church. This was an accomplishment which was profoundly satisfying to the now *The Reverend* Mr. Buell and was to have its effects upon St. George's School.

For the School, it meant that for the first time a Priest/Headmaster was leading it.** Ostensibly, this might be expected to draw St. George's closer to being a church-centered School. This did not happen under Buell. Was it because his experience as a schoolman in a long-established independent school pattern was greater than his new role as a priest? Or was it that the Episcopal Church made no attempt then (or ever) to exert control over its historic and famous boarding schools? What is clear is that St. George's under its new Priest/Headmaster was found at the close of his tenure no more and no less an Episcopal School than it ever was.

Buell dominated the religious life of the School. Retrospectively, the

---

*William P. Elliott was Assistant Headmaster at the time. In a 1986 interview he said that, contrary to some opinions, he had no desire to take the job. His leaving in 1952, he explained, had nothing to do with his seemingly being "passed over" for the Headmastership.

**It is to be remembered that Diman never took priest's orders in the Episcopal Church. (He did, however, become a Roman Catholic priest in 1921 and a Benedictine monk in 1924.)

School Chaplains appeared in a visibly subservient role. (Five came and went during his time – with the Headmaster having the largest role in their appointments – a surprisingly large number.) He enjoyed being in Chapel services, preaching, baptizing, and performing weddings, priestly functions appended to his Headmastering. He had taught Sacred Studies as a layman and permitted laymen without theological training to do so in the 1950's. Buell's personalization of the School's religious life broke the pattern which gave its responsibility to the Chaplains. After he retired, and under a Layman/Headmaster, they resumed the leadership of the School's religious life.*

The turn-around to better days came for St. George's – at long last, after twenty-five troubled years – in the mid-1950's. A confluence of events transpired to aid the Trustees, Buell and everyone else in that turn-around. The nation's economy improved (a factor not to be underestimated). Dwight David Eisenhower's Presidency and the up-swing in optimism which characterized the country was reflected in the life of St. George's School. All aspects of the School's finances were under control by the mid-1960's, building upon the groundwork laid earlier by Eccles. Trustee Morton Goodspeed '14 had been keeping an eagle-eye on raising and expending capital funds and increasing endowment. The Buells became precursors of later "jet-setters," but in prop-planes and by railroad, productively visiting schools, Alumni and benefactors. Students were better off economically and helped establish a buoyancy on the Hilltop which aided in attracting increased enrollments. Their spirits soared when improvements were made in the dormitories. These included converting the "Siberian" cubicles of Arden-Diman into rooms, a better heating plant and the conversion of Auchincloss Gymnasium into a dormitory at a cost of $200,000. This was made possible by the completion of vanBeuren Gymnasium, in use by 1960. The sentimental pain of seeing the ancient Ford station wagon superannuated was eased by its being replaced by "a Chevrolet of recent vintage." The Cabot Memorial Rink, an outdoor, artificial ice rink, provided skaters and ice-

---

*A lapse in the School's institutional memory appears to have occurred in Buell's time. The Trustees in 1917 had reacted against Diman's having a similar dominance over the religious life and established their "Division of Functions," placing a high degree of autonomy in the Chaplains for the School's Chapel and religious studies, with the Headmaster having overall supervision of the School.

hockey players insurance against the vagaries of southern New England's fluctuating winter weather. Its opening in February 1954 was given an especially satisfying twist when, as *The Red & White* reported, "S.G. Tips Priory, 3-1 in Rink Inaugural." (The rivalry, between Diman's older St. George's and younger Portsmouth Priory, would continue to grow.)

Another visible sign of St. George's return to an earlier opulence was the presence of School-owned yachts. "The Big Boat Era" was ushered in. Buell, an avid yachtsman, took pleasure in the gifts of six yachts during his tenure.* Dr. Norris D. Hoyt of the Faculty, was instrumental in helping to obtain these boats. Some were kept and used for week-end cruises for boys with high scholastic standing, and afternoon ones for other students. Yachts were chartered out during the summer to Alumni and/or parents to help defray the expense of their maintenance. The generosity of the donors was thus felt within and beyond the School. These boats laid the foundation for the development of the vital Marine Biology Program which came along in the 1960's.

With the expanding enrollment, need was found not only for additional Faculty but for faculty housing. In the 1950's there were increased numbers of married Faculty with families. A different kind of housing was needed, hence, the expansion in the immediate environs on the Hilltop of "off-campus" faculty homes. Curtin House, 200 Kane Avenue was purchased in 1957; Conover House, 174 Kane Avenue in 1959; the Potter/Vermillion House, 343 Purgatory Road in 1959. Also that year two new houses were built, attached to Auchincloss Dormitory. They were named in honor of Morton Goodspeed '14 and Charles Moran '24, – both "giants" in bringing financial stability to St. George's.

After much had been done to catch up with long-deferred maintenance and improvements, the aesthetics of the School received attention. In his will, Russell H. Nevins had left money for a stained-glass window in the Chapel, in memory of Edward Barry Wall, Senior Prefect of 1912 (killed in World War I). In 1953, John R. Maxwell '24 and his brother, Morris C. Maxwell '27, gave a Van Dyck painting of the Virgin Mother and Child, remembering their father. The painting was all the more

---

*The first yacht was given by Cornelius Wood '13 – "Manatuck," a 46′ cutter-rigged sloop. She was renamed "Sachuest" and kept until 1961. Eventual sale of yachts brought in money to help pay for the expanding physical needs of the Hilltop.

intriguing as the Flemish master included two gentlemen attired in 17th century apparel. Gobelin tapestries were hung in the Ante-Chapel, the much-appreciated gift of John Dorrance '37. King Hall had long been the repository of the flags of the original thirteen United States, together with the flag of St. George. The 1907 set of flags was replaced in the 1960's. In the "Great Hall" atmosphere they remained a tribute to the nation's early history.

It was never far from anyone's mind that still more improvements and expansion of facilities were needed as settings for a boarding school of the type of St. George's. There had been an attempt (in 1951) to return to a greater exclusiveness in admissions. It failed, and by 1952 George W. Wheeler had to report:

> "Many parents and alumni do not yet regard the situa-
> tion at St. George's as having been stabilized, and con-
> sequently they are hesitant and tend to send their sons
> to schools such as Andover, Exeter, Deerfield, Taft,
> Hotchkiss and St. Paul's...many [parents] find our
> plant comparing unfavorably with those of other
> schools."

An improved plant would help, but there was also the unending struggle to keep academic standards high. Interestingly, "The Review of the Year" written by students in *The Lance* for 1952, indicated that "high morale" rather than academic or athletic achievements was the year's highlight. Still and all, something had to be right: over half of the Class of 1952 went on to Ivy League colleges, and this at a time when cutbacks were underway in accepting private school students.

The heartening increases in enrollment after the mid-1950's were traceable in part to a return to a more inclusive rather than exclusive search for students. There was the desire:

> "...to [take] the best all around boys as to character,
> scholarship, and general background. [and] We are firm
> in our conviction that there should always be at St.
> George's a healthy mixture of boys from various eco-
> nomic groups whose homes are widely distributed
> geographically."

This was in line with what Eccles had struggled to bring about; now, however, it was far less the object of controversy.

In an inverse ratio not always understood beyond the private schools, high-spirited (sometimes rowdy) behavior accompanies good times rather than rough times in boarding schools. The return to a greater "normalcy" eased the pressure on the boys to take as heavy responsibilities as had been required in the "tough '40's." Normalcy meant high-jinks and pranks (sometimes later acknowledged in *The Lance*). With some of the stricter Masters no longer supervising dormitories, newer Masters were severely tested as to how they would respond to a variety of jokes and pranks. Buell was a Headmaster not given to ready expulsions and not alarmed at minor departures from behavior which he had seen over his years at the School. The Honor Code, meant to guide honest behavior in classroom and residence hall, came under fire in the mid-1950's. Those leading opposition to it wanted their signatures to be enough (as on checks), to prove that they were truthful; others preferred the traditional system, including turning in classmates if in violation of the Honor Code. By 1958, the traditional "black marks" for misbehavior were abandoned (but not the Honor Code). Buell had never used black marks, indeed, had no use for them. Veteran faculty member, James G. Vermillion, shared their being abandoned and explained to the students:

> "Your entrance to college depends upon the quality of
> your record here...No mark system involving petty
> punishments can be as important to your growth as
> your own knowledge that you are being judged here
> and hereafter by what you do."

The calibre of music improved. Whether aided by students being permitted to play radios (they had a long clandestine existence) and hearing good (or otherwise) music, was never explained. But the School Choir joined with the Lincoln School girls in selections of Handel's *Messiah,* and an interest in classical music was far from absent on the Hilltop.

The 1955 Lance brought national recognition as the best private school Yearbook that year, as judged by the Columbia Interscholastic Competition of Private Schools. James L. Keegan was the Faculty Advisor, with Dan Hutchinson, Editor and Robert Agnew writing the biographical sketches of his fellow graduates. The Yearbook's style was compared favorably with *Life, Look* and the fresh crop of photojournal magazines inspired by the art of candid camera enterprises.

The unforgettable flu epidemic of 1957 found only 70 escaping the malady, 110 being laid low by this temporary scourge.

Headmaster Buell wrote a letter to President Dwight D. Eisenhower asking his observations on contemporary youth. The President's response was proudly published in a February 1961 issue of *The Red and White* in which he offered five points of guidance for young people:

"Be alert and informed citizens.

"Be tolerant and sensitive citizens.

"Be skilled and accomplished citizens.

"Be wise and reflective citizens.

"Be bold and courageous citizens."

The 1950's were a visibly busy time for students on the Hilltop. Buell had a good rapport with them, "slow to chide and quick to bless." A lively Faculty contained some promising younger men, leavening the age factor of senior Masters and an older Headmaster. The later 1950's were, indeed, very good years.

Athletics, expected to rebound to better days after the disappointments of the 1940's, were slow to do so. There were some outstanding individual players and teams in the 1950's, much first-rate coaching, but for reasons never quite clear, St. George's did not develop into an athletic power-house. Given the preoccupation with sports ordinarily found in boarding schools, this offered a measurable amount of frustration. The amount of time, money, energy and spirit expended were not well represented in the "win" columns.*

The Red & White dedicated many of its pages to reporting on athletics. Some writers were openly complimentary of wins, others attempted

---

*Alumni and former faculty members responding to requests for information for the history, have offered some surprising and unsolicited criticism of the School's attention to athletics over the years. Some who were athletes said that the pressures exerted to win neglected the undergirding training needed later in college athletics; others claimed the program "turned them off" from college participation. Those less interested in sports tended to say that they found sports over-exaggerated and far too costly for the limited results. This reverse side of athletics at St. George's stands in contrast to opinions widely communicated by athletes who valued their sports immensely.

to explain losses, a few were frankly critical. A victory over Middlesex in football in November 1951, earned the blackest of boldfaced print: *"Football Team Crushes Middlesex, 45-7, at Concord to Finish Season Undefeated."* In 1953 dual victories in baseball and tennis over this arch rival inspired, "Nine Overcomes Middlesex, 3-1; Netmen Are Also Victorious, 5-4." A tie in soccer was reported in a game with a school bearing a familiar name: "Hilltoppers Tie Diman Vocational, 1-1" in 1953. The sweet victory of a close hockey game spurred the student headline writer to: "Pucksters Nip E. Providence, 3-2; Pete Howe Breaks Tie in Overtime," in January 1956. Hubert "Ted" Hersey introduced track and field, a sport which caught on quickly and remained highly successful under Hersey's coaching. Versatility in athletics became a factor, with athletics a continuing high priority endeavor on the Hilltop.

A reporter from *The New York Times* ventured to the Hilltop in 1959, presumably to investigate the historic rivalry between St. George's and the Middlesex School in football. He did so (it was a 28-26 victory for St. George's under Coach Christopher Corkery, in an exciting comeback). The reporter, however, chose to give his greatest attention to the "Pie Race," a popular sport-for-all-comers, initiated by faculty member Ted Hersey. It was this which was reported on at some length as a novel participatory athletic event, replete with Shirley Hersey's "pie-prizes" (which she was still making in 1986).

The new facilities afforded the School the Cabot Memorial Ice Hockey Rink* for skating (open also to the community) and ice hockey. The roomy new vanBeuren Gymnasium offered new hope for basketball, wrestling and intramural sports. The aging, but still serviceable, swimming pool was the scene of many meets, including those with freshmen college teams. Crew went by the board, to the pain of generations of Alumni who had rowed in many a race on the unpredictable waters of the Sakonnet River and against crews from all over New England. Sailing hurtled into widespread popularity – one of the most successful athletic endeavors of the 1950's.

---

*The first coach of the re-furbished hockey program was Thomas C. Buell, a son of the Headmaster, who returned to the Hilltop to teach English and direct the Theatre Program (1957-1962).

In the inevitable march of time, the loss of people who had given so much substance to St. George's occurred. In a splendid way, the School's maids, janitors, trustees, headmasters, alumni, faculty, students and benefactors were uniquely honored upon their deaths. Russell H. Nevins died in July 1951 and so did Stephen P. Cabot the next December. Their names were engraved on plaques in the Ante-Chapel; for Cabot this meant being honored in the building which (together with his Unitarianism) caused his premature departure in 1928. Touching tributes were paid to Samuel "Old Sam" Ross, son of a slave and a janitor-friend-of-all for thirty-five years, who died in his ninety-ninth year in 1952. Margaret "Maggie" Galvin had often spoken of going to her "big Irish Heaven." Her death, in 1916, elicited another outpouring for a rare personality in the School's life. "Maggie's Pantry" near the Common Room, remains a lasting institution.*

Leonard Bacon '05, Pulitzer Prize winner in Poetry, who had contributed generously in writings at the School's Fiftieth Anniversary, died in 1954; that same year "the other Diman sister, Louise" (author of the School Hymn in 1905) passed away at the Diman home in Providence. Though his official signature was "John R. McLean," St. George's long time Assistant Treasurer, was known affectionately as "Pop." Further human ties were cut with the past by his death in 1955, along with that of Herbert F. Preston, retired since 1947, and remembered as the Founder of the Christmas Festival in 1912. The seemingly indestructible Alan R. Wheeler died in 1956, leaving a legend in contributions incorporated into both people and the grounds of the School. Artist William H. Drury had taught boys an appreciation of art and had adorned places near and far with his paintings. His death in 1960 was the same year as that of the venerable Wallis E. Howe at 93, the architect of Old School and one who had only recently made sketches for new Faculty residences. A. Livingston Kelley '06, died in 1958, deserving battle stars for his yoeman service as a Trustee. Vincent Astor's passing in 1959, brought permission to disclose his many benefactions of buildings, funds and scholarships (delayed by his request until after his death). It would be difficult to find another decade when so many St. George's loyalists left

---

*Well into fifty-years-plus at St. George's in 1986 is Bessie Burns, living in retirement on the Hilltop. She and her sister, Nellie, were "gifts from Ireland" to the housekeeping staff of St. George's.

the scene, all leaving legacies larger than they ever knew.

Buell's eventual success as a Headmaster came in no small measure because, in time, he won over the Faculty. This became most visible when he began to share more and more responsibilities with them. From 1951 until 1956, his most difficult years, he had done without an Assistant Headmaster. With the appointment of George W. Wheeler '27 to that post in 1956, the second "Halcyon Era" for which Buell became justifiably acclaimed, drew closer to reality. Wheeler's work in Admissions was notable at that time in helping the School regain strength.

It was a blow to lose William P. Elliott in 1952 to Browne and Nichols School, Cambridge, Massachusetts. His competency and sensitivity had been demonstrated as a Master, Chairman of the Science Department, dormitory Master, an Assistant Headmaster, and as a friend to both boys and colleagues. A student editorial in *The Red & White* conveyed the boys' deep regrets at his and "Mrs. E's" departure, confirming:

> "...a record of devotion, unselfishness, and genuine interest [which] endeared him to masters and boys alike."

A bright crop of younger Masters came in the early 1950's. Among them were five still on the Faculty in 1986: Hubert "Ted" Hersey and William H. Schenck, who came in 1952; Richard Grosvenor and James L. Keegan in 1953; and W.S.R. Rogers '44 in 1956. Lawrence Goldthwait had come from the University of Maine Faculty in 1952 to give fifteen strong years in Science. Gilbert Burnett, Jr. arrived in 1958 to stay until 1960; returning in 1966 he soon became Chairman of the Science Department and is still active in 1986. Senior Masters, George W. Wheeler and C.P. Beauchamp Jefferys reflected tenures of undiminished loyalty, Jefferys to remain until 1963 and Wheeler until 1975.

Placed in terms of the world of the theatre, which Buell loved so much, his "production" of the 1951-1961 decade offered a classic drama of restoration, and the intimation that the School would be given a long run into the future. He directed that production with persuasive charm; always the convivial host, whether with Lois Buell at "Little Rest" or at

New York's Players Club, he was optimistic and "filled with faith." His incredible ability to impress people was native to him, and it was a strong factor in restoring a patrician image and a network of support to the School. St. George's took the up-swing it so desperately needed under William Ackerman Buell.*

He was aptly described as a "young 65" when he retired in 1961. Being a Headmaster had not so much aged as rejuvenated him. He was ready to go on, he thought possibly to parish life, and become a parish priest – a vocation for which he was well qualified. As it happened, he became a parish priest in St. James' Church, in Taichung, Taiwan and also taught at Tunghai University. Life had drastically changed from the Old China that William and Lois Buell knew, but it was a fulfilling assignment for them. Princeton presented him with an honorary LL.D. in 1961 citing him as a son of that university, with "sterling gifts as an academic leader and ordained minister," and "three stalwart Princeton sons."**

After returning from China, the Buells enjoyed their home, "Little Rest," and entertained their many friends, colleagues and Alumni in their accustomed and welcomed style. His death came in 1976, and in 1982, on the wall above the side chapel in the Ante-Chapel where he had baptized so many babies, the Buell Memorial Window was dedicated during Alumni Weekend.

Early in 1960 when Buell advised the Trustees of his wish to retire in June 1961, they immediately started the search for his successor. Some 200 names of potential candidates were received, indicative of how restored in prestige St. George's had become in the boarding school world. The Headmaster search process had come into a new sophistication. Criteria had been established, and some clear definitions of where the School was and wanted to go were available. The Trustees stated that the new man "must be an Episcopalian though not necessarily an

---

*Asked to write his memoirs, he did so in *My Life and St. George's School,* privately published by the St. George's School Alumni Association in 1967. He also wrote a biography of John Byron Diman printed in 1970 in *Newport History,* the Bulletin of the Newport Historical Society.

**William A., Jr., St. George's '42, Thomas C., and George C. Buell, St. George's '47.

ordained minister." (This criterion, while making certain sense, side-stepped the Charter which made no such provision.) They felt that he should preferably be married; between thirty-five and forty-five years of age; be familiar with the kind of School St. George's was; and have had administrative experience.

Selected a year in advance of his coming, Archer Harman, Jr. met the criteria. A devout Episcopalian layman, he was brought up on the campus of St. Paul's School, Concord, New Hampshire and was a graduate of that school; a Yale man, he came to St. George's having set a notable record as Headmaster of the Peck School, Morristown, New Jersey. Experienced, dedicated, persuasive, he was to take St. George's another giant step forward during yet another time of unique challenge.

Weather Leg

White wings sailing on the blue-white sky,
And the clean tawney body slicing the sea —
The eternal sea —
Gracefully curve together, joined by the silver spars.
She seems alone,
But with others she forms
An ordered design in four dimensions,
Random in three, but with the passage of time —
Dead time, ponderous, yet quick —
They converge on the mark
As Leonardo's lines on Christ's left eye.
Purposefully they strive,
Each in her own way to out-do the other.
Continually they fight, working against the sea
With the life-taste of sun and salt.

The watcher marvels as from South and North
They come and, united, all but one,
Swing around, outstretched their wings,
And strive for another common goal.
That one fouled
And turns away with hanging wings.

Derek Storm '59 in *The Dragon,* May 1959

CHAPTER SEVEN

Charting New Courses In Changing Times
1961 - 1972

Responsible to the past, responsive to the future.

B Y THE early 1960's, St. George's was incontestably identified with the select independent schools of the nation. "Select" implied a school with the academic, financial and social resources to permit it to choose students and faculty with care, students with an accent on upper-income families. It was assumed that a select school had tough admission standards, was strict in its behavioral expectations, conservatively run, and capable of preparing students for major colleges and universities. It helped if a school had been listed in E. Digby Baltzell's, *The Select 16: The Most Socially Prestigious American Boarding Schools.* Formulated in 1958, Baltzell's premise was that such schools served:

> "the sociological function of differentiating the upper
> classes from the rest of the population.*

St. George's was in the "Select 16" and as if to underscore its position, an article in *Newsweek* (26 September 1960) announced the appointment of "Yaleman Archer Harman, Jr." to the Headmastership of St. George's. The article credited William A. Buell as having:

---

*Peter W. Cookson, Jr. and Caroline Hodges Persell used Baltzell's 1958 list, unchanged, in their 1985 book, *Preparing For Power: America's Elite Boarding Schools.* In between, Nelson W. Aldrich, Jr.'s select fifteen included St. George's in his much-discussed *Atlantic Monthly* prep school article (January 1979). Aldrich is a graduate of St. Paul's School (his father was St. George's '30, and was helpful as an architect in developing building plans for the School over the years).

"pushed the Episcopal institution [founded: 1896] into
the front rank of private boarding schools."
Newsweek referred to Harman's interest in a church school and an
emphasis on "the spiritual side of life," concluding with a quote:
"You might say that I'm something of a traditionalist."

The Board of Trustees did a masterful Headmaster search eventuating
in Harman's appointment. In considerable depth and consultation, they
sought the kind of man who might further the School's progress in all
dimensions. The search started nearly a year in advance; aware of
Buell's impending retirement, some two hundred candidates expressed
interest in the position. Enrollment was about capacity (213), the financial situation was improving; little wonder there was no lack of potential
candidates. An experienced man was wanted, preferably a family man,
and one compatible to the various constituencies of the School. In Harman, the Trustees found a man who had spent virtually his lifetime
affiliated with independent schools. The son of a Vice-Rector and Latin
Master at St. Paul's School (from which he graduated in 1941, returning
to teach there from 1948-1954), Harman earned a B.A. from Yale and
an Ed.M. from Harvard. While he was at Yale, he and Mari Brainerd of
Montreal were married. After Yale, they were briefly at the Westminster
School, Simsbury Connecticut, then went on to spend seven productive
years at the Peck School, Morristown, New Jersey – a recognized Country Day School – with Harman as Headmaster. At thirty-seven, an
obviously seasoned schoolman, he, Mari and their four children moved
to the Hilltop.

Appointed in the Summer of 1960 as Headmaster-designate, Harman
visited the School a number of times in the months ahead. An unusually
valuable visit occurred in April 1961 in the form of an orientation meeting between the Trustees and the new Headmaster. The Trustees were
able to define St. George's to Harman as they saw it, and both they and
Harman raised questions concerning the future agenda of the School.
Looked back upon in the light of the years which followed, the challenges ahead came in for close scrutiny.

A number of vital questions were discussed at the meeting.
One was:

"Do we want to be a School that reconstructs boys

who have failed elsewhere?"

This question reflected Willet L. Eccles' attempt to do precisely that, and William A. Buell's move away from the practice. Implicity involved also was the issue of the School's "select" position among its sister schools. Harman's response was a masterful one. He observed that strong schools were in a position to take a variety of students, including those needing "reconstructing," but he felt St. George's was not yet in a position to fulfill that goal. He was frank to assess the School's physical plant as stronger than its academic program. His perceptions proved on target. There was a feeling, by at least some Trustees, that improvements were needed. "We should be more than a trade school for college," was a statement made at that meeting which would permeate curriculum in future years. There was a growing awareness of the need to deal with "the whole student." As a boarding school, this necessitated a responsibility for the growth and development of adolescents usually assumed full-time by parents. *In loco parentis* was declining in some schools, but not at St. George's. While the concept of "the whole student" was somewhat nebulous in 1961, it was accented over the Harman Years as the School sought to reach students academically, socially, culturally and spiritually.

Ever interested in the highest quality Faculty, the Trustees heard their Headmaster-designate candidly opt for a smaller, well-paid, top-quality one rather than a larger, less-well-paid, poorer quality one. (Harman emphasized this during his incumbency, implementing better Faculty salaries, helping put in place a realistic pension plan, improving Faculty housing, and evidencing a superior relationship with his colleagues on the whole.)

One area in which the Trustees and Harman were in congenial disagreement was in his response to athletics. An impressive athlete himself (Captain of crew and hockey at St. Paul's and a member of the Freshman crew and Captain of the Freshman and Varsity hockey teams at Yale), he expressed the belief that it was:

> "...better to err on the side of under-emphasizing than
> over-emphasizing athletics."

This drew from the Trustees a "let's-wait-and-see-how-it-looks-as-time-goes-by response." It was rare to hear even the suggestion that athletics should be "under-emphasized". The Trustees were among the staunchest enthusiasts for school sports; their response could well have been more negative than it was.

The April 1961 meeting touched upon a problem to grow in intensity and to absorb concentrated attention – the pressure to enroll black and disadvantaged students. The Trustees proved cautious about wanting to deal with that pressure saying:

> "The policy of the School is that regardless of race, color or creed, boys who are well-qualified should be given every consideration for admission."

The issue of "well-qualified" was the stumbling block. It raised then, and raised over the ensuing years, many questions as to whether this was to be interpreted academically, socially, culturally, or economically.

That orientation meeting offered the opportunity for a frank and valuable exchange between the Trustees and Harman. This became characteristic of the close relationship which developed between them. The relationship was strong enough to withstand serious disagreements (such as arose over enrolling black and disadvantaged students), and an uninterrupted working pattern existed over the Harman Years.

Significantly, Archer Harman, Jr., soft-spoken traditionalist, was destined to preside over St. George's during eleven years of the most intense change in its history. To his traditional positions he added a deep commitment to human rights – giving his personal example in leading the School in the "rights issues." He wanted to "open up" St. George's to the world beyond itself. There was a sense in which the outlook of the School was bounded by what went on within it. "The Larger World"* was a relative stranger waiting at the gate, one welcomed by Harman and by others wanting St. George's to reach out. He revealed the adroitness of an expert juggler as he managed to keep abreast of the arduous, time-consuming, day-to-day duties of headmastering and still give attention to accepting black students, investigate coeducation, and face the issues of the Vietnam War Era. All these appeared to reflect a spirit of "new occasions teach new duties, time makes ancient good uncouth."**

---

*"The Larger World" became a popular phrase during the 1960's. For a time a column in *The Red and White* was given this title.

**From James Russell Lowell's protest poem against the Mexican War (1845), which became the text for the hymn *Once to Every Man and Nation.*

Between 1961 and 1972, the Board of Trustees took on a new configuration. A mixture of older Trustees, mainly businessmen, and newer ones, with leanings toward *academia,* came into being. Slowly but surely the new configuration affected the strong conservative image reflected in the Board over the years. More Trustees from the Alumni body were added to the now larger Board, providing a "from within the School" perspective. The result was more than a greater diversity of persons; there came also broader concepts of Trustee interest and involvement in the inner workings of the School. The businessmen-academician-alumni mix was a valuable one because of the way the Board had to face both the traditional and emerging non-traditional agendas of the School.

The traditional agenda remained important — monitoring the overall life of St. George's, overseeing new construction and maintenance, raising funds, and lending support to the School in general. The value of the School's plant advanced to $9,000,000 by the late 1960's. Record-smashing amounts of money were raised for endowment which reached $5,000,000 in the early 1970's. More new buildings were constructed[*] than in any comparable period of time in the School's history. The Board was faced with having to "buy out of a chaotic deferred maintenance situation" accumulated over the years. Meanwhile the traditional functions of the Trustees were of on-going significance – always demanding and time consuming.[**]

The untraditional agenda increasingly invaded the Board's deliberations, especially from the mid 1960's on. Under the rubric of having trusteeship over the entire school, there came decisions concerning opening up the School to black and disadvantaged students and the prospect of St. George's becoming coeducational. The Trustees continued for a

---

[*]Between 1963 and 1973, nine faculty homes were either built or acquired. The Francis I. Dupont Science Building, the Edward Sturtevant-Charles Smiley Observatory, a new Library, and the Sacristy-Choir Room addition were constructed. The School Kitchen was improved, the Skating Rink enclosed, and new stained glass windows adorned the Chapel. The bronze dragon sculpture, executed by Henry Mitchell '33 and the gift of Louis C. Madeira, IV '34 and his wife, was placed in "The Dragon Courtyard."

[**]Fiscal affairs always demand attention. Minot Milliken '33 and George Howland '35 have been singled out, in retrospect, for establishing sound fiscal responsibility.

time to be heavily involved in allocating financial aid moneys. This placed them in a position of having a key voice in the admission of black and disadvantaged students. The Board members were in disagreement among themselves on this admission question. It was not a desire to prevent their coming but rather a question of how many and what their presence would do to the quality of the School. The caution of the more conservative Trustees was countered by the desire to move ahead by the more liberal ones. Furthermore, pressure came from Harman and Faculty members (including Faculty suggesting that they might resign if blacks, in particular, were too long delayed in being admitted.)

On the issue of coeducation, St. George's was not in the position of some schools during this period – either go coeducational or close. The School's strength was visible; the pressure for coeducation was manageable. The debate over it could – and did – focus on its feasibility. The cost of adjusting physical facilities, especially dormitories, was the big question. In time, an academician on the Board, William D'O. Lippincott, Dean of Men at Princeton, was among those convincing the Trustees to support coeducation. In 1969 he observed:

> "...within ten years if St. George's were not to offer
> [coeducation] it would cease to be in the forefront of
> schools of its type."

Trustee cooperation came in time, both for accepting black students and for the transition to a coeducational institution.

Bishop James Seville Higgins led the Board for eighteen years (1954-1972). He retired in 1972 but remained as an Honorary Trustee. He had taken his role seriously, and his influence was felt in the Board's decisions. At the close of his long service, the Bishop reminisced that he felt one of his most important functions came in the 1960's and early 1970's – that of mediating the varying viewpoints within the Trustees.

The importance of St. George's Alumni continued to grow in numbers, activity and influence. A series of strong Alumni Presidents* gave impe-

---

*Between 1960 and 1973, Alumni Presidents were: George Howland '35; Hawley T. Chester, Jr. '37; Jonathan T. Isham, '46; and William A. Briggs, Jr. '59. (Alumni Presidents served on the Trustees as well.) In that same period, Development, Alumni Activity and Fund Raising were successively and professionally led by: George W. Wheeler '27; Robert Turcotte; and Howard R. Hall '54.

tus to a vitality in Development and Fund raising efforts, the Alumni being the major source to turn to for such support. They were an essential part of the "Era of Fulfillment" (1966-1969), which raised $4,400,000 for Faculty salaries, scholarship funds, building projects, and the renovation of dormitories. Trustee/Alumni, Charles Moran '24 and Archbold vanBeuren '23, led this impressive venture. The spirit of giving was high, though at times fund-raising was stretched by over-lapping drives. The results were, on the whole, highly gratifying, and in 1965 the American Alumni Council gave its Grand Award to St. George's for improvement in Alumni giving – up 80% in the number of donors and 385% in the amount given. The Alumni Association took action in 1969 to define who the Alumni were:

> "All who attended the School for one academic year
> will henceforth be considered as alumni for Alumni
> Association purposes, no matter what the reason for
> leaving."

The School was growing more sophisticated in its understanding of Alumni and their relationship to the School. Given the divisions in views on the mounting social issues facing the nation and the School in the 1960's and 1970's, the voice of Alumni was sought in crucially important changes, including that of the enrollment of black and disadvantaged students, coeducation and the operation of the School in general as it charted new courses in changing times.

Sylvester Monroe '69 became the first black Alumnus to serve on the Alumni Council, elected while an undergraduate at Harvard in 1970. In 1984 he was elected to St. George's Board of Trustees.

The years 1961-1972 were prime ones in which to teach at St. George's. Harman established with the Faculty a sane and sensible collegiality. It was said of him that he could:

> "both prod and be prodded in return by the Faculty."

The sensitivity he had shown, early in his tenure, toward issues of faculty salaries, housing, pensions and families was sustained. As the

Trustees had had an infusion of new blood,* so did the Faculty. A student (who unfortunately left his comments unsigned) wrote in the 1971 *Lance:*

> "Old Guard or New Frontier, traditionalists or radicals, humanists, scientists, activists – the Faculty face each other and us across the gap of years. The older Faculty find knowledge through the traditional disciplines; the younger seek new tools, new tests, new techniques. The younger make immediate contact with us in dormitories, on fields, or through hobbies. The older organize, systematize, adjudicate."

Student perceptions should never be underestimated; that student deserved a straight "A" for his insight into the Faculty of the time. Harman's early discontent with the academic situation was shared by a cross-section of his colleagues. There were fewer veteran Faculty members than at any time since the earliest days of St. George's. George W. Wheeler '27 had become Senior Master, as versatile as ever in everything from administration to coaching. C. P. Beauchamp Jefferys, as distinguished in his teaching as in his appearance, retired in 1963. His contributions had also been made to the community, especially in his activity with the Newport Historical Society. He had given 33 years to St. George's and, just before retiring, was awarded an honorary doctorate of laws from his *alma mater,* the University of Pennsylvania. James G. Vermillion left in 1966, after 43 years on the Faculty. His long years of coaching crew remain imprinted in the memories of Alumni participating in that sport in his time.

Moving into senior status were: Dr. Norris D. Hoyt (English), who had come in 1946 and retired in 1975; Lawrence Goldthwait, a strong Science teacher and researcher (with unusual summers spent in the Arctic), who came in 1952 and left in 1967; Robert G. Martley (Mathematics) whose 15 years were completed in 1969; and Christopher Corkery from 1958 until 1972 another man-of-many-gifts: teaching, coaching, admissions and resourceful in working with black and minority students. The names Hersey, Schenck and Grosvenor were well known to a grow-

---

*The Board of Trustees was enhanced by two pioneering women: Blanche Gibbs (1971-1979), who was long associated with the Katharine Gibbs Schools, and Carol Guyer (1971-1973) mother of Grant P. Guyer '73.

ing number of graduating classes. It became clear that a "new guard" had assumed increased responsibilities by the mid-1960's, a factor in the changing image of the School. A growing "democratization" of St. George's was visible throughout its total fabric.

If long tenures are a criterion of a School's strength, the 1960's brought an influx of teachers (the designation "Masters" became outmoded) who remained for many years. Dean Blanchard, Jr. came in 1962 (Mathematics and later Dean of Academics): John Q. A. Doolittle '56 returned to teach French in 1962, but became Director of Admission in 1972; Kevin O'Leary (college advising, coaching and Latin) was present 1966-1977. Seasoned schoolman, Roy W. Penny, came in 1966 to spend 19 years (teaching English and later chairing that Department) retiring in 1985. Floride H. Taylor was the first Librarian to be listed as a faculty member, serving from 1966 to 1981; Charles W. "Skip" Howard, II (Mathematics and later Director of Athletics) came in 1968. The first black faculty member, Neville M. Lake (Latin and Spanish) was a resourceful presence during the years 1969-1980. Robert M. Parker taught History from 1969-1980. In 1970, G. Danforth Hollins arrived, to teach English and coach, and he became an Assistant Headmaster in 1975, with Dean of Faculty added in 1985. Charles II. Bodine, Jr. (Mathematics, Astronomy and Director of the Summer Sessions for eight years) came in 1971. Stephen D. Horowitz (French and later chairing the Modern Languages Department and wrestling/bicycling coach), also joined the Faculty in 1971. After leading other schools from 1958 to 1969, Peter F. Rothermel, IV, returned to remain until 1981 teaching History and Economics, also engaged in administration and coaching.

Coeducation brought the first women Faculty since Jane Stormont-Lewis taught Modern Languages at Swann Villa (1897-1898). Faculty wives, Lynne B. Hennion (Mathematics, 1971-1975), Lynda M. Kenfield (German and Girls' Advisor, 1971-1972), Lois C. Buell (Reading Skills, 1971-1973) and Susan S. Hansel (Reading Skills, 1971-1974) joined the Faculty. Kathleen Hall O'Keefe, a non-faculty wife, taught Reading Skills in 1971-1972 (returning in 1976-1978 and for later Summer School teaching). Actually women were intrinsically involved in the areas of Reading Skills and Language Training beginning in 1943; but Faculty recognition was not complete until the 1970's.

School Physicians and School Nurses during the Buell-Harman Years continued their vital services to the Hilltop. For those served by them their names will be recalled: Dr. Louis E. Burns, Dr. James C. Callahan, Dr. Charles L. Hopper, with Dr. James E. Barrett, Jr. consulting psychiatrist.* Nurses Jean Ventura, Helen Gooch, Helen Golden, Bernice Gallagher and Anne Leys staffed Astor Infirmary. Constance Kincade became Head Nurse in 1963, and still does part-time duty in 1986.

When Jean Peirce came from Mt. Hermon School in 1968, she was the first university-trained dietician at the School. She is still feeding the acutely unpredictable tastes of students in 1986.

Buildings and grounds, extensively accumulated over the years, required perpetual maintenance. Robert Knowles was School Engineer from 1955-1974, while Manning "Bud" Worthley was Superintendent of Buildings, 1947-1967.**

Functions of the Business and Academic Offices grew complex over these years with the advent of six-figured budgets, more students and astute fund-raising. Long-timers included J. Halsey Smith, School Treasurer and Secretary of the Board of Trustees from 1951-1963; Cyril Maingot in the Business Office 1943-1965; Richard K. Wallen, Business Manager 1963-1978 to be succeeded by C. Wesley Hennion, III in 1978 (still in that position in 1986). Caroline Carr, Lorraine Nothstine, Margaret W. Howie, Eileen Conheeny, Mary L. Wood and Mary Tracy gave their skilled services to the School over long tenures.***

The history of St. George's could be written from many perspectives. The School has been served well by many categories of people. This account can only motivate readers to remember these, and others, who have contributed their skills to the School's success.

---

*Dr. Robin G. Wallace became School Physician in 1974 and in 1986 still serves the health needs of the School.

**Raymond G. Ottiano came as School Engineer in 1974 and has remained as Director of Plant since 1976. Gordon Snow was Director of Services from 1976-1986.

***Jeanette Connolly, an accountant starting in 1978 and Controller in 1983, is still serving that position in 1986. Gloria Wright became Admission Secretary in 1975 and still serves there.

The 1960's were a time of intense educational ferment. Traditional modes of teaching were questioned; there was a call for better scientific education;* and the recurrent theme "the whole person" took on practical as well as esoteric dimensions. From its earliest days, St. George's had shown concern for science. The laboratory of Nature in moors, seacoast and ocean at its borders had never been matched with an adequate laboratory building. This came with the DuPont Science Building in 1963 fulfilling hopes, as old as those of N. Henry Black in 1895 and Edward Sturtevant over his 41 years at St. George's, for a useable building. A first-rate Science Faculty was in place, and it received the support needed for the new concerns in that discipline.

In 1966** the School was once more accredited by the New England Association of Schools and Colleges. By 1969, however, dissatisfaction with academic performance again surfaced within the School. There was a strong motivation to do some self-evaluation. A Curriculum Committee was established. Its 1970 Report was the result of painstaking, cooperative work, one of the best such efforts undertaken, and had ramifications for many years to come. Faculty members, students and outside experts were involved in its investigations and discussions.

The Report observed that there was a lack of a clearly stated academic purpose in the School. This permitted it "a tremendous flexibility, but at what cost?" Too high a cost it was deemed, in terms of the whole fabric of the School. A dimension entirely new to a school such as St. George's was suggested – involving academics, athletics, the residence situation, and student service in and beyond the School *as curriculum.* Vital to this new dimension were teachers and students joining in a "mutual search for truth," and a Faculty seeking "new tools, new tests, new techniques," was an obvious need in the implementation of such a new curriculum.

In essence, the Report recommended interdisciplinary cooperation between departments, certain modifications in course timing in mathematics, experimentation in curriculum within the boundaries of the current academic requirements, use of audio-visual material, a black faculty

---

*The launching of Sputnik I by the Russians in 1957, stunned the United States, then plunged it into a science and technology program that mounted steadily through the 1960's and 1970's.

**By 1966, the number of younger boys applying had decreased and enrollment of older boys was stabilized. It was voted that year to drop the Second Form and concentrate on being completely a secondary boarding school.

member as a "coach-counselor," understanding and realistic programs for black and disadvantaged students as needed, and the implementation of coeducation.

As an example of its far-reaching intent, the Report stressed that athletics should go beyond competitive teams and include skill training, recreational sports, and an Outward Bound-type of program.*

The assistance of students in the upkeep of buildings and grounds, as prefects, proctors (in the Library, Language Training Room, Computer Room, etc.), and in tutoring students, was held to be a part of, not apart from, the curriculum. The community beyond the Hilltop was envisioned as integral to the curriculum, as it was proposed that students should "move out into the world" and be enabled to deal more realistically in the present and future in the local community, nation and world at large.

Favoring coeducation, the Report recommended gradualism in its implementation. An enrollment of 190 boys and 135 girls was a suggested objective. (There were 241 boys enrolled at the time.) The need for compensatory instruction for some black and disadvantaged students was included, together with recommendations for black Faculty members and more women teachers.

Even in this historical summary, the 1970 Report emerges as one of the most important ever prepared. In a highly realistic manner an educational philosophy emanated from it which offered the School an inclusive curriculum. Edward "Ted" Warren, Senior Prefect for 1972, described his view of the academic relevance engendered:

> "...I think balance is probably the most important part of anybody's life. There's academic balance and there's a balance of using what's learned in the classroom. The tendency is to accumulate and not to apply ...We've got to stop accumulating knowledge and we've got to start using it. That's the kind of delicate balance that has to be reached spiritually, in paragraph structure, in a person's varied interests, and in athletics."

---

*Outward Bound stressed emphasis on wilderness experiences and learning how to deal with individual and cooperative problem solving.

The years 1961-1972, were excellent ones in which to be a student at St. George's. Archer and Mari Harman were close to students and well-liked as well as respected by them. Mari Harman presided at the week-day night coffees for Sixth Formers in the Headmaster's apartment. Well attended during the 1960's, they provided an opportunity to informally talk over all kinds of issues. She served coffee to visiting parents while their sons (and in the Harman's last year, their daughters) were inter-viewed. Her presence made a significant contribution toward an atmos-phere of warmth and caring within St. George's. The "Frostbite Picnics" on the shore at "Whetstone" were continued to the delight of many devoted followers.

Student polls evidenced general approval of the Faculty. The ferment going on in reconstructing student leadership roles offered those inter-ested in effecting change an opportunity akin to that of the boys of the mid-1940's. The upheavals in American Society, however distant they at first seemed from the Hilltop, found a coterie of students impressively engaged in interpreting and supporting various sides of the human rights and Vietnam issues. On the other hand, for boys who were content to remain uninvolved in the changes going on, that option was by no means lacking.

What can be described as a "two-track" student leadership situation developed, with cross-references between them. There was the "official" leadership of Senior Prefects, other Prefects, publications' editors, organ-ization presidents, team captains and committee chairmen. But there was also an "unofficial" leadership. It became particularly prominent and useful in the mid-1960's and into the early 1970's. The center of this leadership came through those editing and writing the "alternative" pub-lications, *Newspeak* and *Counterpoint.* The boys involved in these drew attention to the social issues mounting in the country – racial justice, human rights, the Vietnam War – but also to polls seeking to determine student opinion on life at the School. Originally intended to annoy those who were complacent, the publications became a recognized and accepted expression of minority leadership. Instead of *Counterpoint* being a condemned rival of the official newspaper, *The Red and White,* it was accepted by that paper's editors as a needed "counterpoint" to what could be published in an official, faculty-supervised School paper. By 1969, John G. Harnett '69, long active in social issues, was elected Senior Prefect. Hence, official and unofficial student leadership had its impact upon the School. That helped spare St. George's the damage experienced in other schools in which dissent was stifled and where student apathy and violence each wrought its own harm.*

William Edgar, III '62 remembered in 1986 that the Hilltop had an "in-grown atmosphere," but that he found "tradition as continuity" valuable and received an excellent preparation for Harvard at St. George's. Students like Richard H. Beinecke '67, Michael B. Moore '67, and Sylvester Monroe '69 (later a Trustee) were among those giving initiative and leadership for change. Andrew Fort '70, moved in and out of the traditional and non-traditional roles. He served at Camp Ramleh for three summers, fought Nixon politics and the Vietnam War, worked (against Faculty and peers) to have the 1970 *Lance* dedicated to veteran black custodian, Theo Belcher, and was the first St. George's student to take two Independent Studies. His comment, that he was "uneasy upon arriving on the Hilltop" but felt "a lot of sorrow and nostalgia upon leaving," would be echoed by many over the years.

St. George's was a small school, and its facilities were used to capacity during the Harman Years and after. There was a determined effort to keep the School small, an effort with which the students concurred. Student enrollment grew from 212 in 1961 to 278 in 1971-1972. It grew more costly to attend: tuition rose from $2,300 in 1961 to $3,700 in 1971. However, scholarship aid increased, reaching $90,000 by 1971; the Astor Scholarships still were particularly important in assisting worthy students who might otherwise not be able to come to St. George's.

To catch the changing flavor of the School, one must rearrange earlier social patterns. Where once jazz was the rage, rock and roll became "the new campus sound." While the melodies of the new 1966 pipe organ offered the intricacies of Bach and the crescendos of Couperin, played by Organist-Choirmaster, Winfred E. Johnson (1964-1971);** "The

---

*An example of how "official" student leadership brought change was in the seeking of a greater "School unity." In 1968 (an important year of change) the Sixth Formers proposed dispersing upper Formers throughout the dormitories. The intent was to effect greater student responsibility for the dormitory life and ease the fragmentation found in what was felt by some to be an over-emphasis upon individual Forms. This innovation was a sharp break with past practices.

**The pipe organ was given in memory of veteran Trustee, A. Livingston Kelley '06, by his wife, and it has greatly enriched the services and recitals of the Chapel.

Rainy Day Frogs," the School's home-grown rock band, contributed its more massive decible shattering sounds from other parts of the Hilltop. The Winter Term of 1965 was indicative of the times: two French plays were performed; the Chapel Choir rehearsed for services and ventures beyond the School such as going to St. Peter's Church, Morristown, New Jersey or concerts with girls' School choirs; six dances were planned with girls from such schools as Concord Academy, Dana Hall, the Pingree School and the Newport School. Computers came in the mid-1960's at first to mystify then intrigue students. A newly-formed Student Food Committee undertook the weighty responsibility of arbitrating the gastronomic propensities of students among whom there was a growing interest in the most undernourishing food fads.

Reflecting a side of student life remembered by some with greater zest than epochal events, what went on in dormitories, in recreational sports (which markedly increased), in "bull sessions" and spontaneous meetings with friends remained important. "The Arden Two-Sty" chronicled for a while the pillow fights, romances and on-going life in Arden Two, as remembered in 1986 by Timothy Fort '68, who also recalled the "stunned silence" in response to the assassinations of Martin Luther King, Jr. and Robert F. Kennedy.

Students welcomed their parents to the first Fifth Form Parents' Weekend in 1967. They showed them rooms which they had maintained, a campus also cleaned in part by boys, and demonstrated waiting table with varied skills.

St. George's students were still in exchanges, through the English Speaking Union, with students in British schools. A serendipitous episode occurred in 1966 when Trustee John F. Milliken '38, heard high praise from an ESU official for the high quality of students from St. George's. (He had no idea of Milliken's relationship to St. George's when he said this.)*

Athletics continued to demand time and attention from students in all Forms. By the late 1960's athletic facilities were optimal – a new gymnasium, the ice skating rink covered, spacious playing fields and, while the 1925 swimming pool was soon to be eclipsed by more modern ones, even it served its unique purposes. Students would long remember the

---

*There were also American Field Service students, who came to the campus from all corners of the globe – including Africa, Australia and Sweden.

names of coaches: Corkery, Spranger, Rockwell, Rothermel, Donovan and Howard among them. The Fall Athletic Banquet of 1967 provided a high moment with the visit of Bob Shann '61 returning to the Hilltop, having become defensive halfback for the Philadelphia Eagles football team. In a puzzling manner, despite good coaching and some outstanding players, the School's athletic record was spotty. Football had winning years in 1961, 1964, 1965 and 1970, and 1965 was sweetened by a 42-6 trouncing of Middlesex School. The 1971 season brought a 15-2 ice hockey performance, and wrestling had 0 losses 7 wins and 3 ties. Swimming continued to pile up some impressive seasons. As in the late 1950's, the track and cross country program under Ted Hersey had successful years, especially between 1964 and 1968. Sports such as soccer, tennis and sailing attracted much interest; sailing was boosted by a new fleet of boats and the intrepid leadership of Norris Hoyt. Girls' field hockey made its debut in 1971, bringing yet another dimension to the School's athletic history.

Throughout the late 1960's and into the 1970's, a demand grew among Faculty and students for more recreational, rather than competitive, sports, open to unskilled and skilled students alike.* It became more difficult to attract first-rate athletes to varsity sports – although they were still found in smaller numbers. Given the demands of academics, a proliferation of extra-curricular activities, and the new interest in social concerns such as the civil rights movement, athletics could no longer claim uncontested priority. There remained, nonetheless, strong advocates for competitive teams among the Trustees, Alumni, Faculty, students and townspeople.

Select boarding schools like St. George's had gained a reputation of comporting themselves as gods on Mount Olympus, viewing with detachment the distant and troublesome problems of others. This reputation was applicable to some schools, but St. George's was something of an exception. It had sought to relate to the disadvantaged through Camp

---

*As noted earlier, this was a part of the 1970 Curriculum Report and thus took on a stronger sense of mandate.

Ramleh* and other "missionary work" over the years. There was also Eccles' attempt to enroll students from all economic levels in the 1940's, with limited, but at times individual, success. Over the years a few Oriental students had attended the School. Of unique interest was Yoneo Arai, who graduated in 1908 and who sent his son, Ryo, to St. George's – to graduate in 1939. The Hilltop was marked, however, by an absence of black students. Black employees such as the Rosses – father and son, "Young" and "Old" Sam – Nellie Brown and Theo Belcher, were beloved by generations at the School, but they were treated as trusted servants.

The first black student to be enrolled was Conrad Young from Newport. He entered as a Third Former in 1963 remaining through his Fourth Form year. Viewed retrospectively, his situation became an example, far from uncommon at the time, of a school's good will and best of intentions unsupported by the experience and understanding needed to successfully integrate a black student. St. George's sought to offer Young its quality education and social experience without as great a sensitivity to his needs as might have been desired. He left after two years, although the opportunity for him to stay was given.

The unfortunate experience with Young sharpened the understanding of those desiring to have a racial mixture on the Hilltop. It also raised a cautionary signal to those less convinced. As an independent school, St. George's was not bound by the 1954 ruling of the United States Supreme Court, in *Brown vs. Board of Education,* the case outlawing the earlier "separate but equal" racial composition of the public schools. But as an Episcopal School, St. George's heard Presiding Bishop Arthur Lichtenberger's call in 1960 which reflected the Church's position:

> "There is no place for a school of the Episcopal Church
> which is 'segregated' on the basis of race, or which
> would not meet a full and fair test of the terms of the
> 1954 dictum of the Supreme Court."

There followed a move to bring in more black students but, as specifically articulated by the Board of Trustees, on a highly selective basis. By the mid-1960's black students came in increasing numbers, but there

---

*In 1967 the location of Camp Ramleh was changed from Yawgoo Pond to a location on Indian Lake, South Kingston. At that time additional leadership was provided by St. Luke's Episcopal Church of East Greenwich.

was still much to iron out. Of help was the "A Better Chance" program (of which the School was one of 12 founding members). ABC brought both blacks and disadvantaged students to preparatory schools on the basis of "you take one, we will pay for a second." The screening, especially at first, was thorough and some first-rate students arrived. In the over-all picture, not all black students were from disadvantaged situations, hence, "disadvantaged" had to be separated from only a racial connotation. With the increasing costs of a St. George's education, financial aid had to go to students from a variety of social/economic backgrounds.

Nonetheless, the integration of black students remained on-going agenda. The more liberal Trustees, Faculty members, Alumni and students pushed for more of everything that would incorporate integration more successfully into the total life of the School. The more conservative members of each of these constituencies sought quotas on the number of black students enrolled, a limitation seen as a way of preserving the academic and social qualities believed to be at stake at the time. The "unofficial" student leaders – together with some of the "official" ones – openly sought the elimination of racial slurs and jokes, the admission of more black and disadvantaged students, and compensatory support wherever needed, academically, socially or financially. The Afro-American Association came into being (a group whose name changed over the years but whose purpose remained as a vital support group to minority students). The presence of a black Faculty member, Neville M. Lake, of West Indian origins, provided contact with a man of sensitivity and excellent judgment.

Overall, the efforts to integrate St. George's caused a minimum of disruption (especially if compared to some of its sister schools). There was a "walk-out" by black students on the February day in 1972 when Anthony M. Zane was introduced as the Headmaster-designate at the student Assembly. It resulted from the desire of black students to have more black Faculty members and Trustees, not in protest of Zane's appointment. What made it perplexing for some to understand was that priority attention had been given to the issues at hand; Harman had been personally involved in human rights concerns. The walk-out made its impact, however, and focussed attention more acutely on the still unsolved problems. It was to take time, but the presence of black students, Faculty, and Trustees became an integral part of St. George's, a growing rapport marking their significant relationship to the School.

The discovery of coeducation by sexually segregated independent schools came in the 1960's and 1970's. For some schools, coeducation was a bail-out from pressing financial problems. Thus, merging boys' and girls' schools, with the accompanying influx of students, endowment and sometimes improved facilities, became an undisguised motivation for coeducation. St. George's had no pressing need to become coeducational. In the mid-1960's, however, it began considering that possibility. A concerted effort was made for St. George's to share teas, dances, Choir or Glee Club concerts, and dramatic productions with girls' schools.

In the Fall of 1970, Mary Walsh had the distinction of being the first girl on the Hilltop. A day girl from Newport, she came as a Sixth Former and was awarded a St. George's diploma in 1971. Archer Harman, Jr. remembers her as being an effective proponent of coeducation, "convincing some of the reactionary graduates" at Alumni meetings that coeducation had value.

A "coeducational experiment" took place in January 1971. Nine girls came to the Hilltop from the Shipley School, Bryn Mawr, Pennsylvania, for three weeks while a smaller number of St. George's boys went to Shipley. The girls took a "mini" course in Comparative Religions, were free to visit classes, and joined in social life. The experiment was deemed a success. In the Fall of 1971 twenty day girls were officially enrolled and the Trustees (who had held out the longest) voted to open St. George's to boarding girls as well for 1972-1973. Thus 1972 is considered the time when St. George's officially became fully coeducational with forty day and boarding girls.

By the time St. George's Seventy-fifth Anniversary arrived in 1971 there was much to celebrate. However, for reasons which did not survive the time, the observance was postponed until May 1972. Even then, the celebrating was limited, very much so in contrast to the nostalgic feast of 1946's Fiftieth Anniversary. One notable highlight was a reception for the newly-appointed Headmaster and wife, Anthony and

"Eusie" Zane. Alumni class dinners were arranged and the Annual Meeting of the Alumni Association took place. Those present were given the option of a boat tour of Newport Harbor, watching the varsity baseball team play Tabor Academy (of Marion, Massachusetts), tennis matches or a sailing meet between the Alumni and students.

The Anniversary featured a two-and-a-half hour panel discussion on "Secondary Education of the Future." Featured were: Dr. Chase H. Peterson, Dean of Admission at Harvard; Dr. Ella Cummins, a pediatrician; Mr. Richard W. Day, Principal of the Phillips Exeter Academy; Mr. David L. Evans, a St. George's Trustee;* Mr. Richard W. Mechem, Principal of the Newton (Massachusetts) High School; the Rev. John D. Verdery, Headmaster of the Wooster School, Danbury, Connecticut; and (significantly) Mr. Edward W. Warren, II, the 1972 Senior Prefect of St. George's.

The meeting provided a mix of public and independent school people looking at mutual concerns and to the future. This underscored how far St. George's had come from earlier more provincial and insular concerns. A Seventy-fifth Anniversary service on Sunday brought the occasion to a close in the familiar surroundings of the Chapel.

Concern as to whether or not St. George's was adequately identified as a church school surfaced repeatedly during the Harman Years. Spearheaded by Harman and Bishop James Seville Higgins, the issue was frequently discussed and debated. In his first year the Headmaster observed:

> "I feel that [the religious life of the School] does not
> have the vitality and significance that one would expect
> in a church school of this type."

Harman worked tirelessly to hold up before everyone that:

> "First and foremost we are a church oriented School.
> Our primary obligation is to give our students a tho-
> rough understanding of a particular point of view about

---

*Evans was the first black Trustee; he was Assistant Director of Admission at Harvard. Over his fifteen years on the Board (1971-1986) he was of much help interpreting how St. George's could provide a truly meaningful education for its present and future students.

life, the Christian point of view."

Bishop Higgins took an even stronger stance, including that the School should:

> "have a Christian faculty, teaching history, languages, etc. within a Christian framework."

He made the above statement in 1961 and in 1972 he reiterated:

> "The only excuse I can see for St. George's is that it is a Christian School... The only reason we have Christian schools, not just Episcopalian, is to develop Christian character and we have no business running a humanistic School."

With his natural and generous collegiality, Harman opened up the church school issue to the entire St. George's constituency. He never sought, as were those of Alumni and Faculty members. The students were not intransigently opposed to required chapels; they wanted the eight chapels per week reduced and more "voluntary" ones instituted. Ultimately the number of required chapels was reduced to two, Sunday and a Thursday Headmaster's Chapel; all the others were made voluntary. mately the number of required chapels was reduced to two, Sunday and a Thursday Headmaster's Chapel; all the others were made voluntary.

It was a time of able School Chaplains. The Revs. Hays H. Rockwell, Robert C. Gregg, Robert L. Crawford and Robert R. Hansel, were priests with exceptional teaching skills. During their tenures, advances came which brought not only new life to the services but important revisions in religious studies. The newly-designed Bible and Theology Department (1968) replaced the venerable Sacred Studies.

The scrutiny given to the church-school relationship, during Harman's Headmastership, was the most intense of any given in the School's ninety year history. The results were mixed. St. George's did not join in abandoning required Chapel and religion courses – a phenomenon common to the time. Neither did it tamper with the historic independent school identification by asserting a stronger church-centeredness. As the latest excursion into an area which many felt needed little changing, only an adjustment downward in the number of required chapels and an improved academic level for religious studies were the major results. The Episcopal Church had never questioned St. George's church-school relationship. It recognized the diversity of schools within the Church's fold, from parish day schools to the famous boarding schools, and had always honored St. George's position of being an *independent* church school.

In choosing Archer Harman, Jr. as Headmaster in 1960, the Trustees had hoped to have a man who might remain until retirement age. They and many others were disappointed when, in the Summer of 1971, Harman announced his intention to leave after Prize Day 1972. Archer and Mari had taken a brief sabbatical in the Spring Term of 1970. One of the results of the time away from the Hilltop was his decision to move on to other areas. Between the Peck School and St. George's, he had been a Headmaster for eighteen years. His quiet but determined style of leadership was a great resource to the School as new charts were drawn for the rapidly changing times. The Harmans were greatly loved by a broad company of people. They had been contemporary witnesses in a difficult time. Together they had participated in the Selma, Alabama Civil Rights March in 1965, a demonstration of their concern for human rights. This witness was clearly a controversial one, open to criticism. However, it was consistent with their personal commitment and their desire to "open up" St. George's to new dimensions within and beyond the Hilltop. As Pope John XXIII had sought to throw open the windows of the Vatican to let in fresh new ideas, so had Harman on the Hilltop. On the issue of the Vietnam War, he had been open to student leaders (such as John G. Hartnett '69 and Walter G. D. Reed '70) and Faculty members in free-ranging discussions concerning that troubling war. His unusual blend of conservatism with commitment to human rights was a part of his strength at St. George's and beyond it.

He was forty-eight and at the peak of his powers when he left the School. A significant place in public school administration awaited him in the future. He was Assistant Principal of the Milton (Massachusetts) High School, then Guidance Director of the Wellesley (Massachusetts) Public School System. Later he worked with the independent schools in conveying an understanding of and how to handle the problems of alcohol and drug use and abuse.

Harman has also served two interim Headmasterships, one at the MacDuffie School, a girls' day and boarding school in Springfield, Massachusetts and, one at Sewickley Academy, Sewickley, Pennsylvania. In between, Archer and Mari have relished the time spent together and with their family at Edgartown, Martha's Vineyard, Massachusetts. An avid and expert sailor, his sailing experience seemed a pre-requisite for the way he helped chart new courses in changing times at St. George's.

Once again favored with nearly a year at their disposal to complete their seventh Headmaster search, the Trustees nonetheless moved with dispatch. The list of interested candidates was long and varied. All of the School's constituencies shared in suggesting possibilities. When the selection was made, it was Anthony M. Zane, a veteran St. Mark's School faculty member. Whatever shock was felt because he was a "Middlesex School graduate" (St. George's arch rival in football since 1902) was mitigated by how well he bore that presumed adolescent error by obtaining degrees from the University of Virginia and England's Cambridge University. With Tony and Eusie Zane yet another distinctive texture would be added to the School's history.

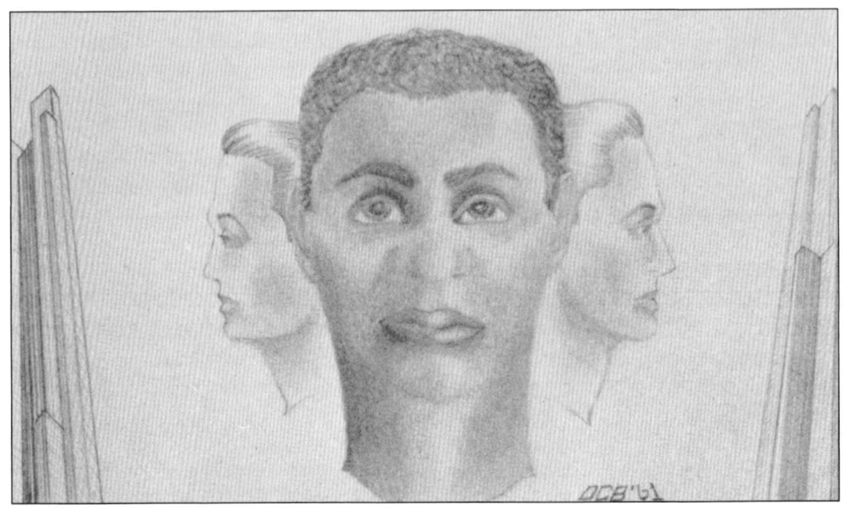

Sketch by Daniel C. Baldwin '61

Consolidation And Further Progress
1972 - 1986

THE YEARS 1972-1986 became years of consolidation but also of progress. There seemed to be a need to bring together the gains made over the previous decade in buildings, the results of coeducation, and to continue to solidify the prestige of St. George's as a premiere boarding school. Any consolidation of the fiscal side of the School was always subject to external forces, such as inflation, and therefore always a difficult area in which to make progress. But during this period, more money was raised and less borrowed than at any other time in the School's history. Fund-raising efforts reached the eight-figure mark, budgets of seven figures were common, and five-figured tuition costs appeared. The effort to consolidate gains outside finances was much easier than in the fiscal area.

The Trustees took responsibility for advancing finances and increasingly drew in the growing numbers of interested parents and Alumni. Consolidated were the lessons of the past which urged financial prudence on the one hand while making strong and successful efforts on the other to progress St. George's financial underpinning. More of everything was asked of all segments of the School, and more was given. Far-flung Alumni became well-organized. It was a productive and participatory era, giving leadership and unparalleled success to such ventures as the Annual Fund. It was also a demanding time for the Faculty and Staff, with increased responsibilities and compensations vying with one another for attention.

In August 1972, *Town and Country Magazine* reported:
> "[St. George's School] resembles an English estate with
> its own magnificent chapel,"

an observation frequently made by those viewing the Hilltop. The School had, indeed, consolidated a striking and valuable physical plant to house its efforts. What was less frequently faced was articulated by Peter B. Freeman, Treasurer of the Trustees and an excellent analyst of the School's life. He reported in 1983:

> "Our plant is both a marvelous heritage and a weighty burden. For every $1.00 we spend on educating the students, we spend $1.50 on our plant."

Freeman's astute comment framed the fact that St. George's had amassed valuable property but needed to be cogently aware of its role in the total life of the School.

From 1896 on, the ever-present "dragon" to be "beaten to the dust"* was the recurrence of unfavorable economic conditions. No decade had been completely free of episodic economic woes. Inflation was the damaging factor throughout the 1970's, complicated by spiralling costs of fuel and electricity. There came the necessity to spend $500,000 on bringing the buildings up to Rhode Island Fire Code standards – an unanticipated blow. By the 1980's, a large increase in some insurance premiums was unwelcome news. The need to subsidize even full-tuition-paying students was a necessity shared by boarding schools everywhere. To consolidate was a strong effort in itself and making progress in the material needs of the School a continuing challenge. This was, if you will, the bad news.

The good news was that the 1972-1986 era found the leadership and resources to create endowment and meet the economic dragons needing to be beaten to the dust. In fact, the challenges were not only met, they were exceeded. It took 85 years to reach an endowment of $5,000,000. By the School's ninetieth year it had reached $14,000,000. The Annual Fund topped $650,000 by the mid-1980's, a tribute to alumni, parents and friends who enabled this to be a budget-balancing factor.**

---

*Those from earlier Hilltop years will especially recognize this line as from Laurence Housman's, *Hymn For St. George's Day,* sung each 23rd of April and at other festive occasions.

**The elements of inflation and good money markets were factors here but in no way compromise the success story of efforts reaching more and more donors. The financial support of parents also became a vital part of fund-raising over the years.

The Headmaster drawn into the mainstream of the consolidation/progress between 1972 and 1984 was Anthony M. Zane (better known as "Tony"). Selected from a wide field of candidates, he had been for 13 years at St. Mark's School, Southborough, Massachusetts. There he had taught History (and became Chairman of the History Department), helped coach baseball, and served on significant committees. Tony was a Philadelphian, educated at the University of Virginia (B.A.) and with a B.A. and M.A. from England's Cambridge University. He and his wife, Eusie, came with their five children to live in the Headmaster's apartment. There was need of a leader committed to strong academics, and Zane met that need. What neither he, nor apparently the Board of Trustees, anticipated was that he would have to become an adroit fundraiser. By his own confession a novice in that field and reluctant to enter it, he proved to be one of the best. Indeed, he became so skilled that in 1983, the year before he left St. George's, Trustee Treasurer Freeman had words of high praise for him:

> "Tony Zane who, while pretending to be an amateur in the world of finance, has somehow managed to make our School a fiscal bulwark. Perhaps he should be studying the Positions Available column in *The Wall Street Journal.*"

A prodigious worker, familiar with the twenty-four-hour-a-day-boarding school life, he was always able to find time and energy to tend the on-going needs of the School. He reflected in 1986 that:

> "coeducation and racial relations were our greatest challenges."

Monitoring life on the Hilltop at the closest possible range, Zane kept in constant touch with students, the Faculty, and the various constituencies of the School.* Eusie Zane was an expert and avid girls' field hockey coach and referee (an enthusiast about sports in general, supporting the Hilltop's teams). Asked what she did, she explained:

> "I coach, have three advisees, cook and entertain and generally nag."

---

*A substantial "constituency" over the years has been the large number of dogs on the Hilltop, a phenomenon in contrast to schools where they are banned. Tony Zane has recalled rescuing them from dumpsters, seeing them wander into Chapel services and otherwise be very much a part of the School.

This was an understatement. She tended a family for many of her years on the Hilltop, accompanied Tony on trips, and added her renowned frank commentaries on life in general.

Students saw St. George's eighth Headmaster as "accessible and caring." He and his wife felt the most "distinguishing characteristic of the School was:

> "the genuine friendliness of the students. It wasn't artificial or phony."

Comfortable with one-on-one conversations, less so in larger meetings, student or Trustee received his undivided attention. He could be tough, as experienced by anyone who strayed beyond the boundaries he established as reasonable. (He had served as a Sergeant in the Army as a younger man.) The 1970's had an undercurrent of unrest among boarding school students; the earlier rebellions of the college and university campuses were now invading preparatory schools. Zane was credited with having the discriminating judgment to bend on tolerating less-essential evidences of adolescent rebellion (such as long haired boys) but being unyielding on major issues. "Constructive tension but never mutiny" defined his impregnable position. His was a strong hand in the life of St. George's; he was disinterested in condoning academic slovenliness, anti-social behavior, alcohol or other drug use by students. His methods consolidated the position of St. George's as a small, caring, but strict, institution.

While Tony Zane's visible devotion to athletics could never quite match the undisguised fervor of Eusie's, he made it a point to "make the rounds" of all athletic contests. He would go from football, to soccer, to field hockey, to lacrosse, to baseball, giving no quarter to his preference for baseball. He could be seen trekking to the wrestling pit, the swimming pool, the basketball court, the ice hockey rink, the tennis courts, in a demonstrated backing of all teams. He managed to work in games of squash and tennis in his own personal fitness program. Students and coaches were cognizant of his even-handed fairness in athletics, appreciating it as one of his strengths.

Faculty colleagues were aware that he had a long legacy as a student and teacher in boarding schools. He made no pretense of embracing the kind of collegiality found in Archer Harman, Jr. (and later in George Andrews). His was more of the "old school," of heavy responsibilities accepted and fulfilled by the Headmaster, with a hand on every aspect of School life. He warned the Trustees that the Faculty was "overworked", with the unfairness and detriment this caused, yet never seemed to complain that he worked harder than anyone else. Fully backed by Zane, increases in Faculty and staff salaries came about, following the eventual successes of the School's financial life.

The Trustees found Tony Zane a congenial colleague. A part of his success in fund-raising was an effortless urbanity relating him readily to people of wealth and power. His unobtrusive cultivation of benefactors resulted from his knowing how to move comfortably in their circles, while holding on to the highest integrity of the School. They (and others) appreciated that he developed strong communication skills. His speeches were models of brevity, as he showed he knew what to say, said it and sat down. His Headmaster's letters had a chatty tone to them more often than not. On occasion he would write, "I worry about...," and proceed to candidly express where he thought the trouble points of the School were to be found. He brought to the multi-faceted word "worry" a dimension, less of uneasiness than, of pertinent concern. His willingness to share these concerns effectively alerted others to them and elicited help in overcoming the problems involved.

St. George's as a church school was not an issue in Zane's time. An Episcopalian layman, he simply accepted the School as related to the Episcopal Church, and found no reason to question the balance between the independent and church school relationship he had inherited. As he personally attended all the required Chapels (and frequently the voluntary ones), he expected the Faculty to do the same. This was in conformity with his Twenty-four-hours-a-day boarding school schedule, as well as believing Chapels to be a part of the corporate community life. Taking responsibility for the brief Thursday evening "Headmaster's Chapel," he opened it up to members of the Faculty or to students who desired to speak.

The leadership of the Trustees had come into the hands of laymen by the time Zane arrived. (Bishops had headed the Board from 1900 on.) Bishop John Seville Higgins had proposed the lay leadership, and a change in the By-Laws of the Charter made laymen Board Presidents.* Bishop Frederick H. Belden (1971-1978) chose a far less active role than his predecessors, and Bishop George N. Hunt, III (1980-   ), with increased ecclesiastical responsibilities, consented to become Honorary Chairman in 1984.

Zane's recognition of the mounting diversity of religious preferences at St. George's was in part behind his appointing (1982) the first other-than-Episcopalian clergyman as Associate Chaplain and a teacher in the Bible and Theology Department – the Rev. Dr. Gilbert Y. Taverner, a Methodist minister and former college chaplain and professor.

A hiatus regarding the church school relationship had occurred and had its own value. It allowed the religious life of the School to consolidate, free from the strong attention it had received earlier. Student polls in the early 1980's, published in *The Red and White,* revealed more interest in obtaining parietals or reviewing the food served in King Hall than in challenging the School's independent church school relationship.

Inflation and rising operational expenses made it more costly to attend St. George's. In 1973 the tuition was $3,900 for boarders, $1,950 for day students, with 296 in attendance, 65 of them girls. By 1975, it cost $6,200 for boarders, $3,850 for day students, with 315 enrolled, 111 of them girls. It was one of Zane's greatest worries that "our tuition was one of the highest" among comparable boarding schools. It was destined by 1986, however, to reach $12,350 for boarders and $7,300 for day students, with 312 at the School, 123 of them girls. Even at these high figures, the tuition represented only part of the total cost to maintain a student at St. George's. Large scholarship and loan fund opportunities, together with funds to meet the actual cost per student, became more vital than ever.

The Admission scene changed. Students wanted "a greater say" in selecting boarding schools, a responsibility earlier left almost entirely to parents. It fell to John Q. A. Doolittle, '56, Director of Admission beginning in 1972, to match the changing patterns with significant new strategies. An expert analyst of the new and growingly complex admis-

---

*Layman Presidents between 1972 and 1984 were: Peter M. Ward '43 (1972-1978), Louis N. Madiera '39 (1978-1980) and Howard B. Dean (1980-1984). In a permanent change of designation Dean became Chairman (1984-1985) and Richard G. Verney '64 (1985-   ).

sion scene, under his direction the School made progress in seeking and admitting students. The change over the years resulted in St. George's being "sought after" more than "seeking" students. Doolittle, with Zane, had to acknowledge that the School's physical facilities lagged behind such schools as Groton, St. Mark's and Hotchkiss. Some students chose other schools as a result. Nevertheless, enrollment at St. George's was at virtual capacity. Its prize-winning, Nature-given seaside location could never be underestimated; even more, a growing academic credibility, rooted in small classes with a high ratio of Faculty. Permeating the School was its extended family environment, another plus-factor in admissions.

A decline in black and minority students in the mid-1970's troubled St. George's leaders. It was a problem, in Zane's words, "getting the black students to feel they were a part of the whole." Urban areas were investigated in an attempt to find students and efforts were made to subsidize them if that was needed. Here was yet more evidence of consolidating an area of particular concern at the School.

Once a student arrived on the Hilltop, what was life like for him or her during the 1972-1986 era?

Photographs of the early to late 1970's, especially from the *Lance,* capture a greater informality than in the earlier years on the Hilltop. The fashion of long hair on boys took over and was condoned.* After the winding down of the Vietnam War in 1973 and a cessation in actually drafting young men into military service, students were less interested in political and social issues.** The Civics Club debated the proposed impeachment of President Richard M. Nixon in 1973. The affirmative debaters won the resolve that he should be impeached. A poll of St. George's students, however, revealed 60% of students opposed to the idea. The intensity of working and re-working the Student Government of the School simmered down to fewer demands. The evidence of a

---

*An alumnus-parent, John L. Welsh '42, recalled in 1985 that the long hair on his son, Edward "Ted" Welsh '72, became almost a family crisis, but one handled by negotiable understanding on all sides.

**The names of those of the School who gave their lives in the Vietnam War appear in Appendix D.

stronger conservatism among students came in the call for abandoning the great equality among students earlier sought and won. The greater interest was in the more traditional privileges for upper formers, especially Sixth Form. There was a negative reaction to the mood of sweeping student rights' reforms found in some boarding schools. A reform, proposed for the Taft School, Watertown, Connecticut for unlimited class cuts, a lawyer present at disciplinary cases, elimination of grades, and "mass student action" to achieve these changes, was met at St. George's with the response that these proposals were:

> "shortsighted in the extreme and have no place at St.
> George's."

Traditionalism did not, however, apply totally. There were growing requests for parietals (visitation rights in the rooms of the opposite sex). The argument was that parietals completed coeducation, that it worked elsewhere, and that the students could both handle the issues and do the self-monitoring required to make it work. Up to 93% of students voted for parietals. Headmaster Zane was unalterably opposed to them and was supported by the Trustees in holding them off. The view of the Faculty was, by and large, less than enthusiastic, with some philosophical approval but an awareness of the added burdens placed upon dormitory supervisors to monitor the practice properly.*

The Afro-American Society invited the black and Hispanic students to find a fellowship within its concern for minority students. A gradual and natural intermingling of all students occurred in the later 1970's and 1980's. It came about as tensions eased around the nation as well as in the schools. James Falcon '73, an Hispanic active in the Afro-American Society, left an indelible statement in his *Lance* comment in 1973. Noting his earlier choice, the Job Corps or St. George's, he wrote:

> "I'm certainly open to any suggestions as to why J.J.
> Falcon remained to graduate from old St. George's."

There would remain an agenda of mutual understanding to be worked upon over the years. The election of Richard A.L. Wayner as Senior Prefect for 1985 brought a black student to that highest of student offices.

---

*As this ninety year History draws to its close in 1986, a compromise solution is in place. "Open houses" at specified hours in the week may be requested of a dormitory supervisor through the Prefects. The granting of the privilege is dependent upon the decision of a supervisor to grant it. Parietals *per se,* however, are not a part of the Hilltop's scene.

With a keen sense of humor, Wayner represented students throughout the total structure of School life.

The *Lance* depicted a good deal of the School's student life as caught up in self-interests. This had a certain validity for the "Youth Generation" of the time; the "Me" and "Now" labels were prevalently used. St. George's was described by some as a "country club," "a party school," in criticism of the devotion of some to recreational life. In a larger context, perhaps the Hilltop's students over 1972-1986 mirrored aspects of their elders who were tired of grueling and exhausting social issues and wanted respite from them.

Students found St. George's a serious academic community whatever external behavior seemed to contradict that image. The high cost to attend a select school such as St. George's helped motivate many parents to focus their money spent on an optimum result of entrance to top-flight colleges and universities. William M. Schenck became the arbiter *par excellence* in guiding students and parents in the selections for higher education. His famous open-door policy allowed students to drift in and out constantly. He thus became very well acquainted with the endless parade of students seeking admission to colleges. There could no longer by any guarantee that, as in pre-World War II days, students could be easily placed in Ivy League colleges and universities. Complicated combinations of College Board scores, academic performance, school citizenship and extra curricular activities, geographical distribution demands by colleges – all of these factors came into play. Unquestionably, the drive for good grades to attain admission at the college of a student's choice (or parental choice) provided motivation and pressure.

In 1975, the first (and through 1986 only) girl to be elected Senior Prefect was chosen – Alexandra Dix '76. That she should serve through a part of the nation's Bicentennial Year, recognizing the results of the American Revolution, was appropriate. Her election and her presence were significantly noted:

> "Skepticism, doubt, excitement, a congratulatory kiss,
> and a dozen roses announced Addie's election ... Fol-
> lowing the initial shock ... came minor tremors: a girl
> leading the Chapel procession, running Council meetings,
> speaking on Parents' Day, representing the Class on
> faculty committees, organizing student advisors, pre-
> senting the honor code responsibilities in Assembly.

"As the novelty wore off, the School recognized the
Addie it had elected. Imaginative, capable, enthusiastic,
talented, personable, Addie leads by example with steady
energy ... The School is proud to add Addie's name
to its list of Senior Prefects."

Addie Dix, female Senior Prefect for 1975-1976, represented the growing maturity of coeducation for St. George's but by no means its full maturity. Throughout the 1970's and into the mid-1980's, student government remained dominated by boys, despite the election of a handful of girls as Prefects. This issue remained on a "back burner", waiting to receive more complete treatment.

For students interested in competitive athletics, the 1972-1986 era offered the largest number of teams in the history of the School. Athletics remained a passionate interest for many students, faculty, Trustees and alumni. It bothered advocates of a strong athletic program that the increased enrollment pushed indoor sports facilities to almost absurd limits. Five basketball teams had to share one court, four ice hockey teams one rink; the swimming pool was becoming obsolete. Hence, interested students and coaches had to cope with somewhat less than ideal conditions for indoor games. Outdoor athletics fared better. The spacious fields of the Hilltop were constantly developed for football, baseball, soccer, lacrosse, girls' field hockey and softball. The tennis courts were adequate but predicted to be too few for the future. Compounding this was a familiar problem: St. George's was off the beaten track (somewhere just west of the Azores, it seemed, after long bus treks to Concord, New Hampshire at St. Paul's School). As if these were not impediments enough, athletes dwindled in numbers. Students wanted a "term-off" to pursue interests outside athletics, or to work in community service, activities granted to larger numbers of students over the years.

The effects of coeducation on competitive athletics at St. George's created a different athletic climate. The number of boys available decreased at the same time the number of sports increased. By 1986 there were 186 boys (about the same number as in 1949) and 123 girls enrolled on the Hilltop. This exemplified the situation at hand. While traditional competitive sports for boys (football, basketball and hockey in particular) were stressed, there was need to mount basketball, ice and field hockey, soccer, lacrosse and softball for girls. Coeducational teams developed in track, cross country, sailing and swimming. It became clear that coeducation was a "trade-off" giving St. George's the kind of academic and social environment desired but dispersing athletics over a very broad territory.

With all of this, there were high moments of athletic victory, good years for teams which Alumni could savor for years, and many individual honors. Jane Humpstone '81 on the coeducational swimming team as a diver, was undefeated in 8 swim meets, and Jane Erdman '85 gave boys in track and cross country a race for honors; she also won the coveted St. George's Medal. The Sailing Team won the National High School Championships in 1985, and victories on field and courts meant much to the athletes participating in them. The Diman Cup was established in 1979. Named for the Rev. John Byron Diman, it is given to whichever school, St. George's or Portsmouth Abbey, accrues the highest number of wins in overall athletic competition in a given year.

Plans begun in 1975 for a Field House and adequate girls' locker room and shower facilities found funding, and in 1985 ground was broken for a building dwarfing the existing vanBeuren Gymnasium. This, in itself, was a reaffirmation whatever the win/loss record, of athletics remaining a visible priority on the Hilltop.

Student-run publications were well-established in the 1972-1986 era. The oldest, *The Dragon,* gave would-be authors, poets, artists and photographers an outlet for their talents. An Anthology Issue in 1978, reprinted contributions to the magazine over a seventy-five year period beginning in 1903. An insight into the changing literary efforts of students was visible in the anthology. The first piece in the magazine was a reprint from a poem by Arthur E. Newbold '05, appearing in 1903. Entitled, *The Battle Hymn of St. George's,* the poet compared athletics with wartime battlefields and claimed confidently "of defeat we have no fear." The last poem of the issue, "Sanity," by Liza Nickerson '80, penetrated the psyche of at least some of the students of the time:

> "...I can't afford to give all
> to someone in control.
> Yet the respect I hold
> overcomes fear
> and creates an honest bond."

The Red and White ubiquitously reported, reviewed and occasionally challenged life on the Hilltop in its journalistic goal of preserving who did what, why, when, where and how. In a spoof on itself, the paper began April Fool's Day editions, including *The Red and What?* in 1982. It reported that the Chapel had simply disappeared, the Tuck Shop had become "Al's Bar and Grille," and that Diman North had become "the first St. George's coed dorm."

The long-abandoned Yearbook custom of a Class reviewing its years was renewed in the 1983 *Lance.* With a candor characteristic of some 1970's and 1980's students, they wrote:

> "When the Class of 1983 started their Third Form Year, they set a stage that would continue until they graduated. They were 'different,' almost odd, in comparison with the rest of the School, and through four years this changed little."

Behind that observation it was possible to detect a different kind of student than was found earlier on the Hilltop. Wanting tradition and its security, there was also a search for an identity apart from the adult community, be it parents or Faculty. Students sought to assert more independence, were more "savvy" about everything from how to spend money to using alcohol and drugs regardless of the illegalities involved. The break from their homes still meant the environment of mandatory "lights," strict rules of personal and social behavior, required Chapels, pressures to produce academically. The talk of "pressures" consumed time and interest. A consulting psychiatrist or psychologist became an important adjunct to the School's life. Programs in Human Sexuality and Substance Abuse were initiated to face (or prevent) problems all boarding schools had.

The Dean of Students' role increased in importance. By 1985, St. George's with 312 students, had two Deans: George W. Maentz, who came from the Hill School, Pottstown, Pennsylvania, and Janet W. Buell,* from Milton (Massachusetts) Academy.

Concentrated attention was given to the organization of student life. To help find places for student participation on and off the campus became agenda, as did the disciplinary aspect of the School. The codification of rules was renewed. In something of a flash-back to the days of "black marks" for infractions, "green cards" appeared. A twenty-five page *Student Handbook* gave tips on everything from School rules to

---

*The wife of George C. Buell '47 and the daughter-in-law of former Headmaster and
  Mrs. William C. Buell.

suggestions as to where to go in Newport and the surrounding communities. The voice of students in disciplinary decisions was carefully written into the on-going operations of the School.

It was an exciting and responsible time to be a Senior or School Prefect. The Senior Prefect's familiar role as a liaison between students and the adult leadership continued to be held up as vital. In the election of Senior Prefects, "Rising through the ranks of the Forms," proven general leadership, became important. Held in somewhat diminished regard was athletic prowess (although this was of some help). In 1986 W. Keyes Edgar was elected Senior Prefect; he represented the fourth generation (in a *direct* line) of his family to attend St. George's.*

Students coming to the Hilltop in the 1972-1986 era found opportunities for creative artistic expression. Music, drama, art and the Dance were available. The Chapel Choir became the most visibly recognized musical group. Under Organist-Choirmaster/Music Department Chairman Franklin G. Coleman, the Choir's *tour de force* was its 1985 Spring Tour to schools, cathedrals and churches in England. Informal musical groups, choral and instrumental, came and went as the indigenous student leadership for it did the same. James Cardom in 1980, an English Speaking Union student, wryly explained that he would never have heard his Headmaster at the Westminster School, London, serenaded with anything resembling *Happy Birthday, Mr. Zane* accompanied by a student punk rock group.

St. George's unusual Architecture courses, taught by Richard Grosvenor, continued to find students learning its basic principles aided by model making. Over the years, major projects included models of the Eiffel Tower, a Geodesic Dome and, out of the unlikely materials of cereal boxes, cardboard, and milk cartons a suspension bridge and a Viking Boat.

Thespians spent their long hours in productions worthy of more seasoned players. The exacting *A Man For All Seasons* won praise reviews; the effervescent musical, *Oklahoma!* was performed with but three weeks rehearsal time. These are but two of a longer list of productions.

---

*His great-grandfather was William Edgar '12; his grandfather, William Edgar, Jr. '37; his father, William Edgar, III '62; and a sister, Deborah '90, joined him in this multigenerational St. George's family as a Third Former in 1986. (This is the only *direct* line-four generation family known, though there are many with three generations.)

John Byron Diman's decision (out of necessity) in 1896 brought day students to St. George's, and they have remained an integral part of the School. In the 1970's and 1980's their numbers increased as did the costs. Tuition for them rose from $1,900 in 1972 to $7,300 in 1986, with more students applying than could be enrolled. While some day-students expressed a sense of "isolation" in a population largely of boarders, their academic and athletic contributions have greatly enhanced the School.

It was a time when students brought a collection of electronic equipment to their dormitories. Stereophonic record and cassette players and computers became standard for many. (Television remained banned in individual rooms). The Electronic Age had arrived. Modern technology aided, but did not replace, the need for students to prove that they had the basic skills to use both in higher education and in being responsible young adults. Theodore P. Sizer* told the Faculty in 1986 that the recent times had been favoring students – and not without reason. He proposed that faculties had been neglected, and were in need of attention.

What was it like to teach at St. George's between 1972 and 1986?

It was to be an integral part of a small, select boarding school, with its demands to teach, advise, coach, be a dormitory supervisor for most, do committee work, and relate to others, whether families, colleagues or friends. For those on the Faculty before coeducation, it was to see the number of women on the Faculty grow so that by the mid-1980's the ratio was 60% men and 40% women – approximately that of the student body.

It was to join a better paid Faculty and one with growing opportunities for professional enrichment. The years were vital and valuable ones to teach with boarding schools presenting challenging situations in encounters with student life-styles. The recognition of the vitality of teaching was underscored by the endowing of Faculty Chairs, signifying support for consistent, high-quality teaching.

A group, to remain ten years or longer, became a part of the Faculty:

---

*Sizer formerly headed Phillips Academy and was author (among other books) of *Horace's Compromise* (Houghton-Mifflin, Boston, 1984), a study of contemporary education.

Rose Bugnet, Stephen Connett, Beth and Sheldon Horton, Dorothy "Dolly" Howard, Conchita Kreisler, Stephen Leslie, Marcia Rogers and the Rev. John S. Rogers. W. S. R. Rogers and James L. Keegan returned having served in other schools. By the mid-1980's Ted Hersey, William Schenck and Richard Grosvenor had been on the Hilltop more than thirty years, now Senior Faculty.

For two of these Faculty members a new and different involvement developed – the Marine Biology Program. Stephen Leslie was instrumental in its advancement, as well as being an outstanding sailing coach, bringing teams into national prominence. Stephen Connett, as captain/teacher of the 54' research vessel, *Geronimo,* began in 1975 taking students to sea to carry out research in cooperation with the National Fisheries Service. The *Geronimo* Program continues to enhance St. George's unusual offering of Marine Biology to secondary school students.

Among the respected Faculty and Staff retiring in the mid-1970's was George W. Wheeler '27 in 1975. In an unprecedented way, he had spent virtually a lifetime at St. George's (save for four years at Yale and short sabbaticals). Throughout the recent chapters of this History his name has appeared repeatedly as he fulfilled varied major responsibilities.* He could be depended upon to meet all ranges of demands upon his time and abilities, as five Headmasters knew well. George and Margery Wheeler moved to a newly-built house on the eastern edge of the Hilltop, and they had eight years together there before George's death in 1983. His passing brought to a conclusion the longest single linkage of anyone to St. George's School (1909-1983). In 1986, Margery Wheeler keeps close contact with a host of St. Georgians from across many years and has served as a member of the Committee overseeing the preparation of this History.

The Board of Trustees grew to twenty-nine voting members (includ-

---

*One responsibility not yet mentioned – he developed the first Summer School in 1944. Serving St. George's students for the most part early on, it tended later to enroll students almost entirely from other schools. From 1960 to 1986 Summer School enlarged and prospered under the able direction of a succession of leaders – William Schenck, Christopher Corkery, Thorne Butler and Charles Bodine, Jr.

ing five women) plus seven Honorary members. Their responsibilities seemed endless. Trustee treasurers took on major roles to interpret the School's ever-interesting fiscal life. George Howland '35 served as Treasurer from 1964-1977, Lewis N. Madeira '39 (1977-1978), John A. vanBeuren (1978-1979), Peter B. Freeman (1979-1984) and Laurance M. Redway '58 (1984-   ).

For some years the Trustees had been drawn increasingly into the in-School affairs. In the 1972-1986 era, their advice was sought on such varied issues as student smoking, parietals, and the problems created by alcohol and other drugs in the boarding school environment. It became customary for them to emerge from their long sessions and sit down at dinner with students and others of the School. Out of this a relationship has been developed with those fulfilling the day-to-day operations on the Hilltop.

As this History attests, vital areas of a school's life are managed by Trustees. Too little recognition of their importance is given to these men and women who literally hold a school "in trust." From the first Trustees in 1900 on, St. George's has had the services of people giving incredible amounts of time and expertise, and money as well. Their greatest reward appears to be seeing the development of the School, throughout the years, to its well-recognized position among boarding schools. To them the thanks of a grateful constituency is given.

Alumni who devote time, attention and money to secondary schools are mainly a phenomenon of independent schools, especially boarding schools. This is related to the years when such alumni were students, transforming schools into "second homes," classmates into close friends, and the environment of boarding schools into time-encapsulated experiences of lasting importance.

By the end of its ninetieth year, St. George's had graduated some 3,000 alumni. In 1986, approximately 2,600 were scattered over the globe, but ingeniously organized and responsive to contacts from the Hilltop.* Alumni Weekends had assumed their multi-faceted roles of

---

*Between 1972 and 1986 professional leadership has been given to the areas of Alumni and Development by Howard Hall '54, Philip M. Reynolds '42, Thorne Butler, William A. Briggs, Jr. '58, Eleanor T. Howard and Jeremy Jones.

bringing graduates back to the Hilltop, citing reunion classes and outstanding individuals, having cocktails, panels, dinners, dances and reuniting friends of past years.

The Alumni Fund grew in accumulated funds and in unique importance to the School. It was crucial to maintaining a balanced operating budget. By the early 1980's it had reached a half million dollars and continued to grow annually thereafter.* In a time when communication became an art form, new techniques were used – including Phonathons, the use of computers, and highly skilled approaches to people resulting in successful drives.

The *St. George's Alumni Bulletin* became the *St. George's Bulletin* reflecting an outreach to the widest possible audience with news of the School. The publication became a prize-winning and visibly professionally produced magazine.

By the mid-1970's Alumnae joined Alumni on the rolls, but it was 1986 before a woman graduate was named to the St. George's Board of Trustees – Elena (Thornton) Kissell '77. A "first" in Alumnae/Alumni weddings was the marriage of Wendy J. Wallen '74 and Richard Gilpin McKee, Jr. '75 in 1979.

Between 1972 and 1984 the permeating presence of Tony Zane was felt. In company with John Byron Diman, his decisions and influence had an unmistakable authority. In 1976, when the *Lance* was dedicated to him, the students called him "The Captain," a leader who gave the School a positive sense of direction and leadership. That was the same year that Zane inquired of the Trustees their views on the direction that St. George's should take:

> "What do you see me doing in the next five years?"
> "What lies ahead in the next five years?"
> "What should we be planning for?"
> "Where are we vulnerable?"

These questions were a clue to the steady manner in which Zane consolidated, then moved ahead, a sign of valid progress. He reflected in 1986 on this pattern:

> "Archer Harman, Jr. and the times took the School

---

*Please see Appendix C for a list of Annual Fund Chairmen.

beyond the gates; the times and I brought the School back within, but not to the degree of other days. That's another complicated question, considered in the light that St. George's is in itself a small town whose needs have to be addressed on the spot by its citizens."

Tony Zane decided in the Summer of 1983 that he wished to complete his St. George's Headmastership after the academic year 1983-1984. St. George's had made measurable progress. The "dragon" of unfavorable economics had been cowed, if not "beaten to the dust" forever. He spent his last year working as hard as ever. Upon leaving in July 1984, Tony and Eusie Zane went to their beloved Northeast Harbor, Maine house, then moved to Charlottesville, Virginia and, for Tony, some relaxed writing. In December 1985 Tony became Vice-president of the Chesapeake Bay Foundation in Annapolis, Maryland, an organization devoted to protection and conservation.

The Trustees began their search for St. George's ninth Headmaster, confident concerning the School's situation. In keeping with the atmosphere of professionalism marking so much in the recent years, an outside consulting firm was retained to help in the Headmaster Search. Thorough contacts were made within and beyond the Hilltop and some 150 names were available for consideration. By February 1984 the Committee recommended the Rev. George E. Andrews, II as Headmaster, and he was duly appointed.

A graduate of Phillips Academy (where he had also briefly taught), Andrews had been for some ten years Dean of Students/Chaplain of the University Liggett School, Grosse Pointe, Michigan. An Episcopal priest, he had graduated from Trinity College, Hartford, Connecticut and from the Virginia Theological Seminary, Alexandria, Virginia. He and his wife Lillian ("Lil") and their three daughters came to live in the Headmaster's apartment in Old School in the late Summer of 1984.

A man of seemingly inexhaustible energy levels, Andrews' early agenda centered on restructuring student leadership, improving the Prefect System, and reassessing the disciplinary area of student life. As a former Dean of Students, he had had much experience with these areas. He increased the number of Deans of Students to two, and within two years the restructuring was complete. Student life became more formally organized and disciplinary procedures more thoroughly codified.

The 1971-1984 period had not been a "bricks and mortar" time.

Zane considered the new Library, with the conversion of the former one into a Student Center, a triumph. But, in the main, he tended to follow the principle articulated in a 1981 Headmaster's letter:

> "The strength of St. George's is something other than
> bricks and mortar...we make do."

For the School to be seen as "shabby," or even in its physical appearance one of "genteel poverty," was not as important to him (or to the other leadership) as consolidating finances and progressing the School's academic image.

Andrews believed it time to spruce up the frayed elegance he found, especially in the interior of Old School and in faculty quarters of the dormitories. Lil Andrews became active in what the students jovially dubbed "the Pretty Committee," but in reality in some well-focussed efforts to make the buildings more presentable. Using the basic architectural settings, the Committee created a refreshed appearance with paint and new furnishings.

The Search Committee had not sought a clergyman/headmaster *per se* but that Andrews was an Episcopal priest was appropriate for St. George's Episcopal School identity. St. George's less "church centered" relationship to the Episcopal Church was an area Andrews wanted reviewed. Recognizing that the issue was one found in the context of decreasing numbers of Episcopalians attending the School,* and where the independent school image of St. George's was vital to its present and future, Andrews moved slowly. He asked for a study of the church school relationship (a study not yet complete as this history is concluded in December 1986).

Andrews showed an early concern for the "gender issue" at St. George's – more inclusive roles for girls and women. As practical steps he led in increasing the number of women administrators and keeping in balance the male/female Faculty ratio. A Gender Committee was established, embracing the School's constituency, to consolidate the gains of coeducation and the participation of women throughout the School.

Encouraging a reaching out to the community at large, Andrews

---

*In the mid-1980's, many Episcopal schools (especially Parish Day Schools) had as few as 25% of their enrollment as Episcopalians. In 1986, St. George's had slightly less than a majority of Episcopalian students (46%) with other denominations or unaffiliated (54%).

made this practical by providing faculty leadership and the opportunities for student participation. Stephen Horowitz and Stephen Leslie of the Faculty and the Prefects from the student body moved in on community service. St. George's was host to the Rhode Island Special Olympics, joined with students from Middletown High School in the Feed a Friend Program for needy people – organized out of Newport's Martin Luther King, Jr. Center, and joined in Blood Drives. Individual students were enabled to participate in other community outreach activities. These, together with the Camp Ramleh program, continued the historic involvement beyond the Hilltop.

In 1986 the School was re-accredited by the New England Association of Schools and Colleges. (Independent schools are not certified by governmental agencies, the Association fulfilling that role.) Virtually an academic year had been spent preparing reports for the accreditation under the leadership of Assistant Headmaster/Dean of the Faculty G. Danforth Hollins. The Visiting Committee from the Association recommended re-accreditation, looking favorably upon St. George's as:

> "an unusually exciting, healthy and energetic community,"

while making recommendations for adjustments here and there, and suggesting that the church school relationship be defined more clearly.

The collegial style of George Andrews was apparent from the beginning. This was expressed in an increase in committees, lengthy Faculty meetings, frequent consultations with all the School's constituency, and a visible intent to involve as many people as possible in the operation of the School. An excellent tennis player and former coach of many winning teams, Andrews revealed a tenacity on the court that seemed to belie his otherwise imperturbable personality. His two-and-a-half years as Headmaster – as this History closes – have been marked by intense activity. Describing himself as "a dyed-in-the-wool-conservative," he has expressed a desire to work toward the presence of conservative values throughout the School's life.

AFTERWORD

Among the best known Episcopal boarding schools, St. George's is a young school. By 1896, St. Paul's and St. Mark's, founded in the mid-19th century, were well established. St. George's is essentially a 20th century School – despite its founding antedating that century by four years. It has acquired traditions and practices forged in the 20th century which have shaped its academic and social development. Along the way, a strong sense of independence became a hallmark of St. George's – as unyielding at times as the rocky cliffs which provide its seacoast boundary.

The School has had the good fortune to have nine uniquely different Headmasters, active Boards of Trustees, Faculty and Alumni, all of whom have contributed to making it an alert and alive community. Each year has taken the School in directions which, while not always visible at the time, have proved to be of immense value. Historically, its best and greatest tradition has been that of a small, caring and concerned School. St. George's "product" is students – become alumni, sent on to colleges and universities and into the mainstream of life – "ready to contend bravely for God and the truth."

This book is a prologue to the School's Centennial in 1996. The tangled skein of its history has been unraveled, clarified and communicated. Building upon its rich and diversified past, the present and future St. George's School can be brought to new and greater heights. □

APPENDIX A

St. George's School Faculty
1896-1986

John B. Diman	1896-1917	Cyril B. Judge	1910-1927
Headmaster		Herbert F. Preston	1910-1947
N. Henry Black	1896-1898	Robert W. Hughes	1911-1914
Frank J. McCloskey	1896-1928	Bernard A. Hoban	1912-1914
James E. Gregg	1897-1900		1926-1934
William Burdick	1897-1901	Walter G. Dawley	1914-1916
Edward Sturtevant	1898-1939	Norman J. Merrill	1914-1917
E. Blake Barton	1898-1899	Noel B. Van Wagenen	1914-1915
Jane Stormont-Lewis	1899-1900	William H. Drury	1915-1953
John S. Galbraith	1899-1902	William N. Dunbar	1915-1916
△Arthur F. Griffiths	1899-1902	Thomas R. Pennypacker	1916-1917
Edward W. Hope	1900-1901	Merton B. Frye	1916-1918
Jesse G. Melendy	1901-1902	The Rev. Israel H. Hughes	1917-1921
Flavel S. Shurtleff Jr.	1901-1903	Charles C. Earle Jr.	1917-1918
Stephen P. Cabot	1901-1926	B. Holt Willard	1917-1918
Headmaster	1917-1926	*Oliver Prescott Jr.	1918-1919
Russell H. Nevins	1902-1936	Raymond A. Crawford	1918-1920
Headmaster	1926-1928	Loring L. Emery	1918-1919
Alan R. Wheeler	1902-1947	Osgood Perry	1918-1920
The Rev. Arthur N. Peaslee	1902-1927	Richard M. Baker	1919-1921
Herman F. Krafft	1902-1907	*George L. Howe	1919-1920
Arthur S. Roberts	1903-1946	Henry M. Spencer	1919-1920
B.L. Henin	1903-1907	Nowell S. Ferris	1920-1922
Robert G. Martin	1905-1907	William E. Shuttleworth	1920-1926
Jay A. Moody	1906-1926	Edward D. Griffith	1920-1921
The Rev. Latta Griswold	1906-1915	Allen H. Gleason	1920-1921
A.S. Gregg Clarke	1906-1907	Willard M. Cook	1920-1932
Karl O. Bertling	1907-1909	Raymond A. Green	1921-1923
Paul T. Christie	1907-1943	Nelson D. Gifford Jr.	1921-1923
Walter R. Cowles	1908-1910	Theodore R. Butler	1921-1923
Leslie P. Thompson	1908-1915	*F. Ogden Nash	1921-1922
Rupert P. Taylor	1908-1915	The Rev. J.H.S. Fair	1921-1924
*The Rev. Harold N. Arrowsmith		Vernon B. Kellett	1921-1926
	1909-1912	Archibald Dudgeon	1921-1926
Harold B. Barton	1909-1910	H. Wood Thompson	1922-1926
Philip B. Eaton	1910-1914	Sinclair W. Armstrong	1923-1928

*Graduate of St. George's   △ Became a headmaster elsewhere

James G. Vermillion	1923-1966	The Rev. Alfred S. Griffiths	1935-1936
*Walter K. Phelps	1923-1924	Wilbur R. Cooke	1935-1936
Wilfred E. Kneeland	1923-1926	*Theodore C. Sturtevant	1935-1936
James H. Barrett	1924-1925	Robert E. Bacon	1935-1942
The Rev. Truman Hemingway		Virgil C. Toms	1936-1938
	1924-1927	The Rev. H. Martin P. Davidson	
Edward B. Blakeley	1924-1928		1936-1951
F. Martin Brown	1925-1927	Adrian H. Onderdonk Jr.	1936-1938
△Laurence G. Leavitt	1925-1926	Walter O. Gollnick	1936-1947
Paul C. Rogers	1925-1926	Leslie D. Bissell Jr.	1938-1939
Robert W. Hughes	1926-1928	Leslie E. Jones	1938-1942
E. Trudeau Thomas	1926-1928	Robert P. Twitchell	1938-1949
*Wellesley Wright	1926-1929	William Law	1939-1941
Donald G. Baker	1926-1928	Benjamin F. Courtright	1939-1941
F. Alton Wade	1926-1927	Winthrop S. Jameson Jr.	1939-1940
Joseph W. Hall Jr.	1926-1928	George G. Hedblom	1940-1941
The Rev. Roger W. Bennett	1927-1932	Keene Shortell	1940-1941
Ashley T. Day	1927-1941	Nicholas Mellen	1940-1941
Edmund P. Coe	1927-1942	Albert R. Dawe	1941-1942
William P. Elliott	1927-1952	Jeremiah Ford II	1941-1952
J. Vaughan Merrick III	1928-1943	Anthony Q. Keasbey	1941-1943
Headmaster		*Jay B. L. Reeves	1941-1942
Ralph E. Langdell	1928-1929	William Green	1942-1943
Mark E. Balis	1928-1929	Kenneth V. Jackman	1942-1943
Alexander M. Neilson	1928-1938	The Rev. Lauriston L. Scaife	
J. Raymond Fritz	1928-1948		1942-1945
*William A. Buell	1929-1961	The Rev. William E. Soule	1942-1944
Headmaster	1951-1961	Willet L. Eccles	1943-1951
(Also a Master 1919-1921)		Headmaster	
Robert S. Lyle	1929-1930	Emily Anable	1943-1946
Carl Thorp	1929-1934	Robert R. Covell	1943-1944
Jesse E. Manley	1929-1930	△*Joseph C. Rennard	1943-1946
C. P. Beauchamp Jefferys	1930-1963	Alexander H. Rice	1943-1946
*A. Lee Y. Ward	1930-1931	△Wilfred W. Clark	1944-1949
*George W. Wheeler	1931-1975	G. Raymond Hicks	1944-1946
Richard L. Kirkman	1931-1932	Richard Knowles	1944-1953
Howard E. Merrill	1931-1933	The Rev. Thomas L. Brown	1945-1947
Henry V. Grattan	1932-1935	George J. Nolan	1945-1947
The Rev. Arthur Rogers	1932-1934	*Reginald Roome Jr.	1945-1951
Joseph D. Wilson	1933-1935	Edward A. Sibley	1945-1947
*Thomas C. T. Buckley	1934-1936	Nancy B. (Eccles) Roome	1946-1951
William R. Strickland Jr.	1934-1936	Carl M. Caspar	1946-1947

*Graduate of St. George's   △ Became a headmaster elsewhere

John H. Emerson	1946-1951	A. K. Cassels-Brown	1952-1955
The Rev. Franklin F. Funk	1946-1947	Hubert C. Hersey	1952-
△Harry J. Groblewski	1946-1949	Floyd A. Couch Jr.	1952-1953
Norris D. Hoyt	1946-1975	Lucile Rogers	1952-1961
△Philip W. Richards	1946-1948	C. Christian Beels	1953-1955
Arthur L. Springer	1946-1948	Robert J. Carner	1953-1954
Margaret A. Spruance	1947-1948	Richard Grosvenor	1953-
*Weyman S. Crocker	1947-1948	△James L. Keegan	1953-1956
David Demaray	1947-1949		1977-
Charles C. Donelson	1947-1948	Howard K. Moore	1953-1954
△Frederick W. Goode	1947-1948	The Rev. Charles W. Nelson	1953-1954
Charles G. Thornblade	1947-1965	Harry C. Allen	1954-1956
The Rev. John C. Dahl	1948-1949	Frederick W. Berg	1954-1959
△Gordon D. Davis	1948-1950	John M. Bergland III	1954-1955
*Roswell C. Josephs	1948-1951	Kimball M. Jones	1954-1957
△Lewis E. Kimball Jr.	1948-1953	William T. King	1954-1962
William W. Minton	1948-1950	Charles S. Knowles	1954-1962
Robert H. Baker	1949-1955	Robert G. Martley	1954-1969
George A. Dinsmore	1949-1950	John W. McAuliffe Jr.	1954-1955
J. Bennett Grocock	1949-1950	Howard A. Jewell	1955-1957
Radcliffe M. Oxley	1949-1950	George B. Ludlow Jr.	1955-1961
△David L. Pratt	1949-1950	*The Rev. William A. Opel	1955-1957
Kenneth W. Thompson	1949-1950	Geoffrey H. Spranger	1955-1972
The Rev. Harold G. Forster		△Samuel S. Stroud	1955-1961
(February)	1950-1953	Harlin A. Sexton Jr.	1955-1957
H. Sanford Brown	1950-1951	△Philip Cutler	1956-1957
Herbert W. Hammack	1950-1952	Rufus King	1956-1961
Anson B. Haughton	1950-1952	△*William S. R. Rogers	1956-1961
The Rev. William Macbeth	1950-1951		1974-
W. Redwood Wright	1950-1952	Richard Bennett	1957-1964
Bessie G. Anderson	1950-1955	Thomas C. Buell	1957-1962
Lois M. Buell	1950-1951	Henry E. Childs	1957-1959
	1970-1973	Charles Elharar	1957-1962
Chauncey H. Beasley	1951-1963	The Rev. F. H. Glazebrook Jr.	
Lyall Dean	1951-1954		1957-1963
The Rev. W. Henry C. Hyde	1951-1953	Harry B. Heneberger	1957-1964
△Peter F. Rothermel IV	1951-1958	△*William C. Prescott Jr.	1957-1958
	1969-1981		1961-1968
Amey Steere	1951-1967	Gilbert Burnett Jr.	1958-1960
Lawrence Goldthwait	1952-1967		1966-
William M. Schenck	1952-	George G. Carey	1958-1960
△Lawrence E. Tuttle	1952-1954	△Christopher C. Corkery	1958-1972

*Graduate of St. George's   △ Became a headmaster elsewhere

Name	Dates	Name	Dates
Guy J. Daney	1958-1959	△Donald M. Sykes Jr.	1965-1972
*Charles Moran III	1958-1960	William Chau	1966-1968
Philip S. Perry	1959-1963	The Rev. Robert L. Crawford	1966-1969
Ronald Richardson	1959-1965		
George Szpinalski	1959-1963	John G. Davis	1966-1970
Frederick Gardner	1960-1961	Marc F. B. Dufour	1966-1968
Jeremiah J. McCarthy	1960-1966	Kevin V. O'Leary	1966-1977
Harold P. Peterson	1960-1961	Roy W. Penny	1966-1985
Peter F. Strauss	1960-1962	Floride H. Taylor	1966-1981
*Bruce R. Burgess	1961-1962	Richard A. Taylor	1966-1971
Frank S. Crenshaw	1961-1963	△*Frederic K. Baldwin Jr.	1967-1972
△Archer Harman Jr.	1961-1972		1974-1976
Headmaster		Robert S. Ballantyne	1967-1969
Manuel Lassaletta	1961-1962	Warren P. Long	1967-1969
The Rev. Hays H. Rockwell	1961-1969	Charles W. Howard II	1968-
Beverley Robinson	1961-1966	William A. Lydgate Jr.	
The Rev. Walter M. Echols			1968-(Feb.) 1970
(October)	1961-1962	C. Lucas Wegmann	1968-1969
Walter K. Beattie Jr.	1962-1971	Robert E. White Jr.	1968-1971
Dean Blanchard Jr.	1962-	Franklin J. Wilkes Jr.	1968-1969
Peter Cook	1962-1966	△The Rev. Robert R. Hansel	1969-1974
*John Q. A. Doolittle Jr.	1962-	C. Wesley Hennion III	1969-
△W. John Friedlander	1962-1965	Michael H. Kenfield	1969-1972
Kenneth G. Geiersbach	1962-1966	Neville M. Lake	1969-1980
*David T. Moran	1962-1965	Robert M. Parker	1969-1980
Manuel Nunez de Cela Pinol	1962-1965	James R. Parkinson	1969-1971
*Howard P. Dodge	1963-1969	The Rev. Thomas W. Wile	1969-1971
The Rev. Robert C. Gregg	1963-1967	Merrill F. Hathaway Jr.	
*Howard R. Hall	1963-1974		(Feb.-June) 1970
Bryant F. Tolles Jr.	1963-1965	G. Danforth Hollins	1970-
Richard K. Wallen	1963-1978	Robert Morris	1970-1973
Robert C. Watt	1963-1966	Peter A. Sila	1970-1976
Michael S. Koleda	1964-1965	Charles H. Bodine Jr.	1971-
Winfred E. Johnson	1964-1971	Lynne B. Hennion	1971-1975
Robert W. Turcotte		Stephen D. Horowitz	1971-
(April)	1964-1965	Linda M. Kenfield	1971-1972
Robert W. McClenahan		Jere L. Lantz	1971-1973
(April)	1965-1967	Timothy H. Tefft	(Sept.-Dec.) 1971
J. Allen Fitz-Gerald	1965-1971	Susan S. Hansel	1971-1974
John McMullan	1965-1974	Ronald D. Varney	1971-1974
Harry M. Robinson Jr.	1965-1966	The Rev. Howard W. White Jr.	
William W. Stork	1965-1971		1971-1974

*Graduate of St. George's   △ Became a headmaster elsewhere

Paul S. Andrews	1971-1973	Beth Smith Horton	1975-
Kathleen Hall O'Keefe	1971-1973	Vicki M. Johnson	1975-1977
	1976-1978	Charles P. Lee	1975-1977
Timothy O. Devlin (Jan.)	1972-1977	The Rev. Darwin L. Price	1975-1978
Suzanne W. Aubois	1972-1973	R. Frederick Seebeck	1975-1977
Stephen D. Carter	1972-1980		1978-1982
Haywood E. Corry	1972-1973	Jane M. Hall	1975-1977
Mary M. Davis	1972-1974	Conchita T. Kreisler	1976-
Stephen B. Leslie	1972-	Katherine Piper	1976-1977
Ronald P. Savoie	1972-1982	Lea C. Reynolds	1976-1979
Gilbert O. Stanley	1972-1974	The Rev. John S. Rogers	1976-
Anthony M. Zane	1972-1984	Claudia Turner	1976-1980
Headmaster		David B. Herter	1976-1981
Day M. Zenker	1972-1973	Henry P. Bristol	1976-1978
Timothy P. O. Zenker	1972-1973	Alan P. Clark	1977-
Stephen M. H. Connett	1973-	Barklie W. Eliot	1977-1981
Sally Lewis	1973-1974	Rosemary B. Fagan	1977-1979
Kim H. Noling	1973-1975	Diana L. Lee	1977-1981
Barbara G. O'Leary	1973-1979	Catherine Pastore	1977-1981
Candace T. Stanley	1973-1974	James A. Purviance	1977-1986
Lydia C. Vine	1973-1975	Mark S. Toher	1977-1980
Dale R. Sparlin	1973-1979	Asheton C. Toland	1977-1980
Lilit M. Zekulin	1973-1976	Allan Whatley	1977-1981
Thorne G. Butler	1973-1978	Ann Kirby	1977-1982
	1979-1983	Suzanne Cruanes	1978-1979
Adela B. Carter	1973-1975	*Peter Drakos	1978-1979
Judythe G. Sieck	1973-1978	*Philip L. Dickinson	1978-
Dorothy B. Howard	1973-	Jerald E. Brown	1978-1986
△David V. Hicks	1973-1975	The Rev. Margaret A. Wilcox	
The Rev. Ian Ogilvie	1973-1974		1978-(Jan.) 1981
(Exchange, Sevenoaks School,		Edward W. Lawrence	1978-1980
Sevenoaks, England)		Jennifer Day	1979-1981
Howard Baetjer Jr.	1974-1978	Jon M. Harris	1979-1985
	1980-1981	Martha Bragdon	1980-1983
Miguel J. Brito	1974-1977	Franklin G. Coleman	1980-
W. Sheldon Horton	1974-	Barbara A. Flynn	1980-1983
*Philip M. Reynolds	1974-1979	Margaret A. Gurren	1980-1983
The Rev. Marshall T. Ware	1974-1976	Elizabeth K. Hollins	1980-
Patricia H. Lazar	1974-1975	Valerie H. McNeil	1980-1983
Marcia Hersey Rogers	1974-	Donald L. Malone	1980-1985
Rose Y. Bugnet	1975-	Gerald G. Morse Jr.	1980-1982
David J. Dupre	1975-1976	Pamela S. Sperry	1980-1982

*Graduate of St. George's   △ Became a headmaster elsewhere

Shirley C. Clark 1981-1983
Lia A. DeRobbio 1981-
Laura B. Lussen 1981-1985
Richard E. Lussen 1981-1985
Yvette Rubio 1981-1985
The Rev. Gilbert Y. Taverner
(Feb.) 1981-
Sandra M. MacDonald 1981-
Linda Cari 1982-
Wendy Goffe 1982-1983
W. Robert Kmen 1982-
Valerie H. Minton 1982-1985
(Feb.-June) 1986
Catherine L. Randall 1982-1983
Jeffrey E. Simpson 1982-
Michael J. Williamson 1982-1984
Russell P. Wilson 1982-1984
Thomas J. Baker 1983-
Sydna G. Budnick 1983-1984
Janet A. Butler 1983-1985
*Richard W. Cooper Jr.
1983-(Jan.) 1986
Christine E. Edler 1983-1984
Eleanor T. Howard 1983-
Denise Hunter-Cooper
1983-(Jan.) 1984
William J. Rushton IV 1983-
Valerie G. Simpson 1983-
Cary T. Gilbart-Smith 1983-1984
(Exchange – Charterhouse School
Godalming, England)

Ann B. Coldiron 1984-1986
Maxwell B. Hall 1984-1986
Amy A. Koontz 1984-1986
Mafalda G. Nula 1984-
Amy O. Wesson 1984-1985
Janet W. Buell 1985-
Peter Bramante 1985-
Melanie N. Broujos 1985-
June Doolittle 1985-
Mace M. Foehl 1985-1986
Marjorie Foster 1985-1986
The Rev. April V. T. Greenwood
1985-
*Nathaniel M. Hemphill 1985-
Anita W. Jackson 1985-
Jeremy Jones 1985-
Elizabeth A. Leslie 1985-
George W. Maentz 1985-
Archibald R. Montgomery IV
1985-
Ellen D. Scully 1985-
Charles M. Stillwell 1985-
George Brownell 1986-
Douglas A. Field 1986-
Jennifer Greeley 1986-
Jean H. Loew 1986-
Lynn Proebsting 1986-
Philip D. Song 1986-
Carrie R. Swigart 1986-

*Graduate of St. George's   △ Became a headmaster elsewhere

APPENDIX B

St. George's School – Board of Trustees
1900-1986

The Rt. Rev. William N. McVickar
  President, 1900-1910   1900-1910
George Gordon King   1900-1922
Thomas G. Brown   1900-1910
Edward Sturtevant   1900-1939
Julien T. Davies   1900-1920
Hugh D. Auchincloss   1904-1913
The Rev. John B. Diman   1907-1917
  Headmaster, 1896-1917
Frederic R. King '04   1910-1939
The Rt. Rev. James DeWolfe Perry, Jr.
  President, 1911-1946   1911-1946
Samuel P. Bush   1913-1919
Stephen P. Cabot   1917-1926
  Headmaster, 1917-1926
Horatio Gates Lloyd '19   1919-1925
  (Also served 1945-1951)
Harford W. H. Powel '04   1919-1931
William S. Sims. RAdm. U.S.N.
    1919-1935
Mark A. DeWolfe Howe   1919-1928
W. Vincent Astor '10   1920-1944
  (Also served 1947-1952)
John M. Bullard '09   1922-1924
  (Also served 1945-1949)
Marion Eppley   1922-1941
Thomas Pierrepont Hazard '11
    1924-1926
Michael M. vanBeuren   1925-1940
A. Livingston Kelley '06   1926-1948
Russell H. Nevins   1926-1928
  Headmaster, 1926-1928
J. Vaughan Merrick, III   1928-1948
  Headmaster, 1928-1943
R. Keith Kane '18   1930-1940
Graham B. Blaine '13   1934-1938
  (Also served 1940-1947)

Barklie McKee Henry '20   1935-1944
Harrison G. Reynolds '13   1938-1941
John Nicholas Brown '18   1939-1971
  Honorary, 1971-1979
Charles S. Cheston '10   1940-1944
Albert J. Redway, Jr. '14   1940-1943
Lucien Wulsin '35   1940-1950
  (Also served 1966-1969)
Archbold vanBeuren '23   1940-1944
  (Also served 1948-1971)
  Honorary, 1971-1975
Graham B. Blaine '13   1940-1947
  (Also served 1934-1938)
Frederic L. Ballard '35   1940-1947
Kenneth S. Safe '20   1941-1943
  (Also served 1947-1956)
Weyman S. Crocker '14   1941-1943
Willet L. Eccles   1943-1951
  Headmaster, 1943-1951
Ashbel T. Wall '33   1943-1944
Rufus S. Frost '12   1943-1945
John R. Haire   1943-1944
Edward S. Noyes   1944-1951
Philip Drinker '11   1944-1947
W. Lawrence McLane '24   1944-1952
  (Also served 1954-1964)
Douglas S. Byers '21   1944-1951
John A. Stevenson   1945-1947
Horatio Gates Lloyd '19   1945-1951
  (Also served 1919-1925)
John M. Bullard '09   1945-1949
  (Also served 1922-1924)
The Rt. Rev. Granville G. Bennett
  President, 1946-1954   1946-1954
Alan R. Wheeler   1946-1947
Morton Goodspeed '14   1947-1956
Howard R. Merriman '24   1947-1956

W. Vincent Astor '10 1947-1952
  (Also served 1920-1944)
Kenneth S. Safe '20 1947-1956
  (Also served 1941-1943)
Archbold vanBeuren '23 1948-1971
  (Also served 1940-1944)
  Honorary, 1971-1975
Henry W. Schereschewsky 1948-1951
Oliver Prescott, Jr. '16 1948-1954
Albert Carey Wall '20 1949-1955
Harrison H. Clement '29 1950-1958
J. Halsey Smith 1951-1963
The Rev. William A. Buell '14
  Headmaster, 1951-1961 1951-1961
William A. Dupee, Jr. '30 1951-1966
Minot K. Milliken '33 1951-1970
James R. Reynolds '19 1951-1971
  Honorary, 1975-
T. Henry Dixon '36 1952-1956
The Rev. Samuel Tyler, Jr. 1952-1965
The Rt. Rev. John S. Higgins
  President, 1954-1972 1954-1972
  Honorary, 1972-
W. Lawrence McLane '24 1954-1964
  (Also served 1944-1952)
John E. C. Hall 1954-1970
Morris C. Maxwell '27 1954-1960
William C. Prescott '20 1954-1970
William D'O. Lippincott '37 1955-1978
Clarke Simonds '35 1956-1965
John F. Ducey, Jr. '32 1956-1969
Lewis R. Page, Jr. '37 1956-1964
Henry H. Patten '31 1956-1971
Charles Moran, Jr. '24 1956-1975
  Honorary, 1975-1978
George Howland '35 1960-1976
  Honorary, 1976-1983
Archer Harman, Jr. 1961-1972
  Headmaster, 1961-1972
Horace P. Beck '39 1962-1966
Richard D. Challener 1962-1975

Sydney Thayer, III '44 1962-1971
  (Also served 1975-1981)
  Honorary, 1981-
John F. Milliken '38 1963-1976
Hawley T. Chester, Jr. '37 1964-1976
Walter Beinecke, Jr. '36 1965-1970
Lewis N. Madeira '39 1965-1980
  President, 1978-1980
  Honorary, 1980-
Elkins Wetherill '38 1965-1976
Peter M. Ward '43 1966-1978
  President, 1972-1978
  Honorary, 1980-
Lucien Wulsin '35 1966-1969
  (Also served 1940-1950)
The Rev. Samuel J. Wylie 1966-1967
John T. Dorrance, Jr. '37 1966-1985
Jonathan T. Isham '46 1967-1980
Albert Wall Merck '39 1967-1976
Edwin C. Donaghy '42 1969-1980
John H. Wulsin '38 1969-1986
  Honorary 1986-
John R. Robinson 1970-1976
Henry F. Colt, Jr. '42 1970-1975
William A. Briggs, Jr. '59 1970-
Graham B. Blaine, Jr. '36 1971-1980
Blanche Gibbs 1971-1979
  (Mrs. J. Gordon)
Carol P. Guyer (Mrs. David) 1971-1973
Frederic S. Mosely, III 1971-1977
The Hon. Claiborne Pell '36 1971-
Jay Derek Reist '63 1971-1977
The Rt. Rev. Frederick H. Belden
  Chairman, 1972-1979 1972-1979
Anthony M. Zane 1972-1984
  Headmaster, 1972-1984
Philip E. Coen 1972-1977
David L. Evans 1972-1986
Charles G. Watson '50 1972-1978
The Rev. C. Blayney Colmore, III
  '59 1973-1980
Nancy Harris (Mrs. John) 1973-1979
The Rev. Edward M. Ward 1974-1977

Sydney Thayer, III '44   1975-1981
  (Also served 1962-1971)
    Honorary, 1981-
John C. Bullard '39   1975-1981
Lee Herter (Mrs. Miles)   1975-1980
Ellen Walton (Mrs. James)   1975-1981
Josiah Bunting '29   1976-1978
Howard B. Dean, Jr.   1976-1985
    President, 1980-1984
    Chairman, 1984-1985
    Honorary, 1985-
Richard W. Angle, Jr. '59   1976-1981
James C. Brady, Jr.   1976-1978
Lawrence Wilkinson '30   1976-1980
Corwith Cramer, Jr.   1977-1982
Henry U. Harder   1977-1985
John Archbold vanBeuren   1977-
William R. Battey, Jr. '71   1978-1981
Richard G. Verney '64   1978-
    Chairman, 1985-
Peter B. Freeman   1979-1984
Hamilton W. Meserve '54   1979-
Mary Robb (Mrs. Edwin)   1979-
Georgia Welles   1979-1982
  (Mrs. David)
Joan Brady (Mrs. James)   1980-1985
Dana S. Bray, Jr. '53   1980-1982
Arthur F. Draper '61   1980-
The Rt. Rev. George N. Hunt, III
                                1980-
  Chairman, 1980-1984
  Honorary Chairman, 1984-

Leslie Barclay   1981-1986
  (Mrs. Rutgers)
The Rev. J. Clark Grew   1981-
Joseph C. Hoopes, Jr. '62   1981-
John W. Lapsley   1981-
Richard N. Sayer '65   1981-
Christopher C. Simonds '61   1981-
Carolyn Alderson   1982-1985
  (Mrs. Irving)
Charles P. Lee   1982-
James W. McLane '57   1982-1985
Timothy Rogers '51   1982-
Laurance M. Redway '58   1983-
William K. Wood-Prince '60   1983-
The Rev. George E. Andrews II
                                1984-
    Headmaster, 1984-
Betsy S. Michel   1984-
  (Mrs. Clifford)
Sylvester Monroe '69   1984-
Francis S. Branin, Jr. '65   1985-
The Rev. John W. Rick, III   1985-
John H. Ariail, Jr.   1986-
Helen P. Dyke (Mrs. James)   1986-
Elena Thornton Kissell '77   1986-
  (Mrs. Michael)
Cynthia H. Shogren   1986-
  (Mrs. Tony)
James M. Stewart   1986-
Meade B. Thayer '70   1986-

APPENDIX C

Alumni Presidents and Chairmen of Alumni and Annual Funds

PRESIDENTS

Samuel Powel '04	1915-1920	Archbold vanBeuren '23	1948-1952
John M. Bullard '09	1920-1924	T. Henry Dixon '36	1952-1956
Thomas P. Hazard '11	1924-1926	John F. Ducey '32	1956-1960
A. Livingston Kelley '06	1926-1930	George Howland '35	1960-1964
R. Keith Kane '18	1930-1934	Hawley T. Chester, Jr. '37	1964-1967
Graham B. Blaine '13	1934-1938	Jonathan T. Isham '46	1967-1970
Harrison G. Reynolds '13	1933-Oct. 1941	William A. Briggs, Jr. '59	1970-1973
		C. Blayney Colmore, III '59	1973-1976
Weyman S. Crocker '14	Oct. 1941-March 1942	Lawrence Wilkinson '30	1976-1978
		William R. Battey, Jr. '71	1978-1981
H. Gates Lloyd '19	March 1942-May 1942	Richard G. Verney '64	1981-1983
		Richard N. Sayer '65	1983-1985
Ashbel T. Wall, Jr. '10	1942-1944	Francis S. Branin, Jr. '65	1985-
Douglas S. Byers '21	1944-1948		

CHAIRMEN – ALUMNI AND ANNUAL FUNDS

T.I. Hare Powel '06	1927-1931	1958-1959 (Suspended, but credited with $40,000 from Development Program.)	
Oliver Prescott, Jr. '16	1931-1932		
John Nicholas Brown '18	1932-1934		
Archbold vanBeuren '23	1934-1937	Clarke Simonds '35	1959-1960
Nathaniel P. Hill '15	1937-1940	Henry H. Patton '31	1960-1962
Kenneth Shaw Safe '20	1940-1942	Charles Moran, Jr. '24	1962-1965
Henry A. Morss, Jr. '28	1942-1944	John F. Ducey, Jr. '32	1965-1968
W. Lawrence McLane, Jr. '24	1944-1948	Henry H. Patton '31	1968-1970
		Charles Moran, Jr. '24	1970-1974
John F. Ducey, Jr. '32	1948-1951	Edwin C. Donaghy, Jr. '42	1974-1977
Hawley T. Chester, Jr. '37	1951-1954	Sydney Thayer, III '44	1977-1980
Morris C. Maxwell '27	1954-1956	Richard G. Verney '64	1980-1981
Clarke Simonds '35	1956-1958	Richard N. Sayer '65	1981-1985
		Francis S. Branin, Jr. '65	1985-

APPENDIX D

St. George's Students
Killed in Wars

As listed in the Plaques in the Memorial Schoolhouse

WORLD WAR I

*Gardner Henry Fuller
Harold Chandler Kimball '07
Ronald Wood Hoskier '14
Henry Brewster Palmer '06
William Smith Ely '13
Richard Cutts Fairfield '11
Caldwell Colt Robinson '13
Welles Bradly Cumings '18

Tolman Douglas Wheeler '10
Philip Newbold Rhinelander '13
William Boulton Dixon '11
Marquand Ward '12
Alexander Rodgers, Jr. '11
Edward Barry Wall '12
Galbraith Ward '11

Faculty: Norman Jesse Merrill

WORLD WAR II

Ethan Allen '38
Hiland Garfield Batcheller, Jr. '41
Harrison Tweed Blaine '38
William Thayer Brown, Jr. '40
*John Bowyer Buckley '40
Peter Tracy Chester '39
Charles Briggs Congdon '40
Greville Cobbett Elliott
    Cumming '40
Chester Coburn Darling, Jr. '34
George Rathbone Dyer '26
John Bedford French, Jr. '33
Charles Lesher Geer '33
Gordon Alward Hardwick, Jr. '39
Thomas Hart, Jr. '40

Phineas McCray Henry, Jr. '32
Jonn Dandridge Henley Kane '16
Henry Horst Kreider '39
Howard Blackwood Ligget, III '36
Archibald Graham McIlwaine, II '39
Edward Morris Murray '21
Frederic Russell Nourse, Jr. '29
John Neville Woodbine Parish '39
Gordon McAlpin Pyle '19
August Alexander Rubel '17
Francis Pugh Thomas '38
William Donald Twining '40
Peter Van Pelt '36
Philip Nicklin Wainwright '37
Charles Dyer Wright '39

THE KOREAN WAR

Stuart Monroe Blazer '45

Charles Ramsay Stapler '34

THE VIETNAM WAR

Clyde Edwin Edgar '58
Arthur Sinclair Hill, Jr. '55

Harold Edwin Gray '49
Robert C. L. Fergusson '62

*Students from England.

APPENDIX E

Senior Prefects

The Prefect System was instituted in 1908 by the Rev. John Byron Diman. Each year since then a Senior Prefect has been elected to lead the students of the School and be a liaison between the students, Headmaster and Faculty.

1908 – Laurance David Redway
1909 – John Morgan Bullard
1910 – Rodney Newbold Landreth
1911 – Robert Burroughs Swain
1912 – Edward Barry Wall
1913 – Prescott Sheldon Bush
1914 – Charles Christian Haffner, Jr.
1915 – Nathaniel Peter Hill
1916 – Arthur Paul
1917 – Thornton Wallace Orr
1918 – Atherton Clark
1919 – James Robbins Reynolds
1920 – Albert Carey Wall, II
1921 – Richard William Ward
1922 – Milton Wilde Alger
1923 – Lee Yates Ward
1924 – Joseph Clifford Rennard
1925 – Walter Howe
1926 – Frederick Evelyn Gignoux, Jr.
1927 – Henry Bogert Clark, Jr.
1928 – Thomas C. Taylor Buckley
1929 – Allison Francisco Fleitas
1930 – Edmund Ambrose Lynch
1931 – Robert Hazard Knapp
1932 – Garrow Throop Geer, Jr.
1933 – Peter Hobart Knapp
1934 – Frederick Martin Hutchinson, IV
1935 – George Howland
1936 – Thomas Henry Dixon, III
1937 – Henry Blair Keep, Jr.
1938 – John Hager Wulsin
1939 – Gordon Alward Hardwick, Jr.
1940 – Charles Briggs Congdon
1941 – Charles Lothrop Ritchie, Jr.

1942 – Philip Murray Reynolds
1943 – Frank Mauran, III
1944 – Sydney Thayer, III
1945 – Philip Milroy Pierson
1946 – Thomas A. D. Champlin
1947 – George Clifford Buell
1948 – Palmer Gavit Jackson
1949 – Wilson Dunbar McElhinny
1950 – John Henry Stein
1951 – John Wood Bolton
1952   Nicholas Hoffman Bayard
1953 – Franklin K. Brown
1954 – Howard Richmond Hall
1955 – Bruce Robert Burgess
1956 – Stephen Cabot Prescott
1957 – John Kremer, III
1958 – Laurance Mitchell Redway
1959 – Peter Hoffman Archer
1960 – John Esher McLeran
1961 – Frederick Winslow Stetson, II
1962 – Allan MacLean Johnson
1963 – Morris Slocum Roberts
1964 – Roderick Ratcliff McKelvie
1965 – Peter Grubb Dearing
1966 – Thomas Stevenson Hackett
1967 – Kenneth Gordon Cross
1968 – Charles Maitland Dean
1969 – John Godfrey Hartnett
1970 – Walter G. D. Reed
1971 – Walter Christopher Gerolmo
1972 – Edward Willard Warren, II
1973 – Jeffrey Faithorn Welles
1974 – John Francis O'Connell
1975 – Glyn Douglas Vincent

1976 – Ann Alexandra Dix
1977 – Peter Nicholson Maduro
1978 – Daniel Carter Walker
1979 – David Elliott Walker
1980 – David Tytus Gardner
1981 – Nathaniel Moss Hemphill
1982 – Augustus Porter Bickford
1983 – Christopher Wadsworth Meserve
1984 – Christopher William Storkerson
1985 – Richard A. L. Wayner
1986 – Edward Duncan Truslow

circa 1906

APPENDIX F

School Prayer – School Hymns
Portraits of School Leaders

THE ST. GEORGE'S SCHOOL PRAYER

Composed by the Rt. Rev. Thomas March Clarke, D.D.,
Bishop of Rhode Island, around 1899.

Almighty God, the Fountain of all Wisdom, without Whom nothing is strong, nothing is holy, we beseech Thee to bless the members of this School with Thy perpetual presence and prosper them in their work. Keep their hearts free from every spot and stain of sin. May they be truthful and reverent in their speech, earnest and faithful in their studies, kind and considerate in their dealings with each other and always ready to help the unprotected and helpless. Bless, we beseech Thee, the teachers of this School and impress upon them a due sense of the responsibilities of their charge. We pray that from these walls young men and women* may go forth, generation after generation, well equipped for the battle of life and ready to contend bravely for God and the truth. And this we ask in the name of Him who died for our salvation, to Whom be glory for ever and ever. Amen.

*The word *women* was added after the arrival of coeducation.

Processional Cross gift of The Reverend Arthur N. Peaslee.

THE SCHOOL HYMN

O, Lord of Truth, and Power and Life,
Whose service makes Thy children free,
Arm these, Thy followers, in their strife,
Who fall, if holding not by Thee.

Fill them with high and holy zeal,
In lonely task or busy throng,
Their souls with heaven-born courage steel,
And in Thy strength, oh, make them strong.

Then, Lord, to every humble mind
Thy wisdom more and more impart,
Till all who seek, in faith may find
The blessing of the pure in heart.

Here let Thy love and Truth abound,
Changeless as yonder changeless sea,
And ever may these walls resound
With grateful voices praising Thee.

For brighter far than sun or star
That shine above this wind-swept slope
Thy greatness and Thy glory are;
Our sun of life and star of hope!

So, Lord, through each successive year,
Till earth's last night for them shall fall,
To sons and daughters who serve Thee here,*
Be thou Beginning, End and All. Amen.

Words by Miss Louise Diman, 1905. Tune: *Duke Street,* by John Hatton

---

*Altered after the School became coeducational

THE ST. GEORGE'S DAY HYMN

Lord God of Hosts, within whose hand
Dominion rests on sea and land,
Before whose world of life or death,
The strength of Nations is but breath,
O King, enthroned all thrones above,
Give strength unto the land we love.

To George our Saint, Thou gavest grace
Without one fear all foes to face,
And to confess by faithful death
That World of Life which was his breath
O help us, Helper of Saint George,
To fear no bonds that man can forge.

Arm us like him, who in Thy trust
Beat down the dragon to the dust:
So that we too may tread down sin
And with Thy saints a crown may win.
Help us, O God, that we may be
Wholly acceptable to Thee. Amen.

Words by Laurance Housman. Tune: *Falkland,* H Lawes

JERUSALEM

And did those feet in ancient time
Walk upon England's mountains green?
And was the Holy Lamb of God
On England's pleasant pastures seen?
And did the Countenance Divine
Shine forth upon our clouded hills?
And was Jerusalem builded here
Among those dark Satanic mills?

Bring me my bow of burning gold!
Bring me my arrows of desire!
Bring me my spear! O clouds unfold!
Bring me my Chariot of Fire!
I will not cease from mental fight;
Nor shall my sword sleep in my hand
Till we have built Jerusalem
In England's green and pleasant land.

William Blake, "Prophetic Books"

Words by William Blake. Tune: *Jerusalem,* by C. H. H. Parry

PORTRAITS

IN KING HALL – HEADMASTERS

The Rev. John Byron Diman, by Alphonse Jongers
Stephen P. Cabot, by Hubert Vos
Russell H. Nevins, by H. Bingham Ballou
J. Vaughan Merrick, III, by Leslie Thompson
Willet L. Eccles, by Marcella Comes Winslow
William A. Buell, by Gordon Stevenson
Archer Harman, Jr., by Nancy Robertson
Anthony and Eusie Zane, by Andrew Festing

IN KING HALL – OTHER PORTRAITS

George Gordon King, copied by William Cotton, from an original portrait by
   Sir James Guthrie
Bishop Thomas March Clark, by Helena Sturtevant

IN THE HEADMASTER'S STUDY

The Rev. John Byron Diman, by Albert Sterner
Arthur S. Roberts, by William H. Drury
Alan R. Wheeler, by David Swasey
George W. Wheeler, by Alden Wickes

IN MISS DIMAN'S ROOM

Emily Diman, by Leslie Thompson
Lois C. Buell, by K. N. Hoyt

APPENDIX G

Chronology of Buildings

Date indicates the year building went into use

1896 – 1901 In Newport, Rhode Island.*
1901 –   In Middletown, Rhode Island:

1901 – "Old School"

1901 – "The Cottage," moved from Purgatory Road to where the swimming pool was built; then to Kane Avenue in 1925, faculty residence.

1903 – Sixth Form House with attached Gymnasium. Gymnasium became a Schoolhouse in 1911, was torn down in 1923 and its timbers used to help build the School's Boathouse on Third Beach (since destroyed).

1907 – King Hall with attached kitchen/servants' quarters; Cloisters 1908.

1907 – Arden, dormitory/faculty residence.

1911 – Little Chapel.

1911 – Temporary Gymnasium; later converted to Twenty House, dormitory.

1913 – Pinecroft, faculty residence/dormitory (demolished, 1965).

1914 – Auchincloss as a Gymnasium; remodeled into a dormitory 1958.

1920 – Twenty House (remodeled 1911 Gymnasium); 1922 – South faculty residence addition; 1929 – North faculty residence addition.

1923 – Memorial School House.

1925 – Behrend Swimming Pool.

1925 – Wyn Wyc; faculty residence/dormitory; Annex 1978.

1925 – Engineer's Cottage; became Ray's House, a dormitory/faculty residence.

1927 – Diman Hall and Diman North; dormitories/faculty residences; 1930 faculty residence added to Diman North.

1928 – School Chapel – The Church of St. George.

1931 – The Infirmary; in 1975 became Astor Hall; dormitory/faculty residences.

1932 – The Headmaster's Apartment in Old School.

1954 – Cabot Memorial Ice Hockey Rink (uncovered); 1968 (covered).

---

*Between 1896 and 1901, the following buildings were occupied by the School but not owned by it (all in Newport):

> 1896-1897, Armistead Cottage, 55 Hunter Avenue,
>
> > Hunter Cottage, 57 Hunter Avenue.
>
> 1897-1901, Swann Villa, 2 Seaview Avenue,
>
> > Sealight Cottage, 45 Dresser Street,
> >
> > Hurst Cottage (now demolished) 47 Dresser Street.

1957 – Curtin House, 200 Kane Avenue; faculty residence.
1959 – Conover House, 174 Kane Avenue; faculty residence.
1959 – Potter House, 343 Purgatory Road; faculty residence.
1959 – Goodspeed House (attached to Auchincloss dormitory); faculty residence.
1959 – Moran House (attached to Auchincloss dormitory); faculty residence.
1959 – vanBeuren Gymnasium.
1963 – Dupont Science Building.
1965 – One James Street; faculty residence.
1965 – Class of 1929 House; faculty residence.
1966 – Brown-Vermillion House, 181 Kane Avenue; faculty residence.
1967 – Reynolds House; faculty residence.
1967 – Little House; faculty residence.
1967 – Smiley-Sturtevant Observatory.
1968 – Verney House; faculty residence.
1968 – Haffner House; dormitory/faculty residence.
1968 – Hill Library (became Student Center 1978); Sacristy/Choir Room.
1969 – 164 Kane Avenue; faculty residence.
1970 – Davenport House, 354 Purgatory Road; faculty residence.
1974 – Alan R. Wheeler House, 346 Purgatory Road; faculty residence.
1975 – Health Center (replacing Astor Hall Infirmary).
1977 – Maintenance Building.
1978 – New Hill Library.
1986 – Field House addition to vanBeuren Gymnasium started (scheduled for completion in 1987).

The Rev. Dr. Gilbert Y. Taverner
is School Historian/Archivist of
St. George's School